TECHNICAL
REPORT

T0195499

Assessing Patient Safety Practices and Outcomes in the U.S. Health Care System

Donna O. Farley, M. Susan Ridgely, Peter Mendel,
Stephanie S. Teleki, Cheryl L. Damberg, Rebecca Shaw,
Michael D. Greenberg, Amelia M. Haviland,
Peter Hussey, Jacob W. Dembosky, Hao Yu,
Julie A. Brown, Chau Pham, J. Scott Ashwood

Sponsored by the Agency for Healthcare Research and Quality

RAND HEALTH

This work was sponsored by the Agency for Healthcare Research and Quality (AHRQ) under contract No. 290-02-0010. The research was conducted in RAND Health, a division of the RAND Corporation.

Library of Congress Cataloging-in-Publication Data

Assessing patient safety practices and outcomes in the U.S. health care system / Donna O. Farley ... [et al.].
   p. ; cm.
   Includes bibliographical references.
   ISBN 978-0-8330-4774-8 (pbk. : alk. paper)
   1. Outcome assessment (Medical care)—United States. 2. Hospital patients—United States—Safety measures—Evaluation. I. Farley, Donna. II. Rand Corporation.
   [DNLM: 1. Medical Errors—prevention & control—United States—Evaluation Studies. 2. Quality Assurance, Health Care—United States—Evaluation Studies. 3. Safety Management—United States—Evaluation Studies. WB 100 A8375 2009]

R853.O87A87 2009
362.110973—dc22

                                                                                    2009029800

The RAND Corporation is a nonprofit research organization providing objective analysis and effective solutions that address the challenges facing the public and private sectors around the world. RAND's publications do not necessarily reflect the opinions of its research clients and sponsors.

RAND® is a registered trademark.

Published 2009 by the RAND Corporation
1776 Main Street, P.O. Box 2138, Santa Monica, CA 90407-2138
1200 South Hayes Street, Arlington, VA 22202-5050
4570 Fifth Avenue, Suite 600, Pittsburgh, PA 15213-2665
RAND URL: http://www.rand.org/
To order RAND documents or to obtain additional information, contact
Distribution Services: Telephone: (310) 451-7002;
Fax: (310) 451-6915; Email: order@rand.org

PREFACE

In 2000, the U.S. Congress mandated the Agency for Healthcare Research and Quality (AHRQ) to take a leadership role in helping health care providers reduce medical errors and improve patient safety. AHRQ is fulfilling that mandate through a patient safety research and development initiative, which is now at the end of its fourth year of operation. In September 2002, AHRQ contracted with RAND to serve as the patient safety evaluation center for this initiative. The evaluation center has been responsible for performing a four-year formative evaluation of the full scope of AHRQ's patient safety activities, and providing regular feedback to support the continuing improvement of the initiative over the evaluation period. The contract also includes a two-year option for analysis of the diffusion of safe practices in the health care system, which RAND performed in October 2006 through September 2008.

This report presents the results RAND's work under the two-year contract option, to assess practice adoption by health care providers and related outcomes. The assessments encompass three analytic components that address different aspects of practice adoption and diffusion across the country. Community studies were conducted of patient safety practice adoption and related activities that qualitatively examined the extent of use of safe practices at the community level, and the experiences of hospitals that used the AHRQ Hospital Survey on Patient Safety Culture (HSOPS) were examined. Finally, recognizing the need for capability to assess practice use quantitatively, a questionnaire was developed to use in a national survey of hospitals to gather data on their adoption of the safe practices endorsed by the National Quality Forum. In addition, this report presents the most recent results from our continued analysis of trends in patient outcomes related to safety.

The contents of this report will be of primary interest to AHRQ, but should also be of interest to national and state policy makers, health care organizations, health researchers, and others with responsibilities for ensuring that patients are not harmed by the health care they receive.

This work was sponsored by the Agency for Healthcare Research and Quality, Department of Health and Human Services, for which James B. Battles, Ph.D. serves as project officer.

This work was conducted in RAND Health, a division of the RAND Corporation. A profile of RAND Health, abstracts of its publications, and ordering information can be found at www.rand.org/health.

CONTENTS

FIGURES

TABLES

EXECUTIVE SUMMARY

In early 2000, the Institute of Medicine (IOM) published the report entitled *To Err Is Human: Building a Safer Health System*, calling for leadership from the U.S. Department of Health and Human Services (DHHS) in reducing medical errors and identifying AHRQ as the lead agency for patient safety research and practice improvement (IOM, 2000). Soon thereafter, the U.S. Congress funded the Agency for Healthcare Research and Quality (AHRQ), in the Department of Health and Human Services, to establish a national patient safety initiative. In its patient safety initiative, AHRQ has funded a portfolio of patient safety research and implementation projects to expand knowledge in this area, provided motivation and guidance for the activities of others, and integrated its work with that of other public and private organizations to achieve synergy through collaboration.

AHRQ contracted with RAND in September 2002 to serve as its Patient Safety Evaluation Center (evaluation center) and evaluate AHRQ's patient safety initiative. This evaluation was completed in September 2006, culminating in a final report that presents evaluation findings over the full four-year evaluation period (Farley et al., 2008b). The final report was preceded by three annual reports, each of which documents the status of the patient safety initiative as of September 2003, 2004, and 2005 (Farley et al., 2005; Farley et al., 2007a; Farley et al., 2007b).

The evaluation center then undertook another two years of work designed to document and analyze the extent to which patient safety infrastructure and practices are being put into place across the nation's health care system. This report presents the results of that work.

FRAMEWORK AND APPROACH FOR PRACTICE-ADOPTION ASSESSMENT

The study results presented in this report are products of the final phase of work for the Patient Safety Evaluation Center. These analyses focus on one component of the overall framework within which the overall evaluation was performed. Called the product evaluation, this component is the assessment of the effects of the AHRQ patient safety initiative on safety activities and outcomes in the U.S. health care system. See Chapter 1 for a full description of how the analyses presented in this report fit into our overall evaluation framework and approach.

Overall Framework

The overall evaluation design was based on the Context-Input-Process-Product (CIPP) evaluation model, a well-accepted strategy for improving systems that encompasses the full spectrum of factors involved in the operation of a program (Stufflebeam et al., 1971; Stufflebeam, Madaus, and Kellaghan, 2000). The core model components are represented in the CIPP acronym:

- *Context evaluation* assesses the circumstances stimulating the creation or operation of a program as a basis for defining goals and priorities and for judging the significance of outcomes.
- *Input evaluation* examines alternatives for goals and approaches for either guiding choice of a strategy or assessing an existing strategy against the alternatives, including congressional priorities and mandates as well as agency goals and strategies; stakeholders' perspectives are also assessed.

- **_Process evaluation_** assesses progress in implementation of plans relative to the stated goals for future activities and outcomes; activities undertaken to implement the patient safety initiative are documented, including any changes made that might alter its effects, positively or negatively.
- **_Product evaluation_** identifies consequences of the program for various stakeholders, intended or otherwise, to determine effectiveness and provide information for future program modifications.

A Nested Process Evaluation Framework

Due to the size and complexity of the patient safety initiative, we identified the need to develop a second logic model within the larger CIPP framework to guide the process evaluation. Such a model enabled the evaluation to "tell the story" of the implementation of the AHRQ patient safety initiative in a way that was intuitively accessible to AHRQ staff and other policymakers who would use the evaluation results. As shown in Figure S.1, the framework consists of five key system components that work together to bring about improved practices and safer health care for patients. We organized our process-evaluation results by these five components and examined the collective contributions of AHRQ-sponsored activities to progress in strengthening each component. The system components are defined as follows:

Monitoring Progress and Maintaining Vigilance. Establishment and monitoring of measures to assess performance-improvement progress for key patient safety processes or outcomes, while maintaining continued vigilance to ensure timely detection and response to issues that represent patient safety risks and hazards.

Knowledge of Epidemiology of Patient Safety Risks and Hazards. Identification of medical errors and causes of patient injury in health care delivery, with a focus on vulnerable populations.

Development of Effective Practices and Tools. Development and field testing of patient-safety practices to identify those that are effective, appropriate, and feasible for health care organizations to implement, taking into account the level of evidence needed to assess patient safety practices.

Building Infrastructure for Effective Practices. Establishment of the health care structural and environmental elements needed for successful implementation of effective patient safety practices, including an organization's commitment and readiness to improve patient safety (e.g., culture, information systems), hazards to safety created by the organization's structure (e.g., physical configurations, procedural requirements), and effects of the macro-environment (e.g., legal and payment issues) on the organization's ability to act.

Achieving Broader Adoption of Effective Practices. The adoption, implementation, and institutionalization of improved patient safety practices to achieve sustainable improvement in patient safety performance across the health care system.

The system component for monitoring progress and maintaining vigilance is identified first and placed on the bottom left side of the figure, reflecting the need for early data on patient safety issues to help guide intervention choices, as well as ongoing feedback regarding progress in developing knowledge and implementing practice improvements. The top row of the figure contains the two components that contribute to _knowledge development_ regarding patient-safety

epidemiology and effective practices and tools. This knowledge is then used in the remaining
two model components, which contribute to *practice implementation*—building infrastructure
and adopting effective practices (in the second row of the figure).

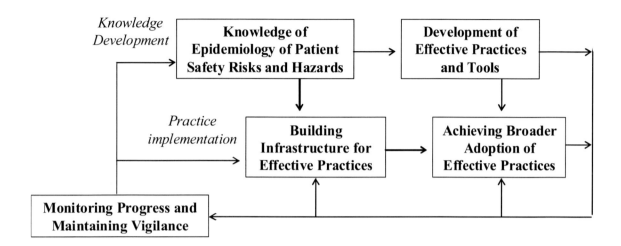

Figure S.1 The Components of an Effective Patient Safety System

Product-Evaluation Framework

In performing the product evaluation, our focus was on stakeholder effects that arise from
actions taken for the *practice implementation* aspect of the system framework identified in
Figure S.1—the two components of infrastructure development and adoption of effective
practices (see also Farley et al., 2008b). Successful implementation of actions in these areas
should lead to outcomes of improved practices by providers, fewer adverse events, and reduced
harm to patients.

To guide our product, evaluation work, we built upon the framework in Figure S.1 to
define the logic model for patient safety effects that is shown in Figure S.2. According to this
model, actions taken in the health care system for development of infrastructure should lead to
adoption of effective patient safety practices by providers (both from Figure S.1) and these, in
turn, should achieve improved outcomes for patients. Both infrastructure development and
practice adoption also affect other stakeholders involved in creating a safer health care system,
including providers, states, patient safety organizations, and the federal government.

This model is a simplified representation of the actual dynamics involved in moving from
actions to effects, which are complex and interrelated, with often-interacting effects of the
various stakeholders involved. While recognizing these limitations, the framework enables us to
explicitly identify the key components of these dynamic processes for consideration in the
evaluation and in future work by AHRQ.

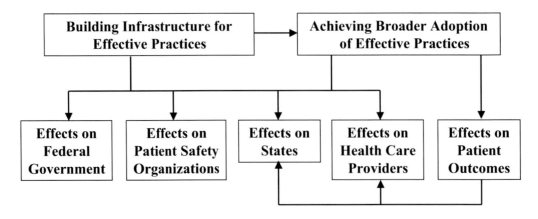

Figure S.2 Conceptual Framework of Potential Effects of National Patient Safety Activities

Analyses Presented in This Report

A product evaluation should consider effects of the national patient safety initiative on health system structures, practices, and stakeholders participating in the system, including effects on patient outcomes. Thus, our product evaluation included analysis of the extent of both adoption of patient safety practices and trends in related outcomes across the United States. We strategically selected our most recent analyses to address the following priority information needs for AHRQ:

- **Provide AHRQ with timely information on what health care providers are doing with adoption of safe practices.**

    What we did. We performed case studies of four communities across the country, using qualitative data collection and analytic methods to examine the extent of use of safe practices at the community level. The case-study approach was chosen because it could generate the most timely data, given that no instrument was available for collecting quantitative data on safe-practice use by providers (presented in Chapter 2).

- **Provide AHRQ with useful feedback on the experiences of providers in using at least one of the major tools AHRQ has developed to support its patient safety practices.**

    What we did. We examined the experiences of hospitals that used the AHRQ Hospital Survey on Patient Safety Culture (HSOPS). We considered also examining use of the TeamSTEPPS package, but it was too early to do so because the product was still being introduced to the field at the time of this evaluation work (presented in Chapter 3).

- **Develop measurement capability to enable AHRQ to collect trend data on the extent to which safe practices are being used by health care providers.**

    What we did. We developed and performed preliminary testing of a questionnaire to use in a national survey of hospitals on their adoption of the safe practices endorsed by the National Quality Forum (NQF). The next step would be to pilot-test the survey, in preparation for AHRQ to perform regular surveys to gather trend data on use of safe practices by hospitals (presented in Chapter 4).

- **Update trend information for patient outcomes for use by AHRQ in monitoring progress in improving safety outcomes, including exploration of methods that AHRQ might use to examine underlying patterns of changes in outcomes.**

 What we did. Much of the outcome trend analysis performed during the third and fourth years of the patient safety evaluation was continued during these two years, adding data for the years 2004 and 2005 to the outcome trends (presented in Chapter 5). These results address outcomes for patients, which is one of the stakeholder groups identified in the framework.

- **Develop a suggested approach that AHRQ could use to regularly monitor progress being made by the U.S. health care system in improving patient safety practices and outcomes.**

 What we did. Drawing upon the full body of work during the evaluation, including the four analyses presented in this report, we developed a suggested approach for ongoing monitoring by AHRQ of progress in the various aspects of effects on stakeholders, including practice-adoption rates and effects on various stakeholders, including patients (presented in Chapter 6). We also identified a number of relevant measurement issues that require attention.

 This report presents the results of each of these five specific assessments designed to develop information on progress in adoption of safe practices in the field, each of which is the topic of a chapter. The results of the assessments are summarized below.

UPTAKE OF SAFE PRACTICES IN FOUR U. S. COMMUNITIES (Chapter 2)

Specific Aims

1. To trace the evolution of patient safety efforts in four U.S. communities that are typical of local health care markets in various regions of the United States. The unit of analysis was the community. The focus of the study was to document patient safety initiatives and trends over time across three specific sectors within each community—hospitals, ambulatory settings, and long-term care facilities.

2. To understand, in particular, how hospitals in those communities made decisions about adoption of safe practices and how they implemented them within their institutions. The unit of analysis was the individual hospital. The focus of the study was to understand how hospitals are implementing the set of Safe Practices established by the National Quality Forum (NQF, 2007).

 Using case study methods, we assessed the uptake of patient safety practices in four U.S. communities, selecting communities from those in the *Community Tracking Study* (CTS) led by the Center for Studying Health System Change (HSC) (HCS, 2009). Since 1996, the HSC has conducted biannual site visits to 12 nationally representative metropolitan areas, to study how the interactions of providers, insurers, and other stakeholders help to shape the accessibility, cost, and quality of health care in local communities. At the time of our study, eight of these communities were also communities in the 2007–2008 regional rollout of voluntary patient safety and quality improvement initiatives by the Leapfrog Group.

 We selected four communities for our study that were both study sites in the HSC *Community Tracking Study* and the Leapfrog Group rollout communities. We studied patient safety activities in the following sites:

Indianapolis, Indiana   Cleveland, Ohio
Seattle, Washington   Greenville, South Carolina

We performed the community-level study to allow us to examine activities across health care settings. Then we did the hospital-level study so that we could obtain more-detailed information on the dynamics of patient safety activities by hospitals, which we already were aware was the setting where most patient safety activity was taking place.

Our data collection was performed using telephone interviews with 76 health care leaders in those communities, as well as site visits with 15 hospitals in the communities. In each hospital site visit, we conducted a series of interviews with hospital leaders knowledgeable about the evolution of the hospital's history and strategy related to patient safety, and we conducted two roundtable discussions about specific safe practices that had been implemented by each hospital. The data were analyzed to characterize the extent to which initiatives to improve patient safety practices have been implemented in the communities, including their use of tools developed by AHRQ.

Key Results—Community Level

The IOM report, *To Err Is Human* (2000), brought attention to patient safety, sparked discussion across the local communities, and stimulated actions by health care providers. The pace at which providers and others built momentum, however, varied widely across communities, in some cases taking years before actions began. Although the communities varied widely in their approaches and experiences, we found a number of common themes that could also be relevant for many other communities across the country.

Patient safety can be "evolutionary" as well as "revolutionary" in nature. It is not always a high-profile adverse event that starts a community or a hospital on the road to change. Even after some progress has been made, there may be tragic events, but they can provide an opportunity to rally around the hospital where the event occurred, reminding everyone that "the job isn't yet done." It also was clear that there is no single "best" approach to addressing patient safety and making local health care safer. In some communities, action was collaborative; in others, the hospitals or hospital systems looked inward.

For all of the communities studied, patient safety activities in the ambulatory care and long-term care (LTC) sectors were much less developed than those in the hospital sector. The ambulatory care or LTC organizations that were part of larger, consolidated health care systems were more likely to have undertaken some actions, compared with independent organizations.

Specific key findings are presented in Chapter 2, addressing the following topic areas:

- Use of community patient-safety coalitions
- Lessons from providers' patient-safety experiences
- Perspectives regarding other stakeholders.

Perhaps the most consistent and urgent message conveyed by providers across these four communities was the immense burden being placed on hospitals by the current state of measurement initiatives by national and state organizations. These reporting requirements have been interfering with the ability of hospitals to focus their attention on improving patient safety issues identified as their own priorities. They saw a need for national and state organizations to coalesce around measures, definitions, and goals for measurement and reporting activities.

Key Results—Hospital Activities

Our findings across 15 hospitals[1] in the four communities focused on their experiences in adoption of patient safety practices. Our review addresses the following dimensions:

- How hospitals set their goals and priorities around patients safety
- How they organize and structure their patient safety efforts
- How the process of implementing safe practices plays out in terms of challenges and facilitators
- Their perspective on the role that wider system-level players and forces (including AHRQ) played in promoting patient safety efforts within their institutions.

Goals and priorities. When asked how patient safety became a priority for their institutions, hospital leaders identified a wide variety of reasons, including a catalyzing event (e.g., a very public death from a medical error), an evolutionary process stimulated by outside influences, a natural outgrowth of decades of work on quality improvement, and stimulus by a new chief executive officer (CEO). After 2000, most hospitals began to develop a more strategic structure around patient safety improvement.

Hospitals also used a variety of processes for determining priorities. For some, there was a strong sense that priorities were based on "doing what is good for the patient"—whether that was the result of a sense of a public mission (e.g., safety-net hospitals) or a faith-based mission. Others described formal priority-setting processes that involved the hospital leadership, and often the Board. It was clear that for some hospitals the process of priority setting was a top-down endeavor—with more emphasis coming from the hospital leadership—while leaders in other hospitals emphasized the role of one or two physicians or nurse champions who had attended either AHRQ or Institute for Healthcare Improvement (IHI) meetings and came back with enthusiasm for change that they then spread to their colleagues.

Organization and structure. Hospital leaders described a variety of organizational structures (e.g., various types and levels of committees and staffing schemes) that were mostly idiosyncratic to their hospitals. There were, however, common themes about leadership, including the imperative for committed CEO involvement, a relatively new emphasis on Board of Director involvement in patient safety endeavors, and designation of a Patient Safety Officer (or someone clearly identified to handle that role) as part of (or reporting directly to) hospital senior management. Interviewees also discussed issues about infrastructure, such as incident-reporting systems and the benefits and challenges of health information technology (health IT).

Implementation process. Leaders from the hospitals pointed to a number of challenges they faced in the process of implementing patient safety practices, some of which already were identified in the case studies. The following key observations were made by the interviewees (in their words):

---

[1] Although we identified and recruited 16 hospitals to participate in the site visits, after repeated attempts we were unable to come to a mutually agreeable date for the site visit for the final hospital. By that point, there was not sufficient time to recruit an alternative hospital, so we report here on the experience of 15 hospitals.

- You can figure out what changes need to be made, but getting people at the bedside to adopt the changes can be a challenge.
- Perceptions of a punitive environment linger, despite assurances to the contrary.
- Counteracting physician skepticism to adopting new patient safety practices is one of the most difficult challenges to overcome.
- Simplify the safety message and focus on a few areas, or risk doing nothing well.
- Health IT can be both a challenge and a facilitator.
- For an effort to work, it takes support of the team to gather reliable data.
- Academic medical centers face some particular issues.
- Leverage community resources to supplement those in the hospital.
- Involving front-line staff in patient safety initiatives is empowering.

Role of systemwide players and forces. Every hospital leader mentioned the importance of external forces to their patient safety efforts. Hospital leaders pointed to AHRQ, the Institute of Medicine, the Institute for Healthcare Improvement, the Leapfrog Group, the Centers for Medicare and Medicaid Services, the Joint Commission, and others as critical to raising awareness and providing tools that have been instrumental in stimulating or supporting their own patient safety work.

Yet hospitals feel that they have no option but to respond to the various regulatory and mandatory programs and other private-sector initiatives. At least some of the leaders are skeptical about the value of some of these reporting initiatives to consumers, purchasers, or the hospitals themselves. Staff at the hospitals complained about conflicting standards, fragmented and duplicative reporting and lack of consideration of the effect of measurement on clinical behaviors, and questionable data.

They saw the need for a lead organization to fill the role of bringing the organizations together to prioritize initiatives in order to focus money, time, and effort on the most significant opportunities for improvement. Many of them named AHRQ as the agency best positioned to serve as a lead organization to bring the organizations together, as well as potentially to develop a national data repository for patient safety data. Hospital leaders thought that AHRQ could fulfill this important role by

- Bringing uniformity to safety and quality measures so that health care organizations would have only one set of measure to report
- Ensuring that all indicators have been tested and actually improve outcomes in order to cut down on meaningless or less effective markers, freeing up energy and resources to focus attention on the most meaningful patient safety activities
- Acting as a clearinghouse to facilitate real-time dissemination of patient safety ideas and innovations.

Summary of Community-Study Findings

Taken together, our findings from the community-level case studies and the interviews with hospital leader suggest that real progress has been made in average communities and average hospitals over the past eight years. Hospitals are building organizational infrastructure to support patient safety work, using data from their incident-reporting systems to determine specific areas for process improvements, and assessing their own progress toward achieving practice sustainability. However, little action was found in ambulatory care or long-term care settings, at least in part due to lack of existing science and tools. Pockets of formal community-wide collaboration can be found, even in very competitive health care markets. Perhaps the most important caution was in the area of measurement. Most respondents reported that current measurement efforts are imperfect and, as "unfunded mandates," may be actually putting patient safety practice at risk by siphoning off resources that could be better spent on addressing safety issues identified as priorities in each hospital. Opportunities for AHRQ leadership are suggested in many of these findings.

USE OF THE HOSPITAL SURVEY ON PATIENT SAFETY CULTURE (Chapter 3)

Specific Aims

1. To develop information on hospitals' motivation and experiences in using the Hospital Survey on Patient Safety Culture (HSOPS).

2. To understand the extent to which the HSOPS has contributed to hospitals' patient safety efforts.

3. To provide feedback to AHRQ on how it might modify the survey questionnaire or offer technical support to enhance the usefulness of HSOPS to hospitals and other users.

One of the major tools that AHRQ developed to help health care providers improve their patient safety culture and practices is the set of Surveys on Patient Safety Culture (SOPS). The first survey developed was the HSOPS. AHRQ also has established a benchmarking database for SOPS data, which is being managed by Westat. Since 2007, annual HSOPS comparative database reports have been published that provide data on HSOPS scores for participating hospitals (Sorra et al., 2007, 2008).

We worked with a sample of 17 hospitals from across the country that had submitted their culture survey data to the HSOPS benchmarking database. We conducted telephone interviews with representatives from these hospitals and two other related organizations, through which we gathered information on the hospitals' experiences in using the survey. We documented the actions or changes that occurred in their organizations as a result of their use of survey information. We also drew upon information from Westat's analysis of survey data to help inform the interpretation of the interview results. As a result of our collaboration with Westat in carrying out this work, our results will be useful for its technical support work as well as for policy considerations.

Key Results

In general, the hospitals we interviewed were pleased with the AHRQ Hospital Survey on Patient Safety Culture: the contents of the survey, ease of administration, usefulness to their patient safety strategies and activities, and availability of the national benchmarking data. Not surprisingly, the hospitals varied in how they administered the survey and used the data, as well as in the extent to which they needed and sought assistance in working with it from Westat and other external organizations. From the perspective of patient-safety strategy, hospitals reported that they used HSOPS as a key measurement and monitoring tool in their patient safety initiatives. These findings suggest that the survey was being put to good use in the field.

The interviews also yielded valuable insights regarding possible actions that AHRQ and Westat could take to enhance the value of HSOPS and the benchmarking database for hospitals. We also identified that an increasing number of hospitals were working with external organizations for survey administration and related technical support, which could reduce future demand for benchmarking and technical assistance from Westat, despite hospitals' positive feedback about the support provided by Westat. This information needs to be considered carefully in planning future roles for national-level technical assistance roles, to find creative approaches for gaining synergy between what is provided nationally with what other support organizations are providing.

NATIONAL SURVEY ON ADOPTION OF NQF SAFE PRACTICES (Chapter 4)

Specific Aims

1. To support efforts to monitor and assess the extent to which safe practices are being adopted in the national health care community by creating a national-level survey on hospitals' use of safe practices.

2. To provide AHRQ with supportive information about the survey that it can use as it adinisters and updates the survey in the future.

The greatest challenge in developing data on the diffusion of patient safety practices in the U.S. health care system has been the inability to measure effectively the extent to which each practice actually is being used by providers. Therefore, we saw development of data collection instruments as the first important step to take in this area. We have developed a survey questionnaire that addresses the majority of the set of safe practices endorsed by the NQF (NQF, 2007), which can be administered to a national sample of U.S. hospitals.[2]

Survey Development and Testing

A 93-item questionnaire was developed, tested through cognitive interviews with four hospitals, and then validated by comparing the survey items for each practice to information from the 15 hospitals interviewed in the community study on how hospitals actually implemented that practice. We first determined which of the 30 NQF safe practices were amenable to assessment with a standardized, self-administered survey of hospitals. We used the standard that a safe practice was not amenable to assessment through a hospital survey if the central component of the practice necessitates observation or chart data to ensure that implementation has occurred. Through a detailed review of each practice, we concluded that 22 of the 30 safe practices could be assessed using an organization survey.

We then created seven groupings of these 22 safe practices based on similarity of topic and hospital function that would use them. This was done for the twofold purpose of providing a framework for organizing the safe practices in the survey and for exploring a modular sampling strategy to reduce data collection burden on hospitals. These groupings were patient safety culture, communication with patients or families, transparency across continuum of care, surgery procedures, medical evaluation and prevention, medication safety management, and workforce.

---

[2] The National Quality Forum is a national organization that reviews and approves health-quality measures, using a consensus process, with the goal of establishing national standards of measurement.

For each safe practice included in the survey, we drafted a set of survey items. Our primary goal was to stay true to the intention, and—as much as possible—to the actual language of each safe practice, as outlined in the Safe Practice Update document (2007). Our core survey-development team consisted of two health services researchers and two staff from the RAND Survey Research Group. Throughout this process, we consulted with clinicians and other RAND researchers with expertise in patient safety, hospitals, and organization surveys.

We conducted cognitive-testing interviews with teams of staff at four hospitals—two in the Los Angeles area and two in the Pittsburgh area. In advance of the interview, each hospital was sent a subset of the draft survey items to be addressed in the interview, which represented approximately two-thirds of the survey. All hospitals received the patient safety culture group, and we divided the remaining practice groups in the survey among the four hospitals.

After revising the draft survey based on cognitive-testing results, we then validated the survey items using data collected in the roundtable discussions with the 15 hospitals that participated in our community study, as discussed above. The goals were to (1) assess how well the survey questions "fit" how hospitals actually implement and use each practice, and (2) solicit specific comments on individual survey items. The written notes from the roundtable discussions were reviewed in detail by a researcher on our survey development team, to identify themes and issues regarding implementation of each safe practice and assess the extent to which the survey questions were consistent with hospitals' actual practice. The core survey-development team then discussed these validation findings as a group.

This questionnaire is now ready for updating and pilot testing before use in a full national survey. The results of this work, presented in Chapter 4, include suggestions for pilot tests and fielding of the survey.

Key Results

Our findings from the cognitive interviews and validation process suggest that, in general, respondents understood the questions and that the questions obtained the desired information about the hospital's patient-safety activities. Hospital responses also identified weak or unclear areas of the survey, which we addressed in subsequent revisions. The pilot test should be used to further examine interpretation of key phrases, definitions, and item intent (e.g., Do terms and phrases have consistent meaning across respondents? Do respondents have uniform understanding of item content?).

Hospitals frequently are asked to complete surveys, and in our discussions with them, many expressed significant resistance to completing yet another survey. Through the testing we conducted, we found that completion of the entire survey requires approximately 2 to 3 hours. However, this preliminary estimate was extrapolated based on hospitals' completion of only parts of the survey, not the entire survey. The pilot study also should test overall hospital and individual respondent burden to complete the survey in its entirety, and determine the survey administration cost per completed survey.

NQF periodically updates its set of safe practices, and indeed it published a revised set of safe practices in March 2009. Therefore, careful consideration should be given to revising the current survey version. It is important to ensure that the survey reflects up-to-date evidence and recommendations; nevertheless, any proposed changes will need to be weighed against the ability to estimate trends, given the importance of being able to conduct longitudinal analyses.

TRENDS FOR PATIENT SAFETY OUTCOMES (Chapter 5)

Specific Aims

1. Continue much of the outcome trend analysis performed during the third and fourth years of the patient safety evaluation, adding data for the years 2004 and 2005 to the trends. Any effects of the patient safety initiative on outcomes might begin to be seen in these two years.

2. Perform additional geographic analyses to identify possible patterns of outcome differences or changes in relation to possible patterns of diffusion of safe practices in the health care system (e.g., in multihospital systems).

Our work in evaluating patient safety outcomes followed two tracks during the two-year assessment focusing on practice adoption. These analyses for patient safety outcomes complement other analyses of changes in uses of safe practices and event-reporting activities, by addressing another key dimension of effects related to patient safety activities.

First, we continued to estimate trends on several patient outcomes measures based on inpatient-encounter or reporting-system data. For the first time in our outcome analyses, this year we also sought to identify changes in the trend lines for the measures used, because we had two years of post-baseline data to examine. We have used 2003 as the end of the baseline period (the earliest time at which we estimate the patient safety activities across the country might begin to show effects on patient outcomes). Second, we pursued several analytic projects, including an investigation of patterns by which changes in patient safety outcomes might diffuse across organizations in the health care system, and an analysis of differences among hospitals in trajectories of change for their patient safety measures.

Key Results

Results of our most recent trend analyses for the AHRQ Patient Safety Indicators (PSIs) as measures of patient outcomes, offer some hope for potentially being able to observe, within a few years, statistically significant reductions in rates for some of the PSIs we have tracked. Our analyses presented in this report now include data for two years following 2003 (the last year in the baseline period we defined). We observed slight downward changes in national rates for four of the PSIs, relative to their baseline trends, but because of the small sizes of changes and limited number of years of post-baseline data, it is too early to tell if those changes are real. Additional years of data will be needed to detect statistically significant changes.

The preferred types of measures for monitoring changes in outcomes over time are those for which objective data are available on a national level, and which can yield estimates that are robust in completeness, validity, and reliability, both in any given year and in trends over time. As we have worked with currently available outcome measures, however, we have found that many of these measures are vulnerable to measurement challenges.

This finding leads us to conclude that, to be effective, the monitoring process for AHRQ's patient safety initiative should track trends in both patient-outcome measures and the implementation of safe practices that are supported by scientific evidence as being effective in reducing harm to patients. As adoption of such evidence-based practices grows over time, it may be inferred that the practices are leading to improved patient outcomes, many of which may not be detectable in the outcome measures selected for national monitoring.

Some important opportunities remain for future action by AHRQ. Ambulatory and long-term care settings continue to be a high priority for measure-development efforts. State-level reporting systems also present a priority for refining and harmonizing adverse-event measures, ultimately in support of the ability to aggregate reported data on a regional or national basis. Inconsistency in coding of administrative data and lack of continuity in measurement definitions for the PSIs remain serious concerns in ongoing efforts to use these data.

SUGGESTED APPROACH FOR MONITORING EFFECTS OF THE PATIENT SAFETY INITIATIVE (Chapter 6)

Specific Aim

1. To provide suggestions to AHRQ regarding the structure and processes for a program of ongoing monitoring of patient safety outcomes, performed either by itself or through an external contractor, after the work of the Patient Safety Evaluation Center is completed.

We anticipate that AHRQ will continue its own monitoring efforts after our evaluation effort ends. Such national monitoring would provide policymakers and the public with transparency regarding the status of patient safety in the U.S. health care system. It also would enable AHRQ to assess effects of its own investments in patient safety and develop a better understanding of which initiatives are most effective in promoting patient safety.

Components of a Suggested Monitoring Program

As a result of our work on the product evaluation, one of our key conclusions is that the monitoring process for AHRQ's patient safety initiative should continually assess

- Implementation of safe practices
- Patient-outcome measures
- Effects on other stakeholders.

The safe practices of interest are those that are supported by scientific evidence as being effective in reducing patient harm. As growth in the adoption of evidence-based safe practices is observed over time, it may be inferred that these practices are improving patient outcomes, many of which may not be detectable in the outcomes measures selected for national monitoring.

A monitoring program should examine, at a minimum, how the nation's patient safety activities are affecting the range of stakeholders involved, in addition to patients. If such an examination is not done, important effects that merit attention could be missed. Further, by tracking trends in adoption of key patient safety practices, it is possible to infer that progress is being made in the right direction, which, eventually, should be manifested in improved patient outcomes (if the practices are evidence-based).

The monitoring program we are suggesting consists of four components: tracking trends in patient safety-practice adoption, tracking trends in relevant patient outcomes, assessing effects on other stakeholders, and assessing how the AHRQ patient safety initiative has been contributing to these three types of effects.

Capabilities Needed for Effective Monitoring

Through our exploratory analyses of effects of national patient safety activities on relevant outcomes, we identified a number of issues that are barriers to achieving valid and reliable measures that can be monitored with confidence. In our discussion of needed monitoring-system capabilities, we examine these issues and possible ways to address them:

Establishing appropriate patient-outcomes measures

- The need for measures for other settings, beyond hospital inpatient care
- Improving measures of adverse events from event reporting systems
- Adding measures of patient and family safety experiences on Consumer Assessment of Healthcare Providers and Systems (CAHPS®) surveys
- Establishing measures of practice adoption.

Establishing valid measures

- Validating existing patient-outcomes rate measures
- Validating event-reporting measures

Consistent definitions and calculation of measures

- Defining *patient safety event* to eliminate conflicting approaches
- Correcting coding issues for the PSIs
- Developing additional data sources, especially in ambulatory care and long-term care.
- Improving measurement consistency across state event-reporting systems.

Appropriate trending methods for the PSIs

We suggest that AHRQ take the following related steps to achieve credible estimates for outcomes trends for the PSIs:

- Any publication of updated PSI definitions or algorithms should include not only a full version history, describing all updates and changes, but also the rationale behind those changes.
- Any longitudinal-tracking effort (e.g, annual *National Health Quality Report*) should state explicitly which version of the indicators is being used, and the effect of any minor updates to the indicators should be examined and published as well.
- When major revisions are made to the PSIs, retrospective analyses may be needed to see how new definitions affect old years of data: major measurement changes may make old years of published summary statistics noncomparable to more-recent years of data.

Transparency in Public Reporting of Trends

From our analyses of trends in the PSI measures, we identified several issues regarding the public reporting that AHRQ has performed for these measures. We believe these issues merit attention. AHRQ has been reporting publicly on health care quality for a number of years through its annual *National Health Quality Report* (NHQR), including trends for some PSIs and other measures of patient safety outcomes. However, recent NHQRs have moved away from providing explanations of how their small set of reported measures have been drawn from the many available measures. In addition, for the patient-safety outcome measures it does cover, the NHQR has not discussed the methods used and limitations for sampling, data, or measure computation. We suggest that future NHQRs could be made more helpful by

- Providing a clearer explanation of which patient safety measures are included in the print version versus online version
- Providing additional technical background information on the sampling, data, and methodological issues that qualify the interpretation of trends in patient safety outcomes

- Presenting more than a few years of data on each measure, to provide a more-accurate perspective regarding patterns of safety outcomes over time.

DISCUSSION

Although it is important for AHRQ to measure effects of its initiative on patient safety activities and outcomes in the U.S. health care system, such measurement has been shown to be difficult for several reasons. One challenge is the limited availability of tools to measure many of the salient effects at a national level—in particular, the adoption of safe practices and effects on a variety of stakeholder groups. The most developed measures are for patient outcomes, but even these are available primarily for hospital inpatient care, with few measures available for ambulatory care or long-term care settings. Further, measurement of patient outcomes remains fraught with issues related to changes over time in measure definitions and coding.

Another challenge is AHRQ's limited funding relative to the magnitude of the patient safety problem, which has limited AHRQ's ability to have a strong influence on outcomes measured at the national level. AHRQ has taken a collaborative approach of working in partnership with many other organizations to effect patient safety improvements. This strategy effectively leverages its limited funding, but it also makes it difficult to attribute any observed changes in outcomes specifically to AHRQ's efforts. Such attribution might be most feasible for effects from the AHRQ-funded patient safety projects; many of these projects would not have happened without AHRQ funding.

AHRQ showed foresight in providing for an analysis on the diffusion of safe-practice adoption at the end of the Patient Safety Evaluation Center contract. The results of this two-year analysis, which are presented in this report, serve as a good "first step" in this assessment process. From the community study, we know that average U.S. communities have indeed been making progress in adopting safe practices, using a variety of approaches, and we have extended the evidence that most of the activity has been in the hospital inpatient sector. Most of this activity has occurred in only the most recent 3 to 5 years, however, and as the providers readily attest, they are still some distance from achieving sustainable safety practices and outcomes. We also have learned that many hospitals across the country are successfully using one of the major tools that AHRQ has developed and supported—the HSOPS—and that this survey is contributing to their patient safety strategies as both a diagnostic and monitoring tool.

Despite this observed progress, our work here has reconfirmed that much remains to be done. More work is needed to develop tools and measures for patient safety in the ambulatory care and long-term care sectors, as well as to establish a national capability to monitor changes in patient safety infrastructure, practices, and effects on a variety of involved stakeholders. Moving forward on future monitoring activities, we encourage AHRQ to use the product-evaluation model to guide its work on tracking practice-adoption activities and their effects on various stakeholder groups. Over time, AHRQ can use the model to ensure that its assessments have considered all of the key system components and stakeholder groups.

ACKNOWLEDGMENTS

We gratefully acknowledge the participation of numerous individuals in the various studies we conducted in assessing the diffusion of safe practices and related outcomes by health care providers across in the United States. The development process for the Hospital Safe Practice Survey questionnaire was enriched by consultation from staff at the Leapfrog Group and the NQF Safe Practices Workgroup, as well as by the thoughtful and candid feedback from hospitals in our cognitive testing and validation of the questionnaire. We have generated a stronger product as a result of their involvement.

Likewise, we extend thanks to the many community leaders we interviewed during the community study, and who provided us with a wealth of information on patient-safety activities and issues in their communities. We also appreciate the generosity of the many staff at the hospitals we visited, who spent a full day with us and candidly shared their experiences, successes, and challenges in their pursuit of patient-safety performance improvements. The rich insights they provided will be useful to other health care providers, as well as to policymakers.

We experienced similar generosity from representatives of other hospitals who willingly participated in our interviews and shared their experiences in using the AHRQ Hospital Survey on Patient Safety Culture (HSOPS), how their survey results led to patient safety improvements, and the role the survey plays in their overall patient safety work. They imparted valuable information that helped us explore how changes in patient safety culture are diffusing in the hospital sector, and they also provided feedback that should help AHRQ and its contractor to refine HSOPS and related technical support.

Thank you also to our AHRQ project officer, James Battles, who has continued to be an active guide and supporter of our work, in both the original evaluation and this two-year work focusing on the diffusion of patient safety practices. We also thank our RAND colleagues Scott Ashwood, Evan Raff, Erin Dela Cruz, and Stacy Fitzsimmons for their indispensable contributions to our data-collection and analysis processes, and to production of this report. Finally, we thank Marjorie Pearson, Veronica Nieva, and Elizabeth Yano for their helpful comments on an earlier draft of this report. Any errors of fact or interpretation in this report remain the responsibility of the authors.

CHAPTER 1.
INTRODUCTION AND BACKGROUND

In early 2000, the Institute of Medicine (IOM) published the report entitled *To Err Is Human: Building a Safer Health System*, calling for leadership from the U.S. Department of Health and Human Services (DHHS) in reducing medical errors, and identifying the Agency for Healthcare Research and Quality (AHRQ) as the lead agency for patient safety research and practice improvement (IOM, 2000). Soon thereafter, the U.S. Congress funded AHRQ, in the Department of Health and Human Services, to establish a national patient safety initiative. This initiative represents one of numerous, important patient safety efforts being undertaken by organizations across the country in which AHRQ has played a leadership role. It has done so by funding a portfolio of patient safety research and implementation projects to expand knowledge in this area, providing motivation and guidance for the activities of others, and integrating its work with that of other public and private organizations to achieve synergy through collaboration.

AHRQ contracted with RAND in September 2002 to serve as the Patient Safety Evaluation Center (evaluation center). The evaluation center was responsible for performing a longitudinal evaluation of the full scope of AHRQ's patient safety activities and for providing regular feedback to support the continuing improvement of this initiative. This evaluation was completed in September 2006, culminating in a final report that presents evaluation findings over the full four-year evaluation period (Farley et al., 2008b). The final report was preceded by three annual reports, each of which documents the status of the patient safety initiative as of September 2003, 2004, and 2005 (Farley et al., 2005; Farley et al., 2007a; Farley et al., 2007b).

The evaluation center then undertook another two years of work in 2007 and 2008 to document and analyze the extent to which patient safety infrastructure and practices were being put into place across the nation's health care system, and the effects they were having on involved stakeholders. The goal of the work was to begin to assess progress in effecting changes in patient safety practices and outcomes. This report presents the results of that work, consisting of four specific assessments that developed information on the country's progress in adoption of safe practices and improving patient safety. In this chapter, we present the framework used to guide the product evaluation, and we introduce these assessments. Subsequent chapters present the results of each assessment.

FRAMEWORK FOR THE PATIENT SAFETY EVALUATION

The study results presented in this report are products of the final phase of work for the Patient Safety Evaluation Center. These analyses focus on one component of the overall framework within which the overall evaluation was performed. Called the product evaluation, this component is the assessment of the effects of the AHRQ patient safety initiative on safety activities and outcomes in the U.S. health care system. We describe here the overall framework for the evaluation and how the product evaluation fits within it.

Overall Framework

The overall evaluation design was based on the Context-Input-Process-Product (CIPP) evaluation model, a well-accepted strategy for improving systems that encompasses the full spectrum of factors involved in the operation of a program (Stufflebeam et al., 1971; Stufflebeam

Madaus, and Kellaghan, 2000). The core model components are represented in the CIPP acronym:

- **_Context evaluation_** assesses the circumstances stimulating the creation or operation of a program as a basis for defining goals and priorities and for judging the significance of outcomes.
- **_Input evaluation_** examines alternatives for goals and approaches for either guiding choice of a strategy or assessing an existing strategy against the alternatives, including congressional priorities and mandates, as well as agency goals and strategies; stakeholders' perspectives are also assessed.
- **_Process evaluation_** assesses progress in implementation of plans relative to the stated goals for future activities and outcomes; activities undertaken to implement the patient safety initiative are documented, including any changes made that might alter its effects, positively or negatively.
- **_Product evaluation_** identifies consequences of the program for various stakeholders, intended or otherwise, to determine effectiveness and provide information for future program modifications.

A Nested Process-Evaluation Framework

Because of the size and complexity of the patient safety initiative, we identified the need to develop a second logic model within the larger CIPP framework to guide the process evaluation. Such a model enabled the evaluation to "tell the story" of the implementation of the AHRQ patient safety initiative in a way that was intuitively accessible to AHRQ staff and other policymakers who would use the evaluation results. Specifically, the model helped the evaluation (1) track a changing mix of activities over time and assess their contributions to the overall initiative, (2) summarize the overall effects of the initiative through the collective contributions of its multiple activities, and (3) examine how AHRQ's initiative contributed to the larger set of patient safety activities undertaken across the country, with AHRQ both as leader and partner.

As shown in Figure 1.1, the framework consists of five key system components that work together to bring about improved practices and safer health care for patients. AHRQ is engaged in all of these system components at the national level, as are numerous other key organizations. In the process evaluation, we organized our evaluation results by these five components and examined the collective contributions of AHRQ-sponsored activities in strengthening each component. The system components are defined as follows:

Monitoring Progress and Maintaining Vigilance. Establishment and monitoring of measures to assess performance improvement progress for key patient safety processes or outcomes, while maintaining continued vigilance to ensure timely detection and response to issues that represent patient safety risks and hazards.

Knowledge of Epidemiology of Patient Safety Risks and Hazards. Identification of medical errors and causes of patient injury in health care delivery, with a focus on vulnerable populations.

Development of Effective Practices and Tools. Development and field-testing of patient safety practices to identify those that are effective, appropriate, and feasible for health care organizations to implement, taking into account the level of evidence needed to assess patient safety practices.

Building Infrastructure for Effective Practices. Establishment of the health care structural and environmental elements (e.g., culture, information systems) needed for successful implementation of effective patient safety practices, including an organization's commitment and readiness to improve patient safety, hazards to safety created by the organization's structure (e.g., physical configurations, procedural requirements), and effects of the macro-environment on the organization's ability to act (e.g., legal and payment issues).

Achieving Broader Adoption of Effective Practices. The adoption, implementation, and institutionalization of improved patient safety practices to achieve sustainable improvement in patient safety performance across the health care system.

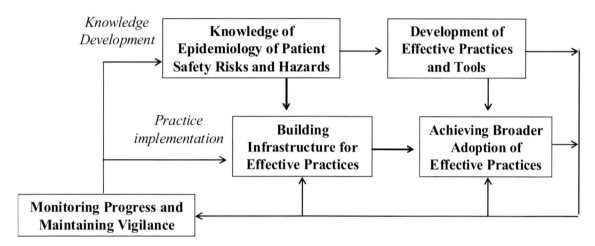

Figure 1.1 The Components of an Effective Patient Safety System

The system component for monitoring progress and maintaining vigilance is identified first and placed on the bottom left side of the figure, reflecting the need for early data on patient safety issues to help guide intervention choices, as well as ongoing feedback regarding progress in developing knowledge and implementing practice improvements. The top row of the figure contains the two components that contribute to *knowledge development* regarding patient-safety epidemiology and effective practices and tools. This knowledge is then used in the remaining two model components, which contribute to *practice implementation*—building infrastructure and adopting effective practices (in the second row of the figure).

Product Evaluation Framework

As described above, the fourth component of the CIPP program evaluation model is the product evaluation, within which we assessed the consequences of the patient safety initiative for various stakeholder groups. Our focus is on stakeholder effects that arise from actions taken for the *practice implementation* aspect of the system framework identified in Figure 1.1—the two components of infrastructure development and adoption of effective practices (see also Farley et al., 2008b). Successful implementation of actions in these areas should lead to outcomes of improved practices by providers, fewer adverse events, and reduced harm to patients.

To guide our product evaluation work, we built upon the framework in Figure 1.1 to define the logic model for patient safety effects shown in Figure 1.2. According to this model,

3

actions taken in the health care system for development of infrastructure should lead to adoption of effective patient safety practices by providers (both from Figure 1.1) and these, in turn, should achieve improved outcomes for patients. Both infrastructure development and practice adoption also affect other stakeholders involved in the initiative to create a safer health care system, including providers, states, organizations involved in patient safety, and the federal government.

This model is a simplified representation of the actual dynamics involved in moving from actions to effects, which are complex and inter-related, with often interacting effects of the various stakeholders involved. While we recognize these limitations, the framework enables us to explicitly identify the key components of these dynamic processes for consideration in the evaluation as well as in future work by AHRQ.

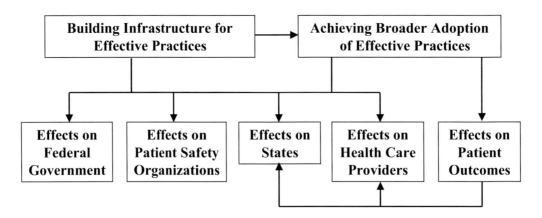

Figure 1.2 Conceptual Framework of Potential Effects of National Patient Safety Activities

To track effects of national patient safety activities on patient outcomes and effects on other stakeholders, identifying measures to be tracked, drawing from sets of already-developed measures, is one of the first steps required. We established the following criteria that should be met by selected measures, to be useful for evaluating changes in patient outcomes and other effects on infrastructure, practices, and various stakeholders:

- Contribute to covering key patient safety issues across the scope of health care practices and settings
- Contribute to covering a range of effects on stakeholders, as well as the practices in the field that yield those effects
- Provide information on a regional or national basis
- Can be measured with data from existing and available sources
- Allow tracking of trends longitudinally, ideally including several years of baseline data preceding the start of the patient safety initiative.

Presented in Table 1.1 are several types of measures that we identified that could be used to track progress in infrastructure development and use of patient safety practices. These measures reflect the activities currently under way by AHRQ and other organizations to establish reliable data on patient safety practices and outcomes.

Table 1.1
Potential Measures of Infrastructure Development and
Use of Patient Safety Practices for the Product Evaluation

Types of Measure	Potential Data Source	Availability
Development of Infrastructure		
Organizational collaboration on patient safety issues and strategies	RAND network analysis	Yes (data for 2004 and 2006)
Adoption of state-based reporting systems using IOM standards	State-based patient safety reporting systems	Yes (Beckett et al., 2006)
Use of NQF patient safety events in state reporting systems	State-based patient safety reporting systems	Yes (Beckett et al., 2006)
Adoption of adverse event reporting systems by hospitals	AHRQ Survey on Hospital-Based Adverse Event Reporting	Yes (survey-data for 2005; again in 2009) (Farley et al., 2008a)
Safe practices for which tools are developed for implementation	Use of TeamSTEPPS (AHRQ, 2007); toolkits developed by AHRQ grantees	No data yet on usage of tools
Improved patient safety culture in hospitals	AHRQ Hospital Survey on Patient Safety Culture (SOPS) (2005b)	Yes (SOPS database)
Legal protections for reporting	Review of state laws; PSO legislation	Yes (2005 legislation)
Use of Effective Patient Safety Practices		
Adoption of NQF safe practices by hospitals	1. Leapfrog surveys of patient safety practices	Leapfrog data reported
	2. AHRQ Survey on Hospital Adoption of NQF Safe Practices (developed by RAND as described in Chapter 4)	AHRQ survey not yet fielded
Adoption of patient safety practices defined in Joint Commission (2007)	Some are NQF safe practices, so data from Leapfrog survey or AHRQ survey	Leapfrog-reported data
Survey data on a variety of safe medication practice issues	Some are NQF safe practices, so data from Leapfrog survey or AHRQ survey	Leapfrog-reported data
Use of risk-assessment methods	TBD: hospitals, ambulatory care, long-term care sources	Not yet
Completed teamwork training	Use of TeamSTEPPS	No data yet on usage of TeamSTEPPS
Patient safety taught in residencies	TBD: hospitals, residencies	Not yet

TBD = to be determined as measurement capability develops
NQF=National Quality Forum; PSO=Patient Safety Organization

One identified measure is the AHRQ Hospital Survey on Patient Safety Culture (HSOPS), which is now being used by hospitals across the country, many of which are reporting data into the HSOPS database (see Chapter 3). Another is the TeamSTEPPS package, developed by AHRQ and the Department of Defense, which has been made available to providers for implementation, and AHRQ also has implemented the Patient Safety Organization (PSO) program under provisions of the Patient Safety and Quality Improvement Act of 2005 (Public

Law 109-41, 2005). The measures also include some that were developed as part of the patient safety evaluation. These include the RAND network analysis (Farley et al., 2008b; Mendel et al., 2009), and the fielding of the AHRQ Survey on Hospital-Based Adverse Event Reporting Systems in 2005 (Farley, Haviland, et al., 2008a).

In our product evaluation work during the four-year evaluation, we specifically focused on patient outcome effects while starting to identify effects on other stakeholders, specifically on organizations involved in the AHRQ-funded patient safety projects (Farley et al., 2008b; Greenberg et al., 2009). Our continued product evaluation work in 2007 and 2008 has expanded to include assessment of practice adoption, and we also continued trend analyses for patient outcomes.

ANALYSES PRESENTED IN THIS REPORT

A product evaluation (the final component of the CIPP evaluation model) should consider effects of the national patient safety initiative on health system structures, practices, and stakeholders participating in the system, including effects on patient outcomes. Thus, our product evaluation included analysis of the extent of both adoption of patient safety practices and trends in related outcomes across the United States. We strategically selected our most recent analyses to address the following priority information needs for AHRQ:

- **Provide AHRQ with timely information on what health care providers are doing with adoption of safe practices.**

What we did. We performed case studies of four communities across the country, using qualitative data-collection and analytic methods to examine the extent of use of safe practices at the community level (presented in Chapter 2). The case-study approach was chosen because it could generate the most timely data, given that no instrument was available yet for collecting quantitative data on safe practice use rates by providers. We selected four communities that have been studied by the Center for Studying Health System Change (HSC) and also are part of the patient safety initiative operated by the Leapfrog Group. We collected information on how local communities are moving forward with adoption of patient safety practices among health care providers, and identified the dynamics and issues that might guide future data collection on practice diffusion for a broader number of providers. We conducted telephone interviews with health care leaders in those communities, and performed site visits with 15 hospitals in the communities.

The data obtained were analyzed to characterize the extent to which the communities had implemented initiatives to improve patient safety practices, including use of tools developed by AHRQ. This approach enabled us to draw upon information already collected by the HSC on the community environments and providers, and to relate choices and progress in practice adoption to characteristics of the providers and the environments in which they deliver care.

- **Provide AHRQ with useful feedback on the experiences of providers in using at least one of the major tools AHRQ has developed to support their patient safety practices.**

What we did. We examined the experiences of hospitals that used the AHRQ Hospital Survey on Patient Safety Culture (presented in Chapter 3). We also considered examining use of the TeamSTEPPS package, but we determined that it was too early because AHRQ still was introducing TeamSTEPPS to the field at the time of this evaluation work.

We worked with a sample of 17 hospitals that had submitted their culture-survey data to the HSOPS benchmarking database, which is managed by Westat under contract to AHRQ. Through interviews with representatives from these hospitals and two other related organizations, we gathered information on the hospitals' experiences in using the survey and documented the actions or changes that occurred in their organizations as a result of their use of information generated by the survey. We also drew upon information from Westat's analysis of survey data to help inform the interpretation of the interview results. Because of our collaboration with Westat in carrying out this work, our results will be useful for its technical support work, as well as for policy considerations.

- **Develop measurement capability to enable AHRQ to collect trend data on the extent to which safe practices are being used by health care providers.**

What we did. We developed and performed preliminary testing of a questionnaire to use in a national survey of hospitals on adoption of the safe practices endorsed by the National Quality Forum (NQF), from which adoption rates for the various practices could be estimated (presented in Chapter 4). The greatest challenge in developing data on the diffusion of patient safety practices in the U.S. health care system is the inability to estimate national adoption rates of safe practices by health care providers. Therefore, we saw development of data-collection instruments as an important first step to take. The Leapfrog Group has fielded a survey on hospital use of these safe practices, but because its primary purpose is for public reporting of hospital performance and information support for hospital quality-improvement efforts, its results are not nationally representative and it does not generate adoption-rate estimates.

We developed a questionnaire that can be used in a national survey to obtain information from hospitals about their implementation of many of the NQF safe practices released in late 2006. We performed cognitive testing of the draft questionnaire, and we also validated it by comparing the questions in the survey to actual practices by 15 hospitals that participated in our community-based study of safe-practice diffusion. The next step would be to pilot-test the survey, in preparation for AHRQ to perform regular surveys to gather trend data on use of safe practices by hospitals.

- **Update trend information for patient outcomes for use by AHRQ in monitoring progress in improving safety outcomes, including exploration of methods that AHRQ might use to examine underlying patterns of changes in outcomes.**

What we did. Much of the outcome trend analysis performed during the third and fourth years of the patient safety evaluation was continued during these subsequent two years, adding data for the years 2004 and 2005 to the outcome trends (presented in Chapter 5). Any effects of the patient safety initiative on outcomes might begin to be seen in these two years. Additional geographic analyses were performed, continuing the analysis started in 2006 to identify possible patterns of outcome differences or changes in outcomes related to possible patterns of diffusion of safe practices in the health care system (e.g., in multihospital systems).

- **Develop a suggested approach that AHRQ could use to regularly monitor progress being made by the U.S. health care system in improving patient safety practices and outcomes.**

What we did. Drawing upon the full body of work during the evaluation, including the four analyses presented in this report, we have developed a suggested approach for ongoing monitoring by AHRQ of progress in the various aspects of effects on stakeholders (presented in Chapter 6). This approach includes tracking trends in practice-adoption rates, assessing effects on various stakeholders, and tracking trends in patient outcomes (the ultimate outcome of patient safety improvements) (see Figure 1.2). We also have identified a number of relevant measurement issues that require attention. Much more work remains to be done to achieve effective measurement of effects on the various stakeholders identified in the evaluation framework.

CHAPTER 2.
UPTAKE OF PATIENT SAFETY PRACTICES IN FOUR U. S. COMMUNITIES

SPECIFIC AIMS

1. To trace the evolution of patient safety efforts in four U.S. communities that are typical of local health care markets in various regions of the United States. The unit of analysis is the community. The focus was to document patient safety initiatives and trends over time across three specific sectors within each community: hospitals, ambulatory settings, and long-term care facilities.

2. To understand, in particular, how hospitals in those communities made decisions about adoption of safe practices and how they implemented them within their institutions. The unit of analysis was the individual hospital. The focus was to understand how hospitals are implementing the Safe Practices established by the National Quality Forum (2003).

This community study directly examines the extent to which U.S. health care providers are adopting safe practices as of the year 2008. The qualitative, case-study methods used in this study were the best available, given that no instrument yet existed for collection of quantitative data to estimate rates of practice adoption by a nationally representative sample of providers. Indeed, the absence of such an instrument led to our work on developing a questionnaire to measure hospital use of the safe practices established by the NQF, as described in Chapter 4.

The practice-adoption actions are, in themselves, a desired effect of the AHRQ national patient safety initiative, and the adoption process also has effects on the various stakeholders involved. Referring to the framework model presented in Chapter 1, we can see that the information collected in this study contributes to the product evaluation by assessing both aspects of practice adoption: status in adopting practices, and hospital experiences in implementing the practices they identified as priorities for action. It also has the added benefit of capturing the dynamics of the implementation process leading to practice adoption, including which safe practices are being adopted, how organizations are making those choices, and implementation strategies used.

SELECTION OF SITES FOR THE COMMUNITY STUDY

Since 1996, the *Community Tracking Study* (CTS), led by the Center for Studying Health System Change (HSC), has conducted biannual site visits to 12 nationally representative metropolitan areas, to study how the interactions of providers, insurers, and other stakeholders help to shape the accessibility, cost, and quality of health care in local communities (HSC, 2009). In 2002–2003, they conducted a special data collection on patient safety, in which HSC investigators contrasted the patient safety experience of five CTS communities that were also Leapfrog regional rollout communities with the remainder of the CTS communities. The Leapfrog rollout communities were Boston, Massachusetts; Lansing, Michigan; Northern New Jersey, Orange County, California; and Seattle, Washington. The remaining cities were Cleveland, Ohio; Greenville, South Carolina; Indianapolis, Indiana; Little Rock, Arkansas; Miami, Florida; Phoenix, Arizona; and Syracuse, New York. Since 2003, Cleveland, Indianapolis, and Greenville also have become Leapfrog regional rollout communities.

9

We used case-study methods to assess the uptake (adoption) of patient safety practices, as of 2007–2008, in four of the CTS communities that were Leapfrog rollout sites. This study period is eight years after the publication of the IOM's *To Err Is Human* (2000) and the start of the AHRQ patient safety initiative, and it is approximately five years after HSC's special data collection on patient safety.

We chose to use the CTS sites because HSC selected them to be nationally representative, and HSC already has developed a wealth of contextual information about these health markets. In addition, we used the Leapfrog regional rollout sites within the CTS communities because they likely would be pursuing at least some patient safety activities, and we had access to Leapfrog contacts within them to assist in identifying potential interview respondents, as well as Leapfrog survey data for hospitals in those sites.

Criteria for Site Selection

To guide our selection of the four sites for our study, we collected data on the eight candidate CTS/Leapfrog rollout sites from a number of sources, including information from the Community Tracking Study Web site, the Area Resource File (maintained by the Health Resources and Services Administration), and internet searches to identify existing patient safety initiatives within the communities. This information was then sorted into a matrix to display the following key parameters to aid in our decision-making:

1. Demographics (e.g., population, ethnicity, median family income, population age 65 or older, major employers, employment rate, persons living in poverty, percentage Medicare/Medicaid, persons without health insurance, percentage in nursing homes).

2. Health system characteristics (e.g., total number of hospitals, staffed hospital beds per thousand population, penetration of health maintenance organizations (HMOs), Medicare-Adjusted per Capita Costs rate (average cost of care per beneficiary), types of hospitals, major hospitals, concentration of hospital systems, percentage in hospital networks, presence of safety-net providers, total skilled nursing facilities (SNFs), dominant insurers, Medicare managed care penetration rate).

3. Health professionals (e.g., physicians per thousand population, physician specialists per thousand population).

4. Health care utilization (e.g., adjusted inpatient admissions per thousand population, persons with any emergency room visit in past year, persons with any doctor visit in past year, persons who did not get needed medical care in past year, privately insured families with annual out-of-pocket costs of $500 or greater).

5. Patient safety initiatives (at the state, community, and facility levels).

6. Penetration of health information technology (e.g., electronic health records in hospitals, ambulatory care settings, and/or nursing homes; medical records and health information technology technicians per thousand).

Sites Selected for the Community Study

Our goal in selecting the four communities for this study was to achieve diversity in community characteristics. Judging from the data collected on the candidate communities, we chose the following communities for the study, defined as the relevant Metropolitan Statistical Areas:

Indianapolis, Indiana   Cleveland, Ohio
Seattle, Washington   Greenville, South Carolina

All of these four sites demonstrated an adequate level of patient safety activity to provide useful information for the study, with sufficient variation in activities to allow comparisons. In addition, they exhibited a diversity reflective of typical communities in the United States on a number of factors of interest, including demographics, types of patient safety activities, and the organization of local health care services and insurance (see Table 2.1). They also represent different regions of the country.

Table 2.1

Characteristics of the Four Communities Selected for the Study[a]

	Cleveland	Greenville	Indianapolis	Seattle
Demographics				
Population 2004	2,240,000	1,005,000	1,700,000	2,501,000
Percentage African-American, 2003	18.8	17.9	14.3	4.8
Percentage Hispanic/Latino, 2003	3.0	3.1	3.0	5.4
Percentage Asian, 2003	1.6	1.3	1.5	10.5
Percentage age 65+, 2000	14.5	12.3	10.9	10.2
Per-capita income, 2003	$32,775	$27,020	$33,357	$41,357
Health care supply and utilization				
Total Active MDs per 1,000 (nonfederal), 2004	3.9	2.3	3.5	3.5
Total number of hospitals, 2003	36	16	27	28
Percentage in hospital networks (total hospitals), 2003	66.7	43.8	37.0	25.0
Percentage with med. school affiliation, 2003	26.7	27.3	33.3	42.9
Short-term community hospital beds per 1,000, 2003	3.3	2.5	3.1	1.7
Short-term community hosp inpatient days per 1,000, 2003	820.9	671.8	715.1	421.1
Total surgical operations per 1,000, 2003	143.0	103.2	101.0	68.3
Nursing Home capacity				
SNF beds per 1,000, 2004	11.0	4.4	7.0	3.5
Nursing facility beds per 1,000, 2004	0.2	0.0	0.7	0.0
Other health care characteristics				
Federally Qualified Health Centers, 2004	11	8	13	21
HMO penetration rate 1998 (enrollees per total population)	26.3	9.4	22.0	26.8
Medicare Managed Care penetration rate, 2004 (enrollees per eligibles)	16.0	0.3	3.8	21.6
Percentage of population without health insurance, 2000	10.8	12.8	11.2	11.9

[a] Each community's geographic area was defined as its Metropolitan Statistical Area.

Other candidate sites considered were Boston, Northern New Jersey, Orange County, and Lansing. Boston was not selected because its preponderance of academic medical centers and other specialty services make it an outlier compared with other community health systems. Northern New Jersey was not a good candidate because much of the patient safety activity appeared to be the result of top-down regulatory action by the state. Orange County had limited apparent patient safety activity, and Lansing had too few hospitals for our purposes.

DATA COLLECTION

Phase I. The Evolution of Patient Safety Initiatives in the Study Communities

Phase I focused on the first aim of the study—to examine community-level patient safety activities. The primary data-collection method was key informant telephone interviews with boundary spanners[3] in the four communities. Our first step was to identify all stakeholder organizations that have been involved in patient safety in those communities, by working with HSC and the Leapfrog Group, searching Web sites, and reviewing our files on AHRQ initiatives and funding. We started with the organizations and individuals we could identify *a priori* and then used snowball sampling[4] until we identified 10 to 20 boundary spanners in each community who were knowledgeable about the relevant stakeholder groups. These included individuals in local hospitals, ambulatory care, long-term care, health plans, safety-net providers, employers, key government agencies, policymakers, and consumer groups (listed in Appendix A).

Using a semi-structured interview guide for the telephone interviews with the boundary spanners, we focused on understanding the community-level activities and dynamics around patient safety. We asked respondents who the actors were, how much and what types of interactions have occurred among them with respect to patient safety issues, what initiatives have been undertaken, in what settings, what progress has been made to date, and what have been the barriers and facilitators to change, particularly at the community level.

Phase II. Adoption of Safe Practices Within Hospitals in the Study Communities

Phase II focused on the second aim of the study—to examine the uptake of safe practices by hospitals in the four communities. We wanted to understand the main sources of information and influences on patient safety for each hospital, how decisionmakers in the hospital prioritize their patient safety efforts and specific practices, which safe practices they have chosen to implement, and their strategies and experiences in implementing different types of practices. The primary data-collection method for this phase of the study was semi-structured interviews, which we performed during a single site visit to each of the participating hospitals.

We used the following criteria to guide our selection of hospitals for study participation:

- Identified by boundary-spanner interviewees as leaders in patient safety within the community

---

[3] Boundary spanners are individuals within organizations who link their organization with the external environment. These individuals are generally considered efficient sources for information on the dynamics of a network or community (Bradshaw, 1999; Williams, 2002; Ansett, 2005).

[4] Snowball sampling is a technique for developing a research sample whereby existing study subjects help to identify future subjects from among their acquaintances.

- Consistently high scores on the 2006 and 2007 Leapfrog surveys for the safe practices covered in the safe practice survey developed by RAND (see Chapter 4)
- At least one academic medical center, one safety-net hospital and one community hospital in each community
- Represent a variety of other characteristics, including pediatric hospitals, hospitals that were part of a national or regional hospital system, and hospitals that were part of integrated delivery systems.

Our goal was to engage a total of 16 hospitals of different types located within each of our study communities, with four hospitals per community. We were successful in confirming 15 hospitals, four in each of three communities and three in the fourth community (Cleveland). The participating hospitals are profiled by type in Table 2.2. Competing demands and schedule conflicts for the candidate hospitals prevented us from engaging a 16th hospital.

Table 2.2 Types of Hospitals Engaged in the Community Study

Hospital Type	Number of Hospitals
Academic medical center	3
Main hospital in local system	5
Community hospital in local system	2
Independent community hospital	3
Safety net hospital	2

General patient safety activities by hospitals. In this portion of the analysis of hospital patient-safety activities, we collected information on the evolution of patient safety within the hospital, the hospitals' current activities, and how other organizations—such as employers, health plans, or peers—may have affected the practice-adoption efforts. This approach allowed us to explore the diversity of strategies used among hospitals and to identify factors that contribute to, or challenge, successful adoption of safe practices. Such exploration of the dynamics of the processes being studied is one of the strengths of qualitative investigations. From the perspective of the product evaluation, the study generates qualitative information on both positive and negative effects on the various stakeholders involved, which also can be used to develop effective tools for collecting quantitative data on these effects.

During each hospital site visit, individual and group interviews were conducted with hospital leaders knowledgeable about the evolution of the hospital's history and strategy related to patient safety. The respondents included the hospital leadership (e.g., chief executive officer (CEO), chief medical officer, chief of surgery, chief of nursing, chief of pharmacy, chief information officer, or their designees) and the Patient Safety Officer or person responsible for or most knowledgeable about the hospital's patient safety initiatives.

The interviews were conducted using a semi-structured interview guide developed for this study. The following questions represent the key topics covered in the interviews:

1. What was the hospital's starting point for awareness of patient safety issues?
2. How have patient safety priorities been determined over time?
3. Who has been involved, including hospital leaders and patient-safety champions?

4. What has been the influence of external forces and market contexts?

5. What have been the major decision points, high points, and bumps in the road in the hospital's patient safety initiatives?

6. What kinds of infrastructure has the hospital developed for patient safety improvement, and how has it evolved?

7. What have been the main issues in implementing patient safety practices, both challenges and facilitators?

8. To what extent has the hospital's patient safety efforts diffused to other settings (such as ambulatory care and long-term care—if applicable)

Adoption of specific safe practices. We also focused on how hospitals approached adopting specific sets of NQF safe practices, and their experiences in implementing them. Each hospital was asked to discuss two sets of NQF safe practices that they already had adopted. To start the selection, we provided them with a list of the NQF safe practices, organized by groups, including four practices in the overall patient safety culture practices as well as six other practice groups. To ensure that all the practice groups were addressed by at least two hospitals, we suggested groups to each hospital, based on what we already knew about practices they had been implementing. Through discussions with the hospital representative, a final selection was made that was acceptable to the hospital and also satisfied our need for practice coverage. The practice groups addressed by each type of hospital are presented Table 2.3, which shows that a variety of hospital types addressed most of the practice groups.

At the site visit to each hospital, we conducted two roundtable discussions through which we gathered data on how the hospital implemented practices in the two practice groups identified for it. One practice group was discussed in depth at each roundtable, with participation by clinicians and other front-line staff at the hospital who are involved in implementing those practices on a daily basis.

A semi-structured interview format was used to guide each roundtable discussion. First, we asked the respondents to describe all safety practices and activities by their hospital that fell into the safe-practices set being addressed. Then, for each safe practice implemented by that hospital, specific questions included:

1. How did the hospital *operationalize* the safe practice in its setting?
2. Does the hospital have a written *policy*?
3. Does the hospital have a standardized *procedure* to implement the policy?
4. *Who* is responsible for compliance (where does "the buck stop")?
5. Does the hospital have a method to *verify* compliance?
6. Does the hospital have a method to *measure* compliance?
7. Does the hospital collect data?
8. With whom are these data shared?

14

Table 2.3
National Quality Forum Safe Practices Examined at Hospitals Studied, by Hospital Type

	Large local integrated systems	Academic medical centers	Safety net hospitals	Independent community hospitals [a]	Total
Safety Culture					
Leadership	2			1	3
Culture Survey	2	1		1	4
Teamwork	1		1	2	4
Safety Risks		2	1	1	4
Total	5	3	2	5	15
Other groupings					
Communication with Patients and Families				1	1
Transparency Across Continuum of Care	2		1		3
Surgery Procedures	1	1	1		3
Medical Evaluation and Prevention	1	1			2
Medication Safety Management	1	1	1	1	4
Workforce	1			1	2
Total	6	3	3	3	15

[a] Includes one pediatrics hospital.

PHASE I FINDINGS—PATIENT SAFETY INITIATIVES IN THE COMMUNITIES

As described above, we interviewed a cross section of key boundary spanners for each of the communities, including respondents from community coalitions as well as hospitals, ambulatory care, long-term care settings, employers, insurers, government agencies and—when we could identify them—consumer representatives. The complete case studies are provided in Appendix B. In this section, we highlight activities and issues identified for each community and then we summarize our findings across all four communities, enumerating some important lessons learned from these case studies.[5]

We used a three-step process to analyze data from this phase of the community study. First, for each community, we prepared a case study that drew upon both data from the boundary-spanner interviews and other information obtained from Web searches and review of relevant written materials. We developed a standard format that we used to structure all the case studies, which provided for presentation of factual information on activities in a community, as

---

[5] Health care market information included in the individual community summaries was obtained from HSC Community Study Tracking Reports (2005) as well as our interviews.

well as for identification of experiences of those involved and issues encountered. Second, we prepared summaries of highlights from these community case studies (presented below). Finally, by comparing activities, experiences, and issues across the case studies of the four communities, we developed a set of key findings and lessons (also presented at the end of this chapter).

Individual-Community Summaries

Indianapolis

The highly competitive environment in Indianapolis has been feeding expansion activity in the four private hospital systems, all of which have been expanding their facilities both within Indianapolis and into the surrounding suburbs. Clarian Health Partners led the expansion into the suburbs, followed by Community Health Network, St. Vincent's Health System, and St. Francis Hospital & Health Centers. Wishard Health Services, a county-owned hospital and network of community clinics, is the principal safety-net provider. As the number of uninsured patients has increased, Wishard has had to implement some cost-cutting measures, such as a reduction in workforce. After experiencing some financial instability for a number of years, Wishard's current financial outlook has improved.

As the insurer for several large Indianapolis-based companies, including Eli Lilly and the Marsh Supermarkets chain, Anthem BlueCross BlueShield is the dominant health insurer in the market. Meanwhile, national insurers UnitedHealthcare, Aetna, and Humana have been gaining membership at the expense of provider-owned local insurers. Employers in the Indianapolis region have struggled with cost containment and are now shifting costs toward employees and focusing on developing tiered provider networks. There is concern that the higher health care costs seen in Indianapolis and the state, relative to those of other regions in neighboring states, may affect business development in the future.

Of our four sites, Indianapolis is perhaps the best example of a truly community-wide, collaborative approach to improving patient safety in hospitals. The key patient safety initiative within the hospital sector is the Indianapolis Coalition for Patient Safety (ICPS). Begun in 2003, the ICPS brings together the six major hospital systems in the metropolitan Indianapolis area (the four private systems plus the VA Medical Center and Wishard Health Services). What grew into the ICPS began in 2001 as discussions between the CEOs of the major health systems, motivated by the IOM report and based on their prior collaboration in the Indiana Health Information Exchange (IHIE).

The initial goals of working together were very broad and largely educational in scope. However, within a short time, and with the assistance of an outside facilitator, the group decided to initiate specific collaborative patient safety improvement activities across the six member hospital systems. In addition to their own involvement, and having set the tone for cooperation and collaboration, the six CEOs brought their high level administrators (chief medical officers, chief nursing officers, and directors of patient safety and pharmacy) into the coalition as active participants. These individuals play a critical role in setting priorities for the Coalition, implementing specific initiatives, and engaging their hospital staff to participate and make the necessary behavior changes.

The ICPS chose an initial set of initiatives that have occupied them since the inception of their coalition:

- A standard practice for surgical site markings and surgical timeouts

- Improving patient safety related to high-alert medications, such as anticoagulants and insulin
- Implementation of a standard policy for "do not use" abbreviations.

For each initiative selected, the hospitals pool resources, each contributing the time of the high-level administrator who is the most knowledgeable about the practice area. These six administrators form the cross-system workgroup. The workgroup meets regularly to review relevant empirical evidence on the practice, as well as the experience of others who have implemented the practice, and to share information about the current practice at their own individual hospitals. The workgroup then determines what the standard of practice should be for all the ICPS hospitals, and each hospital has the flexibility to implement the practice in a way that best fits in its institution.

Another coalition active in Indianapolis is the statewide Indiana Patient Safety Center (IPSC). The Patient Safety Center was formed on July 1, 2006, with the mission of facilitating the development of safe and reliable health care systems that prevent harm to patients across Indiana. The Patient Safety Center is housed at the Indiana Hospital and Health Association's offices. The work of the IPSC spans the state and the range of health care settings. An upcoming focus for the Center will be to work on a pressure ulcer–prevention initiative involving long-term care settings, along with the state health department and Quality Improvement Organization (QIO). Additionally, the Center is working towards developing, or enabling the development of, regional patient safety coalitions through the state.

Seattle

The major hospital systems in the Seattle area include Swedish Medical Center, Virginia Mason Medical Center, University of Washington Medical Center, Overlake Hospital, and Harborview Medical Center (the main trauma and safety-net provider, affiliated with the University of Washington). Hospitals in the Seattle area have been expanding, both in the core urban Seattle area and in the surrounding suburbs. Physicians have been gravitating toward profitable services (e.g., ambulatory surgery centers, sleep centers, vein clinics, laser surgery), partly to cope with financial pressure resulting from increasing operating costs and relatively low reimbursement levels from health plans and public programs. Financial pressures are also encouraging physicians in smaller practices to join larger groups or seek hospital employment. Safety-net providers are struggling to meet demand as the number of uninsured rises.

Premera Blue Cross is one of the largest insurers in Washington state. Others include Aetna, Regence Blue Shield, and Group Health Cooperative (a staff/group model HMO whose direct services focus on ambulatory care). Under pressure from employers to contain costs, health plans are paying closer attention to measuring provider-network performance. Accordingly, health plan products in Seattle are shifting towards tiered networks with preferential cost-sharing for consumers who choose providers in the high-quality/low-cost tier.

As in Indianapolis, Seattle has a diverse group of health care providers, although in Seattle the competition is less head-to-head and more segmented—either by service (e.g., medical specialties and "centers of excellence") or by geography (e.g., urban versus suburban). Despite the competition, the Seattle health care community has a long history of collaboration and, in particular, community coalitions. This culture of collaboration has been partially attributed to a pervasive voluntary ethos (hospitals are nonprofit) and strong relationships among senior leaders across providers, payers, and government agencies (many of whom trained together locally). Leapfrog has been highly active in the Seattle area, receiving strong support from Boeing Corporation and other local employers.

The main collaboration, the Washington Patient Safety Coalition (WPSC), was founded in 2002 after leaders from the State Department of Health and the Health Care Authority (public health care purchaser) attended an AHRQ-sponsored safety conference. They then approached the Foundation for Healthcare Quality in Seattle to serve as a neutral "home" for the initiative. The focus of the WPSC has been on supporting safety improvement among health care providers and sharing of best practices. The coalition was initially formed around hospital-based Patient Safety Officer s, but has since enlisted a range of participants, including government agencies, insurers, and employers.

In addition, the Washington State Hospital Association has pursued an active patient-safety agenda, including sponsoring specific improvement initiatives, as well as advocacy and policy work on safety-related issues (e.g., public transparency requirements, the state's voluntary infection rate-reporting bill). The following are some of the safe practices it has pursued:

- Rapid response teams
- Hand hygiene
- Medication safety.

The other major health collaboration in the Seattle area is the Puget Sound Health Alliance (PSHA). It similarly represents a coalition of multiple community stakeholders, but was formed through the impetus of local county leadership to address health care quality and cost as a public imperative. The PHSA has focused on ambulatory care, and it has embarked on an ambitious community-wide data sharing and public reporting project of quality indicators in medical practices, as a participating site in Aligning Forces for Quality. More recently, the coalition has attracted participants with a stronger patient safety interest.

Cleveland

The health care delivery market in Cleveland has become highly consolidated since the late 1990s into three major systems—the Cleveland Clinic Health System, University Hospitals Health System, and MetroHealth System (the main public safety-net provider). The dominance of the two major private systems in particular makes Cleveland a distinct market. Both the Cleveland Clinic and University Hospitals are large, integrated providers that aim to offer highly specialized services at a national (and international) level. All these systems, as well as the small number of remaining independent hospitals, are expanding. Much of the expansion is being done to develop more-profitable services, such as cardiac or cancer care. However, other services are also being developed, such as emergency departments, primary care service centers, and intensive care beds.

Budgetary issues with Medicaid, and state and local governments have adversely affected Cleveland's safety-net providers, which have seen increased demand from a growing number of the uninsured. Despite these issues, community health centers in Cleveland have found ways to expand their services.

Medical Mutual of Ohio, Anthem BlueCross BlueShield, and United Healthcare are Cleveland's main insurance carriers. Most recently, these carriers have begun offering consumer-directed health plans with high deductibles coupled with either a Health Reimbursement Account (HRA) or a Health Savings Account (HAS). Because of Cleveland's struggling economy and health care's major role as a source of employment, the major health systems have been receiving attention from local civic leaders.

As in Indianapolis and Seattle, most of the patient safety activity in Cleveland is occurring in the inpatient setting. Unlike the other two communities, however, use of community-based collaborations in Cleveland is currently limited, due in part to the dominance of the two large private health care systems, as well as to community experience with the demise in 1999 of the Cleveland Health Quality Choice program, a high-profile local collaboration for public reporting of hospital quality data. Each of the individual systems has tended to work within its own organizations to implement safety improvements. In general, hospitals have been focusing first on Joint Commission core measures, although they also have addressed issues involved in other major initiatives (e.g., Leapfrog Group) as they emerged. The following are examples of patient safety activities undertaken:

- Magnet status (nursing), which requires ongoing process-improvement activities
- Participation in national initiatives (e.g., NQF, Institute for Healthcare Improvement [IHI])
- Executive walk-arounds in hospital units and departments
- Teaching safety techniques to residents and staff physicians.
- Specific patient safety practices that include medication reconciliation, anti-coagulation medication, hand washing at all sites of care, and regular incident reporting.

Much of the major attention to patient safety in Cleveland has emerged within the past two to three years. Although some efforts by individual institutions preceded that time, they were less cohesive than the more recent activities. Some hospitals took action in anticipation of public-reporting requirements. Often, change was stimulated by a new leader (or leaders) who made patient safety a priority for both boards and staff. Typically, when patient safety became a priority, it was part of a larger quality initiative, which included reorganization of the quality/safety activities to make them more central in the organization, reporting to executive management, and often being run by physicians. Some systems tie financial incentives for management to meeting quality/safety goals. Even with systemwide initiatives in place, the systems often reported that safety activities varied across their individual hospitals.

Greenville

The Greenville hospital market is highly competitive, with three major systems vying for market share in hotly contested suburban regions. These three systems are Greenville Hospital System, Bon Secours St. Francis Health System, and Spartanburg Regional Health System. Additionally, hospitals in the area have increased development of profitable specialty-service centers, such as obstetrics, cardiac services, oncology, and orthopedics. Greenville Hospital System is the leading provider of specialty and hospital-based services. Safety net providers have experienced a surge in demand due to declining Medicaid enrollment and reimbursement, high population growth in the Greenville area, and unwillingness of private providers to serve low-income individuals.

BlueCross BlueShield of South Carolina has historically dominated the Greenville insurance market. Competitors, such as Cigna and Carolina Care Plan, have struggled to maintain their positions because of operational issues resulting in the loss of membership. This loss created an opportunity for UnitedHealthcare to make advancements into the Greenville market. Because the Greenville area is home to larger health systems, contracting relationships between providers and insurers can be contentious, because the large health systems hold a considerable degree of leverage.

Greenville perhaps most resembles Cleveland, in that the market is dominated by a small number of health care systems and most of the patient safety activity is occurring within hospital systems rather than through community coalitions. Each hospital system is pursuing its own agenda, while collaborating informally. The evolution of patient safety activities in the Greenville area has followed a steady progression over a long period of time and has not been punctuated by any defining events with a particularly large effect on the agenda. Public awareness of patient safety issues has provided an additional impetus to address patient safety in recent years and there has been more activity over the past 1–2 years, along with a shift from reacting to regulation and external requirements toward transparency and a culture of safety.

Patient safety activities are generally viewed within the context of larger quality initiatives. Executives at the hospitals are generally strong proponents of the quality and patient safety agendas, and pay close attention to how their own hospital system is performing on available metrics. The hospital systems attempt to anticipate future public reporting or other requirements from external organizations, taking a proactive rather than a reactive approach to external requirements.

The hospitals have focused first on the Joint Commission Core Measures (Joint Commission, 2009) and the related Hospital Quality Initiative measures of the Centers for Medicare and Medicaid Services (CMS) as top priorities. The Leapfrog standards are also a priority at the hospitals. The following are examples of other patient safety activities that have been undertaken by Greenville hospitals:

- Participation in national initiatives (e.g., IHI 5 Million Lives)
- Executive walking rounds
- Use of simulation in training
- IHI bundles for process improvements (acute myocardial infarction [AMI], hand hygiene, surgical infection, etc.)
- Universal medication reconciliation
- Infection control
- Computerized physician order entry [CPOE] and bar coding.

Infection control is an area that has been a particular area of focus among Greenville-area hospitals. This is due in part to public reporting of hospital infection rates per the state Hospital Infections Disclosure Act (South Carolina General Assembly, 2006). However, as recognition of the importance of the problem grew in the region and nationally, infection control activities had become a priority among Greenville-area hospitals before public reporting was mandated.

Key Findings from the Community-Level Case Studies

Although the four communities in which we performed this study varied widely in their approaches and experiences, we found quite a bit of similarity in the lessons that can be drawn from them. A number of common themes emerged that also could be relevant for other communities across the country. We summarize here the experiences of the four communities, and we identify some of the specific lessons that emerged from what we found. We start with coalition activities regarding patient safety improvements in hospitals (which were in general more advanced), and then focus on what we learned about ambulatory and long-term care settings. We also discuss the views of stakeholders and the role of external forces (including AHRQ).

The IOM report, *To Err Is Human*, brought attention to patient safety, sparked discussion across the local communities, and stimulated actions by health care providers. The pace at which providers and others built momentum, however, varied widely across communities, in some cases taking years before actions began.

Patient safety can be "evolutionary" as well as "revolutionary" in nature. It is not always a high-profile adverse event that starts a community or a hospital on the road to change. Even after some progress has been made, there may be tragic events – but they can provide an opportunity to rally around the hospital where the event occurred, reminding everyone that "the job isn't yet done." It also was clear that there is no single "best" approach to addressing patient safety and making local health care safer. In some communities, action was collaborative; in others, hospitals or hospital systems looked inward. Specific key findings are presented below, grouped by topic areas.

Use of Community Patient-Safety Coalitions

Regardless of the structure of the health care market in the communities studied, we found a great deal of activity in the hospital sector for improving patient safety practices. In most of the communities, this activity started soon after the Institute of Medicine published its report *To Err Is Human* in early 2000, although there was earlier activity in some communities, and delay in activities in others.

The amount of community-level coalition or collaborative work being undertaken varied widely across the four communities. There appeared to be less use of coalitions in communities with a health care market that was highly consolidated (i.e., dominated by a very small number of large health care systems). The following specific lessons emerged regarding use of community-level coalitions:

- Competition and collaboration are not mutually exclusive, even in very competitive health care markets. It is possible for competitors to sit at a table together and collaborate around patient safety issues (even as they otherwise compete for market share).

- The communities that made good use of coalitions tended to be those in which the hospital CEOs agreed not to "compete on safety" and were therefore more transparent about serious incidents that had happened within their own institutions.

- The presence of a very small number of large, competitive health care systems in a community affects the approach to patient safety activities, with these systems tending to avoid engagement in collaboration with other stakeholders and to resist efforts by others (e.g., purchasers, insurers) to influence their actions.

- Coalitions were of many types: some involved a broad set of stakeholders (e.g., including payers, employers and consumers); others involved just the health care providers. If the goal is change *within* the health care institution, it is not clear that broader coalitions have any advantage over provider-dominated coalitions.

- Although broad, multi-stakeholder coalitions can help achieve community consensus on patient safety goals and progress, they require time to enlist participants and produce results. It may be especially difficult to determine how to actively integrate nonprovider stakeholders (e.g., insurers, consumers)

Hospital Patient-Safety Activities

Health care organizations reported that they adapt as much patient safety information, products, and guidance as possible from other organizations, for use within their own organizations. They also reported that they set their patient safety priorities based, first, on what they are required to do. Therefore, the patient-safety goals and accreditation standards of the Joint Commission are high priorities for them, as are the performance requirements of Medicare. In particular, providers were responding actively to the new Medicare policy of not paying for hospital-acquired events or conditions.

As hospitals' patient safety work developed, they found they were working with so many new practices ("initiative creep") that they experienced safety practice "overload." The hospitals simply could not respond to all of the external organizations and pressures, and they had to set internal priorities for which practices would be the focus of their safety improvements efforts. They still struggle with how to set priorities in the face of conflicting demands.

The hospitals identified a number of challenges involved in their patient safety efforts. They found that it was difficult to build a blame-free culture in which staff felt safe reporting adverse events. As a result, it took a long time to establish the new culture and achieve changes in staff perceptions and actions. Hospitals also encountered resistance from many physicians to implementing new safe practices and bringing about culture change, and it required time and patience to successfully engage them in the process. The following specific lessons emerged regarding hospital patient-safety activities:

- Hospitals in at least two of the communities did not approach patient safety as a separate set of activities but, instead, embedded their patient safety activities within a larger management process (e.g., quality improvement methods). Identifying medical error in these hospitals was part and parcel of a larger focus on streamlining processes and reducing waste.

- The first patient safety priorities addressed by hospitals tended to be those established by external organizations, such as accreditation bodies, Medicare, other payers, and state agencies. As patient safety became more of a priority, hospital systems became more proactive in setting their own priorities and agenda for change.

- Investment by the hospital CEO in patient safety was seen as necessary but not sufficient to make change happen within an institution. This suggests that, to see change happen at the bedside, all levels of the organization must be actively engaged.

- A visible and empowered Patient Safety Officer—i.e., a single person with purview and authority for all patients safety activities—is critical to moving a patient safety agenda forward on a day-to-day basis.

- An emphasis was given to the need to start with a limited number of issues or initiatives, to establish a foothold and some early successes. Providers warned against trying to do too much in too short a period of time.

22

- Key barriers to making "leaps" forward in patient safety are time, money, culture change, and physician resistance. Physicians tend to buy in to patient safety initiatives more readily when they are employees of the hospitals or their compensation is affected by progress (or the lack of it) on patient-safety goals.

- Hospitals have had success in implementing measurement and public reporting, process improvements and technology, but establishing a culture of safety has been more challenging. Staff turnover and competing priorities make it difficult to maintain patient safety gains.

- Greater standardization of practices across hospitals within a local community holds promise for making substantial improvements in patient safety, especially in communities in which patients tend to use multiple providers and the physicians routinely work in more than one health care institution.

Activity in the Ambulatory Care and Long-Term Care Sectors

For all of the communities studied, patient safety activities in the ambulatory care and long-term care (LTC) sectors were much less developed than those in the hospital sector. Experiences appeared to differ according to whether the ambulatory care or LTC organizations were part of larger, consolidated health care systems or independent organizations.

Ambulatory care practices that were in consolidated systems tended to follow the patient safety priorities set by the system. However, the systems were not yet focusing specifically on ambulatory-care safety issues and priorities; their primary focus was on their hospitals. To the extent that there was much patient safety activity in ambulatory care, it tended to be focused on medication reconciliation.

In some communities, community health centers (safety-net providers of ambulatory care) were more active than private practices in addressing patient safety issues, in part because they were addressing standards required for Joint Commission accreditation.

LTC organizations in consolidated systems also tended to follow the patient safety priorities set by the system. Nursing homes, in particular, could adapt some of the standards and practices created for hospital care to the nursing home setting (e.g., practices related to falls, pressure ulcers, and restraints). However, as for the ambulatory care practices, the systems were not yet focusing on LTC, so only limited activities had been undertaken in most systems.

Freestanding LTC organizations varied in the extent to which they were addressing patient safety. Generally, activities were limited, with some variation among communities. Seattle stakeholders, in particular, reported greater levels of patient safety activity within the long-term care sector, mainly attributed to the state's combination of strong oversight and technical assistance (e.g., visiting quality-assurance nurses), and an active quality and safety improvement program for LTC providers by the state's QIO.

The following specific lessons emerged regarding patient safety activities in ambulatory care and long-term care settings:

- Patient safety activity in ambulatory and long-term care settings, in general, lags behind the hospital setting.

- Multi-institutional health care systems are well positioned to transfer some lessons and practices among their hospitals, ambulatory care, and long-term care facilities, although even in these systems, more attention has been paid to the hospitals than to the other institutions.

Differing Perspectives of Stakeholder Groups

The various stakeholder groups (e.g., providers, patients, purchasers, insurers) in the communities studied tended to have differing perspectives on local patient safety issues and progress being made in addressing them. It appeared that the extent to which the groups agreed (or disagreed) on whether hospitals were improving depended on how much communication existed among the groups. In communities with more coalition activity, the stakeholder groups had shared information and tended to have more similar views on safety progress.

The health care providers tended to focus on their own work as the important focus of patient safety improvement, downplaying the roles of other stakeholder groups. Again, this perspective tended to be stronger in communities with large consolidated systems (and less use of coalitions).

The following specific lessons emerged regarding perspectives of stakeholder groups:

- For communities in which other stakeholders were not involved in patient safety coalitions, and had limited knowledge of what the health care systems are doing, the stakeholders tended to perceive that providers were focusing on "marketing" rather than taking substantive actions to improve safety. This issue highlights the need for active public communication about safety activities by local health care providers.

- Consumer organizations, in particular, were notable by their absence in local patient safety activities. Activism by national consumer organizations was not mirrored at the local level in these communities.

- The media could be a powerful facilitator in increasing awareness of patient safety issues or an adversary. Hospitals may need assistance (e.g., toolkits, training) to work effectively with the media, especially during times of crisis.

Effects of External Factors on Providers' Patient-Safety Activities

A variety of external factors were found to affect how health care providers were approaching patient safety and the action priorities they set. Health care organizations set their patient safety priorities in part on what they are required to do by external organizations. Therefore, the patient safety goals and accreditation standards of such organizations were high priorities for them. In particular, providers respond actively to requirements of the Joint Commission and Medicare.

The role of state-driven coalitions or initiatives varies across communities. Although it is not clear what factors affect involvement in state activities, some possible factors may be the size of the community, the extent of health care consolidation in the community, and the nature of state-local relationships.

AHRQ appears to be both a direct and indirect resource for local health care organizations. The interviewees usually did not identify AHRQ spontaneously as they thought about patient safety resources, but with prompting on a specific product or activity, they generally recognized its importance as a resource. They also reported using a variety of AHRQ products and tools.

Multiple measurement and reporting requirements from various entities (e.g., Medicare, Joint Commission, Leapfrog, state agencies) mean that hospitals spend substantial time on compliance activities that otherwise could be spent in improving safety performance. Hospitals have found conflicts between some of the standards and measures, so they have to choose which of the conflicting standards they should use and which they should ignore. Such conflicting requirements may be harming, rather than improving, safety. Even with these frustrations, the health care organizations reported that they strive to use each reporting process as constructively as possible as an opportunity to learn and improve.

Providers identified national patient safety improvement initiatives (e.g., the 5 Million Lives Campaign of the IHI) as very important for them. Such initiatives focus on priority safety issues and practices, provide structure within which providers can participate, and offer products and tools ready for use by the providers.

Leapfrog has been a primary vehicle for employers to become involved in promoting patient safety in their communities. Hospitals credit the initiative with stimulating change within their organizations, but many view it as extremely unfocused (mixing too many high- and low-priority issues) and are skeptical of the survey data (i.e., self-reported and not audited), of the validity of some of the indicators, and of the general usefulness of the measures for driving behavior of purchasers, health plans or, especially, consumers. For these reasons, some hospitals have begun questioning the value of future participation in the Leapfrog survey, even though most providers consider Leapfrog to have greater staying power than similar past initiatives by employers.

The following specific lessons emerged regarding the influence of external factors on local patient safety activities:

- Accreditation bodies, Medicare, other payers, and state agencies (e.g., public reporting requirements) were important external forces in stimulating safety improvements, as reflected by hospital reports that practices and measures required by these organizations were their first priorities for safety improvement actions.

- A significant evidence base on safety practices and tools needs to be available for each health care setting, to support providers' safety improvement actions. Hospitals are largely adapting patient safety practices developed by other organizations, when they can find them. Such resources are not yet available for ambulatory care and long-term care settings which, to some extent, explains the lack of progress in those areas.

- Both providers and purchasers would like to see a well-documented business case developed for safe practices in all settings, but particularly in ambulatory and long-term care.

- A high priority should be given to integrating current knowledge and best practice on patient safety into medical-school and nursing-school curricula. It was observed that it is easier to "build it in" than to "build it on later."

PHASE II FINDINGS—ADOPTION OF SAFE PRACTICES IN HOSPITALS

As described above for the four communities, we studied practice adoption in 15 hospitals that represented a range of hospital types (e.g., academic medical centers, community hospitals, safety-net hospitals). During the site visits, we conducted interviews with hospital leaders, including chief executive officers, chief medical officers, chiefs of surgery, and chiefs of nursing and pharmacy, as well as the designated Patient Safety Officer or person responsible for or most knowledgeable about the hospital's patient safety initiatives. We also conducted two roundtables at each hospital, at which we discussed the hospital's actions taken to implement each of two sets of NQF safe practices that they already had adopted.

We summarize here our findings across the 15 hospitals in the four communities.[6] The first set of results focuses on their experience in pursuing improvements in patient safety practices. The second set of results examines how the hospitals had implemented each of the specific NQF practices selected for discussion.

Overall Experiences with Patient Safety Practices

Our review of overall experiences will touch on how hospitals set their goals and priorities around patient safety, how they organized and structured their patient-safety efforts, how the process of implementing safe practices played out in challenges and facilitators, and their perspective on the role that wider system-level players and forces (including AHRQ) played in promoting patient safety efforts within their institutions.

Patient Safety Priority-Setting

We asked hospital leaders to describe how patient safety became a priority for their institutions. While some described a catalyzing event (e.g., a very public death from a medical error), many said that there was no particular event but, rather, an evolutionary process that was often stimulated by outside influences (such as the publication of *To Err Is Human* -- which put a national spotlight on patient safety). Many said that their patient safety work was a natural outgrowth of decades of work on quality improvement—and for some hospitals there is no separation between quality and patient safety efforts. However, some described the process before the year 2000 as fairly haphazard and driven mainly by regulatory and compliance issues. After 2000, however, most hospitals reached a tipping point of momentum in progress and began to develop a more strategic structure around patient safety improvement.

Interestingly, a number of hospitals reported that the hiring of a new CEO (and a reorganization) was the most important stimulating event. Other hospitals described the prioritization of patient safety as embedded in a larger process of developing strategic goals— and the placement of patient safety among the four or five institutional "pillars" that drive the activities at the hospital. Others have embedded their patient safety improvement processes within a larger management change process employing Toyota Production System/LEAN methods to "drive to zero defects." State public-reporting mandates also had an effect, as did media reports and publicity and the fear of falling behind competitors in a tough health care market. For others, becoming nationally recognized as a health care quality leader motivated their efforts.

The leaders with whom we spoke described a variety of processes for determining priorities. It was clear that for some hospitals the process of priority setting was a top-down

---

[6] We identified and recruited 16 hospitals to participate in the site visits, but after repeated attempts, we were unable to come to a mutually agreeable date for the site visit for the final hospital. By that point, there was not sufficient time to recruit an alternative hospital, so we report here on the experience of 15 hospitals.

endeavor—with more emphasis coming from the hospital leadership. Leaders in other hospitals emphasized that the stimulus had come from one or two physicians or nurse champions, who had developed enthusiasm to pursue improvements.

For some, there was a strong sense that priorities were based on "doing what is good for the patient"—whether that be the result of a sense of a public mission (e.g., safety-net hospitals) or a faith-based mission. Others described formal priority-setting processes that involved the hospital leadership and often the Board. Still others told us that they do not make any changes to practice without involving the medical staff. Leaders at one hospital reported a lack of consensus among leaders and front-line staff. They indicated that front-line staff and senior leaders have their own ideas about what is important, and they are not always the same ideas.

Many hospitals told us that their priority setting process is data-driven. They use data on sentinel events and near misses (often generated from their internal voluntary incident-reporting systems) to understand where the risks are in their hospitals and to determine which areas need attention. Others reported that the AHRQ Patient Safety Culture Survey has been useful in helping them identify critical areas. For others, "patient-safety rounds" have brought issues to the forefront that might not have shown up in administrative or survey data.

Once issues are identified, hospital leaders agreed that it was critical to assess them, come to consensus on priorities, develop an operational plan and a scorecard to drive performance, and then implement and monitor over time to assess progress and sustainability. Several of our interviewees emphasized the need to "pick a handful of priorities and not try to work on everything at once." Finances are also an issue: because hospitals do not have unlimited resources for patient safety initiatives, they need to be strategic in choosing areas in which they can make sustainable improvements.

The issue of balancing a hospital's own internal priorities with external reporting requirements and other mandates was raised frequently in the hospital site visits. Leaders in one hospital stated that they prioritize areas that they believe have a direct effect on their patients, noting that national priorities do not always line up with their own experience. At the same time, they are inundated with external initiatives that are all "top priority" for some group and they feel they cannot "choose not to do" any of them, which becomes overwhelming. Some leaders with whom we spoke looked forward to a day when they would be able to (or allowed to) move from a reactive to a more proactive approach based on their own assessment of need and not just responding to external mandates. Several referred to the current environment as one of "initiative overload" that prevents a more targeted effort on high-impact areas and may impede the sustainability of their existing initiatives.

Organization and Structure

Hospital leaders described a variety of organizational structures (e.g., various types and levels of committees and staffing schemes) that were mostly idiosyncratic to their hospitals. Interviewees discussed issues about infrastructure, such as incident-reporting systems and the benefits and challenges of health information technology (health IT). Within these various structures, there were common themes about leadership, including the following:

- The imperative for committed involvement by the hospital CEO
- Involvement of the Board of Directors in patient safety performance and related issues (a relatively new emphasis)

- Designation of a Patient Safety Officer (someone clearly identified to handle that role) as part of (or reporting directly to) hospital senior management.

As mentioned above, some of the leaders with whom we spoke saw the hiring of a new CEO as the turning point for patient safety in their hospitals. Still others emphasized the importance of leadership "from the top of the organization" as crucial to senior and middle managers' ability to make change "at the bedside." For example, CEOs at some of the hospitals participated in leadership rounds to listen directly to front-line staff, or they made patient safety goals a part of the compensation package for managers (and sometimes physicians)—clearly communicating to hospital staff that patient safety is an issue of importance to the organization and not the "flavor-of-the-month" initiative.

With regard to hospital Boards of Directors, many hospitals reported that only recently (within the last 2 to 3 years) have their Boards become fully engaged in safety and quality efforts. In years past, the Boards primarily reviewed finances. Now, according to our interviewees, most Boards, either as the entire Board or through a standing patient safety or quality committee, review "dashboards" that summarize progress on patient safety initiatives, and they also review all critical incidents. Some Board members even participate in leadership rounds. Some interviewees noted that Board members (especially community members) have varying degrees of knowledge and comfort with data and wondered whether it was a reasonable expectation that they would be well-versed enough to make use of the data. Some thought that training for Board members (such as that offered by IHI) might be useful.

All of the hospitals we visited could point to a single person whose role it was to manage patient safety for the organization. From what they described to us, that would not have been the case five years ago. Several interviewees mentioned that the Patient Safety Officer at their hospital had been through the IHI Patient Safety Officer training, which they found very useful (although probably too advanced for those without one or two years of experience as a Patient Safety Officer before taking the training).

The Patient Safety Officer's position in the organization reflected the structure the hospital used for its quality and safety structures. Not all of the Patient Safety Officers were part of the senior management team, although all reported directly to a member of the team. In hospitals that organized patient safety as part of a larger organizational unit (for example, with Quality or Risk Management), the Patient Safety Officer worked within that larger unit. In other hospitals, where the functions were separate, the Patient Safety Officer often headed a separate unit. Again, it was not clear that one type of organization was superior to another, as long as patient safety was clearly a priority of the organization.

All of the hospitals reported having an incident-reporting system, although some still were paper-based systems, which reduced their utility. Senior leaders in a number of the hospitals acknowledged that many staff continue to be fearful of reporting, despite their various attempts to educate staff and support a blame-free culture. On the other hand, some hospitals with online reporting systems have robust reporting and are able to estimate trends in events. Administrators at one hospital, however, reported that they believe that some staff were using their reporting system to "settle scores" among staff that are not related to patient safety. It has been difficult for them to determine how to limit that kind of inappropriate use.

The extent to which hospitals have electronic medical records varies, and even those hospitals that report utilizing health information technology often have health IT "silos" so that one database cannot be integrated electronically with others. A number of hospitals reported that they are in the advanced planning or early implementation stages of a new EMR or CPOE system that they hope will allow them to lighten the load on patient safety staff by, for example, making chart audits unnecessary.

While all hospitals reported that they had patient safety infrastructure in place, some reported the need for additional resources, especially as patient safety mandates grow. To the extent that hospital leadership reported safety infrastructure to be lacking, it was often in the area of staffing for data acquisition and analysis.

Challenges and Facilitators for the Implementation Process. Leadership from the hospitals pointed to a number of challenges they faced in the process of implementing patient safety practices. Some of these challenges and facilitators have been discussed already in this chapter (lessons from the case studies). Therefore, we will focus on a few key observations (in the words of our interviewees) here:

- *You can figure out what changes need to be made, but getting people at the bedside to adopt the changes can be a challenge.*

Our interviewees noted that making change is costly in time and resources—and not only the resources devoted to patient safety activities but also resources required to educate staff and involve them in process-change activities. In addition, they noted that attitude change is often as important as teaching a new skill. One interviewee said that if employees understand the value of patient safety and are confident that they will not get fired if they report near misses, the hospital will be more successful in improving patient safety. Others were more skeptical about their ability to change either attitudes or behavior in the short term, especially among physicians. One person noted that there were still many people in their hospital who do not believe that problems exist in their hospital or that it is possible to have zero defects, which affects their motivation to change. Another interviewee suggested that interventions will be most successful if they are designed to minimize effort on the part of clinical staff, because work-arounds are "human nature."

- *Perceptions of a punitive environment linger despite assurances to the contrary.*

A number of interviewees noted that they were surprised by findings from the AHRQ Patient Safety Culture Survey that staff in their institutions continued to fear retribution for reporting and consequences for medical errors despite all their attempts to educate staff to the contrary. They noted that culture change takes a long time to take hold, and some felt that nurses in particular were also sensitive to the hierarchical structure of hospitals and took that into account in their willingness to make incident reports. One hospital reported instituting a zero-tolerance policy for "disruptive physician behavior," which seems to have enhanced culture change.

- *Counteracting physician skepticism to adopting new patient safety practices is one of the most difficult challenges to overcome.*

According to one interviewee, physicians need to be involved in making patient safety process improvements all along the way, rather than excluding them from the planning process and presenting the new process to them at the end. Information will be most readily accepted if it comes from other physicians, which is why physician champions are critical. Some suggested that executive "you will…" mandates are required. A few interviewees took exception to the notion of physicians as a problem, however, suggesting that the problem was "information overload" on busy physicians. They said, "If you present something to them that is obscure or difficult to understand, their response is going to be to question the data behind what you are presenting. That was their first response to the IOM data. The challenge is getting the education across in a way that speaks to physicians—is based in the scientific model, as they are."

- ***Simplify the safety message and focus on a few areas or risk doing nothing well.***

Communicating patient safety information can be challenging. Staff are bombarded with messages, so if you are not communicating well, what you are saying will come across as "noise." Leadership from one of the hospitals also noted the need to pick a small number of initiatives so as not to dilute the effort. They suggested that "high energy" staff, if not given sufficient direction will run off in too many directions and run the risk of not doing anything well by trying to do too much. Others expressed concern about the sustainability of successes, noting that staff members assigned to an intervention make improvements but then get distracted by the next issue and sometimes the staff revert to baseline processes and performance.

- ***Health information technology can be both a challenge and a facilitator.***

Many interviewees expressed hope that new health IT systems would solve many of their problems, but others noted that health IT can be both a facilitator and a challenge. One interviewee wondered if the external forces pushing health IT on hospitals (especially small community hospitals and safety-net hospitals) have truly considered how cash-strapped hospitals can manage to implement their recommendations. Others noted the resource and implementation challenges of implementing an electronic medical record. EMRs have not always been a boon to hospitals: some have had to scrap their systems and start over; many piecemeal electronic systems do not interact, and information still resides in silos.

- ***For an effort to work, it takes support of the team to gather reliable data.***

One hospital reported that now that they have data systems in place to collect incident-report information, they have so much data to look at that they are in "data overload" and are challenged by trying to figure out what needs attention and what does not. Several other interviewees expressed concern about the reliability of the data that underpin some of their efforts. For example, one hospital found that measured mortality rates were unexpectedly high in their administrative data compared with the rate from chart reviews. They discovered that the admissions staff were entering every person as an elective admission—skewing the data— because every time a death occurred as a result of an elective admission, it was registered as a Level 1 mortality (a hospital-based event). So the data indicating a quality-of-care issue were totally inaccurate. Some respondents also expressed concern that standards to which they are being held by outside organizations sometimes are not fully supported by evidence and/or lag behind the science.

- ***Academic medical centers face some particular issues.***

On the one hand, affiliation with a medical school means that some of the medical staff are younger and more amenable to change. On the other hand, the fact that medical staff rotate in and out of the hospital on a monthly basis creates a challenge for standardizing safe practices. In communities (such as Indianapolis) in which hospitals have agreed to standardize practices across a community, such problems are reduced.

- ***Leverage community resources to supplement those in the hospital.***

Several hospitals reported that they were able to access LEAN and Six Sigma experts from outside organizations to work collaboratively within their hospitals. The benefit to the hospitals was access to expertise that they did not have in-house. The benefit to the outside organizations was to provide them with a real-world setting in which to work.

- *Involving front-line staff in patient safety initiatives is empowering.*

Hospitals that involve front-line staff directly in identifying the problem and determining what change should be implemented (e.g., those using Toyota/LEAN methods) have observed that it is very powerful and engaging for staff when they see that they are in a position to change something that has been irritating them. It is a much more effective process in developing a culture of change than "educating" staff.

The Role of External Players and Forces. Every hospital leader emphasized the importance of external forces to their patient safety efforts. Hospital leadership pointed to AHRQ, the Institute of Medicine, the Institute for Healthcare Improvement, the Leapfrog Group, the Centers for Medicare and Medicaid Services, Joint Commission, and others as critical to raising awareness and providing tools (such as safety practice "bundles") that have been instrumental in their own patient safety work.

On the other hand, as noted earlier in this chapter, hospitals feel they have no option but to respond to the various regulatory and mandatory programs, including publicly reportable databases, as well as Leapfrog surveys and other private-sector initiatives. At least some of the leaders are skeptical of the value of some of these reporting initiatives to consumers, purchasers, or the hospitals themselves. They believe that it is difficult for consumers to understand much of the data, and that the measures often do not clearly differentiate hospitals (for example, in one city, the three largest hospital systems have indistinguishable Consumer Assessment of Healthcare Providers and Systems (CAHPS) Hospital Survey scores). They reported that employers and insurers occasionally discuss indicators but do not use indicators to set reimbursement rates, and insurers seem more concerned with collecting indicators than understanding the underlying issues. Hospital leaders are also concerned that the measures themselves can yield conflicting results for a single hospital.

Measurement of Processes and Outcomes. Staff at the hospitals we visited were very vocal in their frustration over the current state of affairs in measurement of patient safety processes and outcomes. They complained about conflicting standards, fragmented and duplicative reporting, and lack of consideration of the effect of measurement on clinical behaviors. Perhaps most important, they noted that measurement initiatives are not "synched up" at the national level. Different organizations sometimes use the same definitions but require the same things to be reported in different ways, which is costly and undermines a hospital's ability to focus its resources on improving safety. They questioned the integrity of various initiatives because the data used to compare hospitals is often questionable – and dated – which makes the findings less relevant. They also complained that certain standards (such as Leapfrog Group's intensivist standard) are difficult for some hospitals to achieve because of a shortage of intensivists.

Perhaps the most consistent and urgent message conveyed by providers across these four communities was the immense burden being placed on hospitals by the current state of measurement initiatives by national and state organizations. These reporting activities currently are so burdensome that they are interfering with the ability of hospitals to focus their attention on improving patient safety in the areas they have identified as their real priorities.

Hospitals saw an urgent need for national and state organizations to coalesce around measures, definitions, and goals for measurement and reporting activities. There was widespread agreement that too many measurement organizations exist and too many measures are being proliferated. They saw the need for a lead organization to fill the role of bringing the organizations together to prioritize initiatives as a way to focus money, time, and effort on the most significant opportunities for improvement. Some also felt that a national data repository for patient safety data should be developed under the auspices of a trusted organization.

Many people we interviewed named AHRQ as best positioned to step in to harmonize these requirements and to establish a national data repository that would obviate the need to submit patient safety data to multiple organizations. Hospital leaders thought that AHRQ could fulfill this important role by

- Bringing uniformity to safety and quality measures so that health care organizations would have only one set of measures to report
- Ensuring that all indicators have been tested and actually improve outcomes (thereby cutting down on meaningless or less effective markers)
- Managing the future measurement agenda so that measure development is focused only on the most meaningful patient safety activities
- Acting as a clearinghouse to facilitate "real time" dissemination of patient-safety ideas and innovations.

Implementation of NQF Safe Practices in Hospitals

We conducted two roundtable discussions at each of the 15 hospitals to examine a limited number of NQF safe practices in depth. In each hospital, one roundtable focused on an aspect of the development of patient safety culture and the second focused on a grouping of other safe practices (see Table 2.3 above). Roundtable respondents consisted of individuals most familiar with and responsible for implementing the specific sets of safe practices. At most of the hospitals, these roundtable discussions included clinicians and other front-line staff who are involved in implementing the practices on a daily basis.

We first asked the respondents to describe all the safety practices and activities by their hospital that fell into the relevant safe-practices category. Then we talked specifically about safe practices corresponding to items in the draft RAND survey (see Chapter 4). We focused the discussion on three basic themes: the goals the hospital had set for the safe practices; how the hospital had operationalized and implemented the group of NQF practices in the specific context of their hospital; and the major challenges and facilitators they had experienced in their implementation of the group of practices. The results of these discussions for each practice grouping are summarized in the tables in Appendix C. We report here the overall highlights of our findings, aggregated across the practice groups.

Goals. All practice groupings were considered important to some extent, although some groupings were viewed as higher priority than others—in particular Surgery Procedures and Medication Safety Management. However, there was greater variation among practices within the groupings. For instance, NQF safe practice no.10 (on proper labeling and patient identification) was generally considered higher priority than the other practices in its grouping (i.e., Transparency Across the Continuum of Care). Similarly, NQF safe practice no. 30 (related to contrast media-induced renal failure) was perceived as having relatively low priority within its grouping (Medical Evaluation and Prevention). In some cases, roundtable respondents reported focusing on issues not included in the NQF safe practices but which they considered of at least equal importance, such as a number of practices related to surgical procedures (e.g., use of blood products, proper positioning of patient, room temperature, and hand-offs between surgical and intensive care unit [ICU] staff).

Implementation of Practices. We devoted one roundtable at each hospital to an aspect of the development of patient safety culture. These aspects included the role of leadership, the use of culture survey and measurement, teamwork development, and systems for identifying and mitigating risks. For many roundtable participants, these cultural elements were fundamental to driving and sustaining the patient safety agenda and specific other safety projects throughout their respective organizations. Much can be done with designing safer technical systems and organizational procedures, but even these require the commitment and awareness of people within the organization to use them as intended. It was also noted that patient safety culture is integrally related to a hospital's wider organizational culture. Thus, developing a particular patient safety culture is not wholly separate from, and needs to take into account, the wider organizational culture and history of the institution.

Similarly, the four sets of practices for developing patient safety culture were observed to be integrally related to each other. For example, one objective of leadership systems was to encourage a sense of teamwork, and integration of different risk-identification and risk-mitigation systems was considered an exercise in teamwork across units and professionals within the organization. This interrelationship among the practices was common among the other practices as well (e.g., the heavy use of reporting systems to identify adverse medication events).

As a result, it is not surprising that a number of themes were shared in the roundtable discussions for the different culture practices. These themes included working to instill a sense of ownership and accountability for safety practices among individuals throughout the organization, creating a "proactive" mentality in which staff attempt to identify problems and improve processes before an incident occurs, and an emphasis on a culture of open communication, including a nonpunitive, nonblame climate for reporting errors.

Likewise, there were a number of common elements across the implementation of the other practice groupings. The use of multidisciplinary and cross-functional teams to lead safety-improvement efforts was particularly prominent in the areas of Transparency Across the Continuum of Care and Medication Safety Management. The reliance on technology was emphasized for both Medication Safety Management (e.g., CPOE) and Identification of Risks (e.g., electronic error-reporting systems). There was an especially strong emphasis on communication practices across a number of groupings, including the role of leadership in establishing mechanisms both up to the Board and down to the front lines, principles of communication embedded in models of teamwork, and internal marketing and communication to promote error reporting. Education and training was also strongly emphasized across a range of groupings, such as various training programs on teamwork that hospitals had used, training of safety professionals and staff in risk-identification and risk-mitigation techniques (e.g., root cause analysis [RCA], failure mode and effects analysis [FMEA]), and continuing education and cross-training as part of workforce practices.

Hospitals have been working to implement many of the practices for several years, from when guidelines were first being developed, even before the publication of the NQF standards (e.g., most practices under Medical Evaluation and Prevention). However, the NQF safe practices, as well as other external initiatives, such as Leapfrog, IHI's 5 Million Lives Campaign, and CMS' never events, have refocused and renewed attention on these areas. Moreover, although having made progress and laid important foundations for patient safety, the hospitals still tended to report being in fairly early or nascent stages of development in many areas. Results of patient safety culture surveys frequently indicate that the hospital is not as far along in nonpunitive climate and hand-offs as patient safety staff and administrators had thought from anecdotal experience. There is also a widespread belief that reporting systems, even well-developed and introduced electronic platforms, are not capturing the majority of events, and that communication on safety issues across levels and units of the organization often remains problematic.

Implementation Challenges and Facilitators. A general theme across the hospitals was the difficulty inherent in changing patient-safety systems and culture. This challenge, not surprisingly, is prominent within the practices related to patient safety culture, especially in light of the point raised above that patient safety is embedded within deep-seated mind sets and expectations within the hospital's wider culture. As a result, changing patient safety culture is necessarily a long-term endeavor.

Physician attitudes were both a challenge (in terms of clinician resistance) and facilitator (in the form of medical leader support). But of greater prominence was general staff resistance to perceived additional workload, changes in routine, pro forma performance of new practices, and a tendency to find work-arounds for new systems. These challenges were particularly noted for Safety Culture Survey, Identification of Risks, Transparency Across the Continuum of Care, and Surgery Procedures.

Another oft-mentioned challenge was difficulty in disseminating information and practices across different groups of professionals, boundaries between organizational units within and outside of the hospital, and especially among academic and attending staff who hold multiple affiliations or who practice only intermittently in the hospital. As one might expect, these issues were emphasized in cross-cutting areas, such as Transparency Across the Continuum of Care, and Medication Safety and Management. Implementing and managing technology, such as incompatibilities and interfaces among complex information systems—a commonly cited challenge to quality and service improvement—were primarily emphasized in discussions of Safety Culture Survey, Transparency Across the Continuum of Care, and Medication Safety Management.

Roundtable respondents also discussed a number of facilitators to implementing safe practices. The most noted facilitating theme was flexibility: not expecting strict uniformity in implementation across units, allowing small changes in safety procedures that can make a large difference in reducing workload burden on care providers, encouraging inclusion of a wide range of stakeholders in the implementation process, and methods by which stakeholders can participate. Another noted theme was the role of leadership, particularly in establishing coordination and networking mechanisms (e.g., patient safety governance committees, multidisciplinary programs to share experiences) and providing tangible resources for safety efforts (e.g., investment in new hospital beds and mattresses to reduce the incidence of pressure ulcers). An equally prominent facilitator across the groupings was communication and feedback to front-line staff. Investing time to explain patient safety issues, and to "close the loop" with care providers on safety priorities, incidents, and results of error reporting and corrective actions taken, were described as highly motivating to hospital staff for committing to and implementing patient safety practices.

CONCLUSIONS

Taken together, our findings from the community-level case studies, the interviews with hospital leaders, and the roundtables on patient safety practices suggest that real progress has been made in average communities and average hospitals over the past eight years. Hospitals are including patient safety among their highest institutional priorities and are putting in place Patient Safety Officers, leaders and Board infrastructure to effect change. Hospitals have incident reporting systems and are using those data, along with RCAs, FMEAs, and findings from culture surveys to determine specific areas for process improvements. They are assessing their own progress and are focused on achieving sustainability of their efforts.

There are pockets of formal community-wide collaboration, even in very competitive health care markets. But even in communities that lack formal collaborations, hospitals are looking to outside organizations to acquire information and expertise to help them with internal activities. Unfortunately, we found little evidence that these patient safety efforts have diffused beyond hospitals and into ambulatory and long-term care settings. The rate-limiting step appears to be a lack of existing "bundles" of practices—something AHRQ can readily address.

Perhaps the most important caution, which was almost universally expressed by our respondents, was in the area of measurement. Most reported that current measurement efforts are imperfect and, as "unfunded mandates," may be actually putting patient safety practice at risk by siphoning off resources that could be better spent making improvements rather than measuring them in repeated ways against different standards and with different measures. Many of our respondents value the leadership that AHRQ has shown in the patient safety arena and suggested that AHRQ was the trusted agency that could step in to address this critical need.

CHAPTER 3.
USE OF THE HOSPITAL SURVEY ON PATIENT SAFETY CULTURE

SPECIFIC AIMS

One of the major tools that AHRQ developed to help health care providers improve their patient safety culture and practices is the Survey on Patient Safety Culture (SOPS). The first survey developed was the Hospital Survey on Patient Safety Culture (HSOPS). We gathered and assessed information on hospitals' experiences to achieve the following aims:

1. To develop information on hospitals' motivation and experiences in using the HSOPS

2. To understand the extent to which the HSOPS has contributed to hospitals' patient safety efforts

3. To provide feedback to AHRQ on how it might modify the survey questionnaire or technical support to enhance the usefulness of HSOPS to hospitals and other users.

As described in Chapter 1, this part of our product evaluation work focuses on one of the major patient safety tools developed by AHRQ to furnish resources to providers as they work to achieve safer health care for their patients. We limited this analysis to only one tool—the HSOPS—because of budget limitations. However, we suggest that AHRQ undertake similar inquiries with users of other key tools it develops (e.g., TeamSTEPPS), both to document how the tools are contributing to improving safe practices in the field and to obtain feedback from users for improving the tools.

THE SURVEY QUESTIONNAIRE AND PROTOCOL

Early in the patient safety initiative, Quality Interagency Coordination Task Force sponsored the development of the AHRQ-funded HSOPS to provide hospitals a measurement tool to help them assess how well their cultures emphasize patient safety, as well as to facilitate open discussion of error, encourage error reporting, and create an atmosphere of continuous learning and improvement. The survey contains 51 questions that combine into composites that assess 12 dimensions of patient safety culture: communication openness, feedback and communication about error, frequency of events reported, handoffs and transitions, management support for patient safety, nonpunitive response to error, organizational learning/continuous improvement, overall perceptions of patient safety, staffing, supervisor/manager expectations and actions promoting safety, teamwork across units, and teamwork within units.

AHRQ partnered with the American Hospital Association, Department of Defense, and Premier Health Systems to support initial release of the HSOPS in 2004 to U.S. hospitals and health care systems. A growing number of hospitals are using the culture survey. Feedback from these hospitals suggests that the dimensions measured on the survey are relevant at the operational level, and are being used for quality-improvement work. However, quantified data are not yet available to verify this assessment.

AHRQ contracted with Westat to build and manage a benchmark database, into which hospitals can submit their survey data and obtain information on how they compare with others. Westat produces annual reports summarizing the HSOPS data submitted by hospitals to the benchmarking database. These reports provide information segmented in a variety of ways, including hospital characteristics (e.g., bed size, teaching status, region), as well as by respondent characteristics (e.g., work area/unit, staff position, patient contact). Hospitals that submit their data to Westat receive customized reports comparing their survey results with the other results in the benchmarking database.

The first benchmark report, entitled *Hospital Survey on Patient Safety Culture: 2007 Comparative Database Report*, was released in March 2007 (Sorra et al., 2007). A second benchmark report, *Hospital Survey on Patient Safety Culture: 2008 Comparative Database Report,* was released in March 2008 (Sorra et el., 2008). The 2007 report contains comparative results for 382 participating hospitals in which 108,621 hospital staff completed the culture survey. The 2008 report contains comparative results for 519 hospitals, with 160,176 hospital staff completing the survey. Additionally, the 2008 report contains a chapter showing changes in the survey results for 98 hospitals that had submitted their survey data for both benchmarking periods.

METHODS

In FY 2008, we conducted telephone interviews with representatives from 17 hospitals that had conducted HSOPS one or more times and had submitted their data to the national benchmarking database operated by Westat. We used a semi-structured interview protocol for the interviews, to ensure that we collected consistent information from those interviewed.

The confidential nature of hospitals' participation in the national benchmarking database meant that we were not able to recruit participants in the study directly. Rather, we collaborated with Westat in this process. Westat contacted potential participants to introduce them to the study and offer them the opportunity to participate. Only those hospitals interested in participating identified themselves to RAND, thus protecting the confidentiality of those who did not choose to participate.

To select the sample of hospitals, we provided Westat with a list of criteria describing the optimal sample characteristics. We wanted roughly half the sample to be hospitals that submitted survey data to the database only once and half to be hospitals that submitted data twice. We also wanted the sample to be relatively equally distributed across bed size, geographic location, teaching hospitals, and system ownership. Given these criteria, Westat identified approximately 90 hospitals and sent them invitations to participate in the study. The invitation instructed those who chose to "opt in" to participation to send RAND an affirmative response email. To schedule interviews, we then contacted those who responded.

Eighteen hospitals contacted us to indicate their interest in participating, and we completed 17 interviews. One hospital that initially expressed interested subsequently did not respond to repeated requests to schedule an interview after their initial contact with us. After scheduling an interview, we provided each hospital representative a short version of the discussion protocol so that they would know in advance the topics we were covering in the interview. We also requested that the hospital provide consent for Westat to release the hospital's customized database report to RAND, so we would have background information on the hospital-survey results for the interview. Twelve hospitals provided consent to have Westat send us their customized reports.

In addition to interviewing the 17 hospitals, we spoke with representatives from one hospital association and one Quality Improvement Organization. These two organizations, and others like them, are playing a role in the diffusion of HSOPS through a range of activities:

promoting awareness of the survey, facilitating the administration process and submission of data to the benchmarking database, and providing technical assistance for interpreting the data and taking action on the results.

Two members of our research team conducted all the interviews. Twice during the interview process, the interviewers met with the project director to assess the information obtained, identify areas where questions needed to be refined, and ensure that the interviewers were asking the questions consistently.

To analyze the interview data, each of the two interviewers independently reviewed all the interview notes to determine trends in responses and identify the most prominent themes or lessons described by the interviewees. They then compared their results and, when they found differences, they together examined the relevant interview data to reach a final consensus on findings. The researchers also looked for any differences in responses across individual hospitals or types of hospitals. For example, one trend identified was that smaller or rural hospitals tended to benefit more than the larger or more urban hospitals from assistance with the survey, such as support provided by QIOs to administer the survey and to analyze and report the data.

FINDINGS REGARDING HOSPITAL EXPERIENCES WITH HSOPS

Characteristics of the Interviewed Hospitals

The 17 interviewed hospitals were a relatively diverse group of hospitals. Eight were stand-alone hospitals and nine were part of larger hospital systems. Seven were teaching hospitals. Four hospitals had submitted data to Westat for the 2007 national benchmarking report only, five submitted data for the 2008 report only, and eight submitted data in time to be included in both reports. We note that several of the hospitals only reported data in one year or the other, while many of them actually administered the survey more than once. Table 3.1 shows the distribution of hospitals in the sample by bed size, and Table 3.2 shows their distribution by geographic region.

Table 3.1 Distribution of Interviewed Hospitals, by Bed Size

Bed Size	RAND Sample	2007 Database Report	2008 Database Report
Small (0–99)	6 (35%)	217 (59%)	287 (55%)
Medium (100–299)	2 (12%)	106 (28%)	143 (28%)
Large (300+)	9 (53%)	59 (15%)	89 (17%)
Total	17	382	519

NOTE: Percentages may not sum to 100 because of rounding.

Table 3.2 Distribution of Interviewed Hospitals, by Region

United States Region	RAND Sample	2007 Database Report	2008 Database Report
Mid Atlantic/New England (NY, NJ, PA, ME, NH, VT, MA, RI, CT)	2 (12%)	20 (5%)	32 (6%)
South Atlantic (DE, MD, DC, VA, WV, NC, SC, GA, FL)	4 (24%)	60 (16%)	89 (17%)
East North Central (OH, IN, IL, MI, WI)	3 (18%)	100 (26%)	113 (22%)
East South Central (KY, TN, AL, MS)	2 (12%)	26 (7%)	29 (6%)
West North Central (MN, IA, MO, ND, SD, NE, KS)	4 (24%)	83 (22%)	92 (18%)
West South Central (AR, LA, OK, TX)	0	31 (8%)	37 (7%)
Mountain (MT, ID, WY, CO, NM, AZ, UT, NV)	1 (6%)	35 (9%)	57 (11%)
Pacific (WA, OR, CA, AK, HI)	1 (6%)	27 (7%)	70 (13%)
Total	17	382	519

Motivations for Using HSOPS

Initial impetus. The interviewees reported a variety of factors that motivated their organizations to conduct HSOPS and submit data to the benchmarking database. Interviewees identified the following motivating factors most frequently:

- Initiative of the Patient Safety Officers, who pursued approval for the survey
- Desire by senior leaders to know the patient safety culture in their hospital
- Need for data and feedback on progress in patient-safety improvement activities
- Inquiries by external organizations to work with the hospital to administer the survey
- Requirements of the Joint Commission to do a safety culture survey
- Inclusion of a patient safety culture survey in the safe practices established by the NQF.

Initiative by the Patient Safety Officer was the primary stimulus for the survey for about half the interviewees. Several Patient Safety Officers reported that they brought the survey to the attention of senior leadership and lobbied for its use. For example, one Patient Safety Officer who was new in the position thought it was critical to get a baseline measurement and hear about staff's perceptions of culture. She wrote the survey into the patient safety program.

In a few cases, senior leaders determined that the hospital would conduct the survey. This decision often was made by senior leaders who were highly interested in patient safety or who had learned about the survey at a patient safety–related conference or other educational activity. For example, one CEO heard about HSOPS at an Institute for Healthcare Improvement conference and made it a priority for the hospital to conduct the survey. In another case, previous employee surveys identified that employees were concerned that the hospital did not take actions to follow up on incident reports. The decision to administer HSOPS partially grew out of that survey's findings. However, even when senior leaders initiated use of the survey, a committed person at the mid-management level (e.g., Patient Safety Officer) was needed to spearhead the effort and keep the project on track.

Administering the survey was one aspect of the hospitals' plans to place a greater focus on patient safety, including providing better feedback to employees who report safety concerns. For example, one hospital, which was very active in patient safety initiatives, decided to implement HSOPS as a way to measure the effects of those activities.

Several hospitals reported that the impetus for doing the survey came from being approached by other organizations, including QIOs, hospital associations, and university researchers. A number of interviewees also cited Joint Commission requirements and the first NQF safe practice as motivating the hospital to conduct the survey.

Several interviewees reported that their organization had considered other culture surveys but chose the AHRQ survey for several reasons: they liked the topics the survey covered, the questionnaire was available in Spanish and English, results could be used to guide actions, and it was free. They also liked the availability of both the national benchmarking database and the technical assistance for data collection and analysis.

Leadership support. In the majority of cases, hospital leaders were supportive of the survey activity, even when they had not initiated it. This support was shown in a number of ways, including provision of adequate resources and staff time to conduct the survey. Some senior leaders also assisted in publicizing the survey by discussing it at meetings and setting expectations for participation. Many interviewees thought that this support made a big difference in increasing their hospital's survey response rate.

In a handful of cases, senior leaders resisted approving the survey, not so much for resource reasons but because they did not understand or perceive the value of the survey. In these cases, the person leading the effort (usually a Patient Safety Officer) had to educate the leadership about patient safety and the value of the survey. In one case, the Patient Safety Officer conducted a pilot project in which the survey was administered in just one unit of the hospital. After seeing the low cost to administer the survey, and the value of the information it yielded, the senior leaders then approved conducting the survey hospital-wide.

Survey Administration Process

Administration strategies. The interviewees chose one of the following three basic strategies for administering the HSOPS at their hospitals—self-administration, partnering with an external organization, contract administration to external organizations (Table 3.3) Of the interviewed hospitals that plan to repeat the survey in the future, most do not plan to change their administration process.

Table 3.3 Distribution of Interviewed Hospitals on HSOPS Administration Approach

Type of Survey Administration	Number of Hospitals
Administered the survey entirely in-house (self-administered)	9
Worked jointly with external organizations to administer the survey	6
External organizations did the entire survey administration	2

Most interviewees at hospitals that self-administered the survey reported that the entire survey process was handled by one person, usually the Patient Safety Officer. This could be a very labor-intensive process, particularly when the survey was administered on paper. For example, some Patient Safety Officers did everything from making photocopies of the survey to stuffing the envelopes and hand-delivering them to individual units. In a few other cases, most often with larger hospitals, several people assisted the lead survey coordinator, or a committee was formed that prepared a plan of action for the survey and guided the data-collection and analysis process. These committees typically included leaders in the organization involved in process improvement and the marketing department.

Partnering organizations identified in the interviews included Quality Improvement Organizations, hospital associations, or universities. For the six hospitals that conducted the survey as a joint effort between the hospital and a partner organization, the required tasks were divided between the hospitals and the partners. For example, the hospital may have distributed the survey and performed all the publicity activities, while the partner organization collected, analyzed, and reported the data back to the hospital. The hospitals reported that the support offered by partner organizations was key to the success of their efforts, including provision of needed resources. In addition, when the partner did the data collection, the comfort level of some survey respondents regarding their privacy increased, because they knew their responses were not being seen by anyone at the hospital.

Sample design. The majority of our interviewees defined the HSOPS sample as the entire employee population, including all clinical and nonclinical staff. They generally made this choice for two reasons: simplicity in survey administration and ability to obtain a large number of responses. Interviewees reported that, although surveying all employees may result in more data entry work, it actually simplifies the administration process substantially, because it avoids the need for a complex methodology for tracking respondents.

Some hospitals started with smaller samples and then expanded their sample to the entire population. Reasons reported for expanding their samples were to move to a full survey from a pilot (the first administration), to simplify the administration process, to increase the number of completed surveys, and to reach a segment of the employee population that was not included the first time they administered the survey.

Some interviewees felt that it was not appropriate for nonclinical staff to receive the survey, whereas others believed it was critical to include nonclinical staff because they have a different perspective from the clinical staff. Additionally, hospitals that include all staff, not just clinical, did so because they believed and wanted to emphasize the idea that patient safety is everyone's job, not just that of those who have direct interaction with patients. One reason that a few interviewees cited for not including nonclinical staff was that the hospital had multiple employee surveys and they were concerned about survey fatigue for employees.

Survey format. The hospitals we interviewed used both paper and Web-based modes for collecting the HSOPS data. Their choice of mode was related to the modes they normally used to communicate with staff. Of the hospitals that conducted the survey more than once, many began by using paper surveys, and then, for subsequent administrations, either used both paper and Web-based modes or moved entirely to a Web-based mode. The smaller, more resource-constrained hospitals tended to just use paper data-collection modes.

Survey promotion. Hospitals employed a variety of methods to publicize the survey to the hospital staff. Several hospitals involved mid-level and senior-level managers in discussing the survey at meetings. They also provided the managers with the paper survey to give directly to their staff and to personally encourage them to complete the survey. Other publicity methods included posting flyers around the hospital, placing stories about the survey in employee newsletters and video broadcasts; using payroll stuffers, sending organization-wide email messages about the survey; creating a screen saver for all hospital computers, reminding employees to complete the survey; and discussing the survey at staff meetings.

Response rates. The response rates achieved by the interviewees' hospitals varied greatly, ranging from 12 to 90 percent.[7] Interviewees' feelings about the response rates also varied, with some interviewees extremely pleased with their response rate and others very disappointed. There was no clear relationship, however, between the interviewees' feelings about the response rate and the actual response rate (i.e. some interviewees whose hospitals' response rates were low were pleased whereas others were disappointed). For every hospital interviewed that conducted the survey more than once, the response rate increased in their subsequent surveys. They attributed the increase to a variety of potential reasons, including increased publicity for the survey, greater awareness of the survey since it had been administered previously, and incentives provided to complete the survey, such as gift certificates or tickets to local events.

Factors affecting survey administration. The issue mentioned most frequently by the respondents was the challenge of getting physicians to complete the survey. One hospital representative reported that the physicians did not think the survey was clinical enough. However, the hospital liked the general nature of the survey, which allowed it to be used by every type of staff member, and they were concerned that modifying the survey for different types of respondents could create unwelcome challenges when trying to analyze the data and compare their results to other hospitals' results.

Another challenge that respondents identified as affecting response rate was survey fatigue. Many of the hospitals interviewed said HSOPS is one of several employee surveys they routinely conduct throughout the year on a variety of topics. Examples of other employee surveys used included satisfaction surveys, surveys related to performance evaluations of themselves or their supervisors, and surveys used in quality-improvement or measurement activities.

Even though the AHRQ HSOPS is free to use, it requires substantial resources to administer the survey in-house. However, the majority of interviewees said that they did not face resource barriers to conducting the survey. Interviewees from hospitals that used a web-based data-collection mode reported that they depended on their information technology departments to construct the Web pages, link them to a database for data collection, and address other technical requirements related to conducting the online survey. Often, they had to work

---

[7] Overall, it was reported in the 2008 *Comparative Database Report* that average response rates for participating hospitals varied by mode, with response rates of 60 percent for paper surveys, 44 percent for Web surveys, and 52 percent for mixed-mode administrations (Sorra et al., 2008).

hard to elevate the priority of the survey on the work schedule of the IT departments, which often led to delays in getting the online survey ready to use.

FINDINGS REGARDING USE OF SURVEY RESULTS

Perceptions of the HSOPS Culture Survey Results

All 17 of the hospital interviewees reported that, for the most part, the culture survey results accurately reflected their hospitals' patient safety culture. All respondents reported that the results generally confirmed what they had learned through other data-collection efforts or through informal information gathering (e.g., informal reports from front-line staff, issues raised during staff meetings).

Of the 17 hospital representatives interviewed, 11 respondents indicated that their HSOPS results included at least one or two surprising findings. Most of the unexpected findings were low scores, but in some cases they were scores that were higher than expected.

For many of the hospitals in our sample, *communication openness*, *handoffs and transitions*, and *teamwork across units* were three areas on which they scored low. This was not a surprise to most of the interviewees, who reported that the HSOPS results confirmed their sense that these were problem areas. In many cases, they reported they already were taking action to improve in these areas. Some respondents said that the results gave them additional evidence to show senior leaders (and in some cases, front-line staff) to strengthen the case for making improvements (and for the resources needed to do so).

The results revealed a disconnect in some hospitals between the perceptions of senior leaders and those of front-line staff. In those hospitals, the survey results filled an important information gap for senior leadership, providing information about problems (or at least *perceived* problems) of which they previously were unaware. Staff working on safety and quality issues (such as a Patient Safety Officer) were not surprised by low scores in certain areas, whereas senior managers were reported to be "shocked" or otherwise very surprised by the results. For example, in some hospitals, senior managers were quite surprised by low scores on the *nonpunitive response to error* composite.

In many cases, the most surprising finding was low scores on the *nonpunitive response to error* composite. Almost all of the hospitals interviewed scored low (in absolute terms) on this composite, and most of the interviewees had expected to see a higher score. The results highlighted the pervasive impression among staff that they might be punished for mistakes or errors in which they were involved, and that their mistakes are documented in their personnel file. Patient Safety Officers, other administrators, and hospitals' management teams realized that they had work to do to promote a nonpunitive culture around event reporting.

Various other unexpected findings were reported. Some respondents reported surprise at their low scores on the *communication openness* and *management support for patient safety* composites. A few respondents noted that they had unexpected results for particular units. For example, the Patient Safety Officer in one large academic medical center stated that the results for some HSOPS dimensions were lower than expected for a few hospital units. Further investigation into those units shed light on the previously unknown problems underlying the survey results.

Sharing of HSOPS Results

The interviewed hospitals varied in how they shared HSOPS results with groups within the hospital. As shown in Table 3.4, all hospitals said that they reported results to senior managers and 15 of them (88.2 percent) also shared results with department heads. Fewer of them (7 hospitals, 41.2 percent) reported results to hospital governing boards or front-line staff.

Table 3.4 Distribution of HSOPS Results Within the Interviewed Hospitals

	Hospitals That Shared HSOPS with Group	
Hospital Groups	Number	Percentage
Hospital governing board	7	41.2
Senior hospital leadership	17	100.0
Department heads	15	88.2
Front-line staff	7	41.2

The seven interviewees who said they provided HSOPS results to front-line staff indicated that they gave the staff a high-level summary of the results, often indicating the areas for which scores were particularly high or low. Those who did not directly provide the results to front-line staff made the results available to department heads or unit supervisors and left it up to them to pass the results on to front-line staff.

The format in which the hospitals shared the results also varied. The hospitals reported that they used one or more of the following formats:

- The customized reports they receive from Westat or a partner organization
- PowerPoint presentations or similar kinds of presentations
- Summaries of the results in employee newsletters
- Posting of results or summaries of them on the hospital's intranet.

The level of results reported depended on the available survey sample size. The majority of hospitals reported hospital-level results, and when they had a sufficient sample size, they also presented unit-level results. For some smaller hospitals (with fewer employees), there were not enough respondents to be able to report unit-level results. In at least one hospital, unit-level results were shared hospital-wide, and a healthy competition emerged between units to improve their survey results.

A few of the hospitals we interviewed did not collect data at the unit level; therefore they were only able to report hospital-level data. Interviewees that reported this expressed some frustration at not being able to see more detailed data. They are encouraging the hospital to enable unit-level data collection and reporting in the future. This situation was not more prevalent in the small versus large hospitals interviewed.

Interpretations of Changes in Results

For those hospitals that administered HSOPS more than once, the extent to which (and the direction in which) the survey results changed over time varied. Several interviewees reported that their results improved across many items and composites. When asked to speculate about the reasons for these improvements, most of them pointed to specific interventions that they believed were bearing fruit, such as SBAR (Situation-Background-Assessment-

Recommendation Communication), TeamSTEPPS®, new systems for administering medications, and homegrown processes and solutions. Some credited the survey itself with helping to raise awareness of patient safety issues (see below).

A few respondents noted, however, that their scores declined for a number of items and composites. These respondents typically attributed such changes to specific changes in leadership, systems, or processes. For example, one hospital had recently implemented an EMR system, and the implementation process had been difficult and disruptive for staff. This respondent believed that the negative effect this change had on staff was reflected in the latest culture-survey results. A respondent from another hospital pointed to frequent changes in leadership as a possible reason for declining scores.

Other respondents reported that their scores have changed little over time. Several of these hospitals have administered the survey annually, and the respondents in these hospitals tended to believe that changes in the culture are too slow-paced to be captured by the survey one year later. These interviewees hoped to see improved scores in future years.

Acting on the Results

How actionable the results were. We asked respondents whether they found the survey results to be usable in guiding actions to improve safety practices (actionable). Although their responses varied, most of them believed that the survey results were actionable to some extent. There was wide agreement, however, that the results do not point directly to specific actions to take. Rather, the results point to problem areas that need to be addressed, which most interviewees thought was quite helpful. With these problem areas identified, it was up to the management team or other staff to identify possible courses of action.

Some respondents noted that they would like to see more detailed results that are more actionable. For example, some hospitals that did not have results at the unit level felt they were missing the more detailed information needed for action. In addition, for some hospitals with partner organizations (e.g., QIO or state hospital association) that collect and analyze their survey data, the reports they received from these parties only provided data at the hospital-level.

The interviewed hospitals that received assistance in administering the survey or analyzing the results from a partner organization (QIO, state hospital association, or university research team) reported that these partners often helped them determine actions to take based on the survey results. Specifically, the partner organizations analyzed the results and drew connections between those results and best practices or other actions. These hospitals stated that they greatly valued this assistance and viewed the survey results as being very actionable.

Those hospitals working with the partner organization also benefit from obtaining their survey results very soon following the survey period. By contrast, other hospitals that only submit data to the national benchmarking database may wait nearly a year before getting their hospital's customized results. Some of these hospitals do not have the resources to perform the types of analyses done by the partner organizations or the benchmarking database, or they do not want to use their resources for performing analyses that will eventually be done by Westat or another partner organization.

Some interviewees noted that the results for certain items and composites are open to interpretation. For example, the scores on the *staffing* composite for one large urban hospital were relatively low, but management was unsure how to interpret these scores. The scores could indicate a general inadequacy of staffing levels, or they could indicate problems with the work assignment of staff or with needed support across units. An interviewee from another hospital stated that management was unsure of how to interpret its low scores on the *nonpunitive response to error* composite. They were interested in knowing whether staff were concerned about formal punishment or more informal punishment (e.g., receiving poor or unfair treatment from a supervisor). The survey does not distinguish between these two types of punishment.

Actions taken by hospitals. Although the hospitals varied in the actions they reported taking in response to the results, some common actions emerged from our interviews. The actions or interventions identified included:

- Identification of priorities for performance improvement
- Development and implementation of action plans to improve patient safety
- Changes made to hospital policies and procedures
- Patient safety walk-arounds
- Training of staff on patient safety
- Implementation of SBAR Communication.

In some cases, the actions were taken in direct response to the survey results. However, in most cases, respondents noted that the HSOPS results were one of several influences on the decision to take these actions.

In addition, the interviewed hospitals had taken actions to improve patient safety and the culture around safety, but not in response to the survey results (i.e., the actions were taken before the survey was ever administered or were otherwise not influenced by the survey). Many of these actions included those listed above. Other common examples were implementation of TeamSTEPPS™, establishment or modification of relevant hospital goals and priorities, and the formation of committees to focus on patient safety. In some cases, these actions or activities influenced the decision to administer the culture survey. For example, a few hospitals made patient safety a higher hospital-wide priority, which, in turn, stimulated interest by senior leaders in assessing the organization's patient safety culture.

In a few hospitals, specific units or departments had taken the initiative to develop and implement interventions aimed at improving patient safety (without direction from senior leaders or the Patient Safety Officer). The culture-survey results often influenced their decisions to take these actions.

Many of our respondents stressed that their hospital's use of the survey was part of a larger effort to improve patient safety and the culture around safety. Rather than being the driving force behind changes, the survey was simply one of several components of an overall strategy. Respondents often had difficulty pinpointing specific actions or interventions that had resulted directly from their review of the survey results. However, almost all respondents identified actions that had been at least partly influenced by survey results. Moreover, even if the survey results did not lead to certain interventions, interviewees emphasized that they saw the survey as a key piece of their overall efforts, alongside the actions taken, and they saw value in continuing to administer the survey in the future.

EFFECTS OF HSOPS ON PATIENT SAFETY CULTURE

A large proportion of the interviewees indicated that the survey has not directly affected patient safety culture in the hospital. Rather, the survey results helped to determine priorities or inform decisions about actions to take, thereby indirectly influencing eventual culture change. Several respondents noted that it was too early to tell from the survey results whether actions taken had affected safety and the hospital's culture. Many of the interventions reported to us had been started only in the past year or two.

Several of the interviewees reported, however, that simply using the survey and reporting of the results had raised staff awareness of the importance of patient safety and the specific safety issues addressed by the survey (e.g., handoffs, transitions, communication). As a result, HSOPS had helped to improve the hospital patient-safety culture.

Virtually all of the interviewed hospitals used the survey results both as a monitoring tool to identify and track trends and as a diagnosis tool to learn what actions the hospital should take to improve its patient safety culture. The hospitals that had administered the survey only once planned to administer it again and to use the results for assessing trends in their culture status.

In addition to administering the survey organization-wide, a few hospitals planned to use it in conjunction with patient safety initiatives. For example, one hospital was planning to provide teamwork training to a single, individual unit of the hospital. Prior to the training, and following the training, the participants would complete the survey, and the survey would be used in evaluating the training program results.

FEEDBACK TO AHRQ

Several culture surveys currently are available to hospitals. The interviewees have used other surveys in addition to HSOPS, and some developed their own surveys before adopting HSOPS. There seems to be a growing perception among hospitals that HSOPS is the best survey available. First, interviewees like the content of the survey. Second, the survey is free to use and free to access results. Third, the availability of the national benchmarking database played a role in more than one hospital's decision to use HSOPS over another survey. Finally, having technical assistance available (provided by Westat) is an important feature.

Suggestions to Improve the Survey

A few respondents suggested that AHRQ could make the survey more relevant to physicians, either by asking different questions or by wording the questions differently. For example, rather than asking physicians who their "supervisor" is, they could be asked who their "department chair" is. These respondents noted, for example, that, in many hospitals, physicians do not work in a particular unit and do not report to a particular unit supervisor. Therefore, physicians find the survey instructions to be confusing or irrelevant to them.

Some interviewees recommended that AHRQ change negatively worded questions to positively worded questions. The combination of both types of questions on a survey can be confusing for staff. A few respondents also felt that it would be useful to have a separate version of the survey for nonclinical staff.

The large "other" category for staff position in the reported data was problematic for some of the interviewees. They would like to know more about the staff who fall into this large category, and would like AHRQ to add more or better staff labels to reduce the size of this residual category.

Use of the National Benchmarking Data

The AHRQ national SOPS benchmarking database generates annual reports on hospital culture-survey results, as well as customized reports for participating hospitals that compare their survey results to results from all hospitals participating in the database. Most of the hospitals interviewed were very positive about the database and found the comparative information helpful as they interpreted their own results. Those who represented hospitals that received customized benchmark reports from other organizations (e.g., QIO, hospital association) had similarly positive views of those reports.

Many interviewees reported that they analyzed the details of the benchmarking data in detail, to compare themselves to hospitals with similar characteristics. Interview responses were mixed on the relative importance of comparisons based on hospital size or geographic region.

One hospital reported that it used the benchmarking report to set goals and expectations for improvement in the survey results in specific areas the next time the survey is administered. Particularly when a hospital's survey results showed the hospital scoring higher than the national average in a particular domain, or average for similar hospitals, this information was shared with hospital employees to give them positive feedback and to show that their participation in the survey was a valuable activity.

Some respondents, however, did not think the benchmarking reports were very useful because they were focused internally on their own results and did not get much utility from benchmarking themselves to others. As one respondent stated, "…when you are looking at the issue of culture, you should only be benchmarking against yourself." Others found that they were struggling with the same issues as hospitals similar to them and, thus, they did not feel that the report added useful information or provided any guidance.

Regardless of the specific ways that hospitals are using the benchmarking reports, we heard numerous times that the existence of the benchmarking report was a key factor in getting senior leadership's buy-in for doing the survey, and was also an important factor for hospitals that had considered multiple culture surveys but chose HSOPS because it included availability of information from the benchmarking database.

Ideas for Technical Assistance

Most respondents reported that the technical assistance they have received from AHRQ and Westat has been very useful. However, some found the assistance Westat provided to be limited, particularly compared with the assistance they were receiving from other organizations. In particular, one theme that emerged was that support provided by other organizations was especially important for sustaining the survey activity of smaller, rural, and other resource-restricted hospitals.

Some interviewees offered ideas for additional or improved technical assistance. There was a desire for guidance on actions to take in response to the results. Although some of the hospitals obtained this guidance from their QIO, state hospital organization, or a university-based research team with which they partnered, most hospitals did not have external organizations to which they could turn.

Some respondents would like to receive their customized reports from Westat (and the comparative database reports) in a more timely manner. In some cases, the lag time between submitting survey data and receiving their results was longer than a year, which limited the usefulness of the data. A few respondents were not aware that a customized version of the benchmarking database report was available.

A few interviewees would like AHRQ to prepare communication-media templates as tools they could use to publicize the survey and results to staff. Ideas included brochures, posters, flyers, and similar materials. A promotional kit with publicity materials that the hospital could adapt to its own use would be very helpful, particularly for hospitals in which one person has the full responsibility for the survey-administration process. In addition, some respondents suggested the development of different report templates for different audiences within the hospital (e.g., Board of Directors, quality committee, nonclinical staff), reflecting their differing information needs.

Some respondents were interested in comparing their culture survey results with the results of other surveys they administer, such as employee-satisfaction surveys or CAHPS surveys. They wanted to know whether AHRQ or Westat could provide assistance in this area.

One respondent suggested that Westat provide a summary that allows people to compare the pros and cons of the different culture surveys currently available. Hospitals that are deciding which patient safety culture survey to use for the first time could benefit from having this information. In addition, the information could help hospitals that have already administered a survey and want to assess whether they are using the one that matches their needs.

One interviewee who administered a Web-based version of the survey would like to be able to submit the data directly to Westat, rather than having the intermediate step of submitting it to the hospital, which must then submit the data to Westat. This capability would reduce the labor burden on hospitals and also potentially make it possible to get faster benchmarking feedback from Westat. It could also improve response rates if respondents knew their survey responses were not being seen by anyone in their hospital, an issue that is particularly relevant to small hospitals in which data on personal characteristics quickly identify survey respondents, even though the survey is completed anonymously. Although data on respondent characteristics, such as unit or staff position, is useful for acting on the results, respondents may not respond, or may not respond honestly out of concern for being identified.

Implications of Other Support Organizations for National Support Roles

During our interviews, we found that a number of hospitals have worked with external organizations that have helped them with the survey-administration process. These organizations included QIOs, state hospital associations, and universities. From interviews with representatives from two of these organizations, we learned that they were playing a number of roles including assisting hospitals with data collection, analysis, and submission to the AHRQ benchmarking database. In some cases, they also were assisting hospitals in interpreting their results and developing plans of action to respond to the results. The hospitals using these external organizations identified several advantages to working with them:

- The resources provided by the organizations were critical to some hospitals' ability to administer the survey.

- Some hospitals got customized feedback from the organizations that was highly personalized to their type of hospital, including benchmarking their results to those of other hospitals within their market, state, or region.
- These organizations provide survey results very quickly to their participating hospitals. In particular, when a Web-based survey was provided by the external organization, hospitals got survey results immediately after each survey field period closes.

Under the new Ninth Statement of Work for the QIO contracts with CMS, QIOs are expected to work with community access hospitals (CAH) and rural PPS (Prospective Payment System) hospitals in administering HSOPS surveys and initiating actions to improve patient safety culture results. Thus, because an increasing number of hospitals use QIOs as external organizations, the demand for benchmarking and technical assistance from Westat may decline. We emphasize that the feedback about the support from Westat has been positive, but demand will decline if hospitals find they can get higher value from working with other organizations. This factor should have less effect on the benchmarking database, however, because it is unique in having the capability to provide comparisons with hospitals across the country.

Linking Results with AHRQ Tools and Best Practices

Several of our interviewees mentioned that they were able to connect the survey results with specific AHRQ tools and best practices (whether associated with AHRQ or not). Many respondents were aware that specific tools have been developed for patient safety areas in which hospitals tend to score poorly. Examples of such tools include SBAR Communication, TeamSTEPPS™, and rapid-response-team models.

However, a few respondents reported that it can be difficult to connect specific problem areas or composites in the survey with tools and best practices. These respondents suggested that AHRQ provide guidance to help them link the survey results to tools and best practices. One interviewee suggested that AHRQ provide an online toolkit that hospitals can use in initiatives to improve their patient safety culture. The toolkit could be organized by the survey composites, and, for each composite, links to tools and best practices could be provided. With this resource, a hospital that scored low in a particular survey composite could get specific recommendations online for actions to take in response to its results.

One interviewee called for more research on correlations between patient safety culture and improved outcomes. This person gave the example of one physician in his organization who had excellent leadership skills that promoted a strong culture of patient safety, and the interviewee would like to be able to link this to outcomes data to see if that physician's skills affected outcomes.

CONCLUSIONS

In general, the hospitals we interviewed have been pleased with the AHRQ Hospital Survey on Patient Safety Culture's contents, ease of administration, usefulness to their patient safety strategy and activities, and availability of the national benchmarking data. Not surprisingly, the hospitals varied in how they used the survey data, as well as in the extent to which they needed and sought assistance in working with it from Westat and other external organizations. From a patient-safety-strategy perspective, hospitals' reports that they use HSOPS as a key measurement and monitoring tool in their patient safety initiatives suggest that the survey is being put to good use in the field. These interviews also yielded valuable insights regarding actions that AHRQ and Westat can take to enhance the value of HSOPS and the benchmarking database for hospitals. In particular, the information obtained on the growing use of external organizations needs to be considered carefully in planning future roles for national-level technical-assistance roles, to find creative approaches for gaining synergy between what is provided nationally and what other support organizations are providing.

CHAPTER 4.
NATIONAL SURVEY ON ADOPTION OF NQF SAFE PRACTICES

SPECIFIC AIM

An important part of AHRQ's patient safety initiative is monitoring and assessing the extent to which safe practices are being adopted in the national health care community. Yet the greatest challenge in developing data on the adoption of patient safety practices in the U.S. health care system has been the inability to measure effectively the extent to which each practice actually is being used by providers. Therefore, we saw development of a data-collection instrument as the first important step to take in this area. The specific aims of this survey-development work are as follows:

1. To support AHRQ's efforts to monitor and assess the extent to which safe practices are being adopted in the national health care community by creating a national-level survey on hospitals' use of safe practices.

2. To provide AHRQ with supportive information about the survey that it can use as it administers and updates the survey in the future.

We have developed a survey that can be used to document the extent to which U.S. hospitals are adopting safe practices and are tracking their own performance in using them. The questionnaire is designed to gather data on structures and processes that hospitals have in place that indicate they have implemented each safe practice addressed by the survey. The survey does not focus on outcomes, nor does it judge the actual practice performance of hospitals.

The survey items address the majority of the set of safe practices adopted by NQF in its *2006 Update* (NQF, 2007), which was the most current NQF document available at the time we developed the survey. Our development process included testing of the draft questionnaire, using cognitive testing methods, as well as validating it by comparing the questions in the survey to actual practices by the 15 hospitals that participated in our community-based study of safe-practice diffusion.

CONTEXT

The NQF Safe Practices

In 2003, the NQF endorsed a set of 30 safe practices to be utilized in applicable clinical care settings to reduce the risk of harm to patients (NQF, 2003). These safe practices are a set of voluntary standards established through the NQF consensus process, which are intended to serve as a tool for health care providers, purchasers, and consumers to identify and encourage practices that reduce errors and improve care. In developing the safe practices, the NQF selected 30 practices from an original pool of over 220 candidates based on each practice's specificity, evidence-based effectiveness, and potential benefit (NQF, 2007). The NQF also considered each practice's generalizability (i.e., applicability in multiple clinical-care settings or multiple types of patients), and readiness for implementation. The set of safe practices was carefully reviewed and endorsed by a diverse group of stakeholders in keeping with the NQF's formal Consensus Development Process.

NQF updated the original set of safe practices in 2006, through the work of its Safe Practices Consensus Standards Maintenance Committee. The updated set developed by the

Committee also included 30 practices, all but a few of which had been in the original set; they were refined in the 2006 update (NQF, 2007). This Committee has the responsibility of reviewing the practices periodically and recommending additions or changes for consideration by its members. Based on review of the 2006 set of practices, NQF released a revised set in March 2009.

Leapfrog Group Survey

The Leapfrog Group ("Leapfrog") has developed a survey to assess hospital performance on practices that are proven to reduce preventable medical mistakes. The practices, which have been endorsed by the NQF (The Leapfrog Group, 2008), encompass computerized physician order entry; intensive care unit physician staffing; evidence-based hospital referral; and many of the remaining NQF-endorsed safe practices.[8] Now known as the "Leapfrog Group's Hospital Survey," this survey was first released in 2001, is voluntary, and may be completed by any hospital in the United States. The Texas Medical Institute of Technology, a medical research organization under subcontract to Leapfrog, developed the "Safe Practices Scores" section of the survey, which addresses the NQF Safe Practices. The 2006 and 2007 surveys addressed all 27 NQF practices (in addition to the three Leapfrog practices). In response to feedback from hospitals regarding data-collection burden, this section was substantially shortened in the 2008 survey to address only 13 of the NQF practices.

In an effort to promote transparency in health care, the survey data are publicly reported on Leapfrog's Web site (www.leapfroggroup.org). Consumers (e.g., individuals and larger purchasers) are the primary intended audience, and all employer members of Leapfrog make the survey data available to their enrollees. These data are also used in Leapfrog's Hospital Rewards Program, which assesses and rewards the quality and efficiency of hospital performance.

RAND's Collaboration with Leapfrog

Given the basic motivation to document the status of U.S. hospitals in the adoption of the NQF Safe Practices at a given point in time, a survey instrument is needed that generates data that can be used to estimate valid rates of adoption by hospitals of key aspects of each practice. Although the Leapfrog survey addresses the same NQF practices, its survey items are not designed for use in estimating rates of practice adoption. Many of the Leapfrog items capture stages in the practice-adoption process that precede full implementation (e.g., planning stage, small-scale testing, partial implementation), and Leapfrog gives them credit for progress through these stages, which increases hospitals' reported scores. In addition, for many of the Leapfrog items, the denominator data needed to calculate rates of practice adoption are not collected. In examining data from the Leapfrog 2006 and 2007 surveys, we found that we could obtain basic frequencies of positive responses, but its data were not coded for "no" responses.

The design of the Leapfrog survey reflects the purposes for which it has been used—for public reporting on individual hospitals to achieve the transparency goal of informing health care consumers, and for encouraging hospital quality improvements for these practices. We were advised by Leapfrog that, because hospitals are now accustomed to the Leapfrog survey, it may be challenging to get them to respond to a survey that does not allow for such "partial credit,"

---

[8] The first three areas listed comprise the "Leapfrog Safety Practices," known as the first three "leaps." They overlap in topic area, but not exact content, with three of the 30 NQF Safe Practices.

even if it is anonymous. (In fact, we did encounter such responses in the cognitive testing and validation steps of our survey-development process.)

Given the existence of Leapfrog's hospital survey and the potential for shared learning in our survey-development efforts, we approached Leapfrog's survey team early in our process for consultation and collaboration opportunities. Our two teams agreed to work together throughout our process, seeking opportunities to achieve consistency and mitigate redundancy between the two surveys. As our survey-development work progressed, and Leapfrog became engaged in significant revisions of its own survey, it became apparent to both teams that there would be fewer opportunities for shared survey items than we initially had anticipated. Given the significant differences in the purposes of the two surveys, the focus and design of individual items also differed. As such, our two teams continued working independently, but also shared draft items and sought input from each other at appropriate junctures.

SURVEY DEVELOPMENT

At the start of our survey-development process, we held discussions with key individuals who could provide us with valuable historical and contextual information. They included the Leapfrog staff, the co-chairs of the NQF Safe Practices Consensus Maintenance Committee and Joint Commission staff. The information they provided allowed us to understand as clearly as possible the nature of related work performed to that point, and how it could provide a basis for—or differed from—the survey and sampling strategy we aimed to develop.

Discussions with the co-chairs of the NQF Safe Practices Consensus Maintenance Committee—Gregg Meyer, M.D. and Chuck Denham, M.D—enabled us to learn about their experiences developing the NQF Safe Practices. In particular, they shared their thoughts on survey design to document practice implementation. Both of them emphasized the need to reduce the response burden for hospitals by keeping the survey as short as possible, and to word items precisely to capture accurate data and reduce gaming of responses.

In discussions with representatives from the Joint Commission, we sought to learn whether their data could be used to develop national estimates of the adoption of some of the safe practices. If so, data for those practices would not have to be collected in the survey we were developing. We found that, because the Joint Commission relies heavily on data collected through in-person observation at site visits, its review process does not generate data that could be used to develop national estimates of adoption rates for the safe practices. Therefore, we would have to address all the NQF practices in designing the survey.

The first step in our item-development process was to determine which of the 30 NQF Safe Practices were amenable to assessment with a standardized, self-administered survey of hospitals. To accomplish this task, a team of RAND researchers—including staff from our Survey Research Group (SRG) and two practicing physicians with patient safety experience—reviewed in depth each of the 30 safe practices. We generally determined that a safe practice was not amenable to assessment through a hospital survey if the central component of the practice requires observation or chart data to ensure that implementation has occurred. We concluded that 22 of the 30 safe practices could be assessed using an organizational survey.

We grouped these 22 safe practices into seven groupings based on similarity of topic as well as by hospital function to which practices were relevant. Our intention in developing the groupings was twofold: (1) to provide a logical framework by which the safe practices could be organized in the survey, for ease of use by responding hospitals; and (2) to explore a modular sampling strategy based on the groupings, in which hospitals in the sample could complete survey questions for a subset of the practices in the survey, which would reduce data collection burden for them (see Survey Sampling subsection below). These groupings were patient safety culture, communication with patients or families, transparency across continuum of care, surgery procedures, medical evaluation and prevention, medication safety management, and workforce. Table 4.1 presents the 22 practices that are included in the survey, listed by group, along with the expected areas of hospital jurisdiction that would complete items for each group. The list of eight excluded practices, and the reasons for their exclusion, is presented in Appendix D.

Table 4.1 NQF Safe Practices Included in the Survey

Safe Practice Groups	Hospital Jurisdiction
Patient Safety Culture 1. Create, sustain a health care culture of safety	Executive management, Patient Safety Office
Communication With Patients or Families 3. Ensure written documentation of patient's preferences for life-sustaining treatments 4. Provide timely and clear communication to families about serious unanticipated events	Quality Management, Patient Safety Office
Transparency Across Continuum of Care 10. Implement policies, processes, systems for accurate labeling of diagnostic studies 11. Prepare discharge plan for each patient at time of discharge, with summary given to receiving caregiver and confirmation by him/her 13. Standardize list of abbreviations "not to be used" 14. Develop and communicate accurate medication list throughout continuum of care	Patient Safety Office
Surgery Procedures 25. Implement universal protocol for wrong site, procedure, person surgery for all procedures 26. Evaluate patients with elective surgery for risk of acute cardiac events; consider prophylactic treatment	Chief of Surgery
Medical Evaluation and Prevention 23. Immunize health care workers and patients who should be immunized against influenza annually 27. Evaluate patient for pressure ulcers upon admission and regularly thereafter; implement preventive methods 28. Evaluate patient for risk of VTE/DVT upon admission and regularly thereafter; use appropriate thromboprophylaxis methods 29. Monitor patients on long-term oral anticoagulants by qualified health professional using a careful strategy 30. Use validated protocols to evaluate patients at risk for contrast media-induced renal failure; use appropriate method to reduce risk based on kidney-function evaluation	Chief of Medicine, Medical Administration

Table 4.1 NQF Safe Practices Included in the Survey (cont.)

Safe Practice Groups	Hospital Jurisdiction
Medication Safety Management 12. Implement CPOE on foundation of re-engineered, evidence-based care, staff readiness, and integrated IT infrastructure 15. Have pharmacists participate in medication management systems with other health professionals 16. Standardize methods for labeling and packaging of medications 17. Identify "high alert" drugs and have policies and procedures to minimize risks associated with them 18. Dispense medications in unit-dose or unit-of-use form whenever possible	Pharmacy, Patient Safety Office
Workforce 5. Implement critical components of nursing workforce that reinforce patient safeguards 6. Ensure that non-nursing direct care staffing levels are adequate, competent, trained 7. Manage ICU patients by physicians with training in critical care medicine	Nursing Administration, Medical Administration, Human Resources

NOTES: VTE=venous thromboembolism; DVT=deep vein thrombosis

The next stage of our survey development process involved drafting the individual survey items related to each safe practice included in the survey. Our primary goal was to stay true to the intention, and—as much as possible—to the actual language of each safe practice, as outlined in the *NQF Safe Practice Update 2006* document. Our core survey-development team comprised two health services researchers and two staff from RAND's SRG. Throughout this process, we consulted with other RAND researchers and clinicians with expertise in patient safety, hospitals, and organizational surveys. We also shared draft items with the Leapfrog survey team and NQF co-chairs for their feedback. Our core survey-development team methodically reviewed and discussed each comment and made determinations as to whether to incorporate suggested edits.

TESTING OF DRAFT SURVEY ITEMS

The testing of the draft items for the safe practice survey consisted of two steps. The first step was cognitive testing of the items to ensure that the items written to address each practice were clear and reasonable to users. This step was followed by validation analysis to assess how well the set of items for each practice "fit" how hospitals actually implement and use that practice. Following revisions made to the draft survey as a result of these two testing steps, the survey was ready for pilot testing with a larger sample of hospitals before being used to collect national data from a full sample of U.S. hospitals.

Cognitive Testing

Our first step in testing the draft survey items was cognitive testing interviews conducted with four hospitals. The goal of the cognitive testing was to seek input from front-line hospital staff about the face validity, applicability, understandability, and response burden of the draft survey items.

Cognitive-testing methods. We conducted cognitive-testing interviews with two hospitals in the greater Los Angeles area and two in the Pittsburgh area. We purposely recruited different types of hospitals, including two large academic hospitals and two community hospitals, one of which was rural. We identified hospitals according to our survey team's knowledge of hospitals in these areas, and in consultation with clinical experts in both cities. We recruited hospitals by approaching the Patient Safety Officer (or equivalent), and inquiring about their interest in providing feedback on this survey.

Each testing interview was conducted by RAND staff at the hospital, with a team of representatives from the hospital. We worked with our primary contact at each hospital (typically the Patient Safety Officer) to identify the most appropriate hospital staff to attend the interview. In most cases, the following types of individuals were present: the Patient Safety Officer /risk manager; the chief medical officer; and the directors of pharmacy, nursing, and performance improvement. In some cases the CEO and key clinical department heads (e.g., surgery) also attended.

The interviews usually lasted two hours. We used a standardized cognitive-interview protocol that included scripted probes to guide the interviews, which allowed us to analyze data across the four hospitals. A RAND team member recorded notes of the discussions. In advance of the testing interview, each hospital was sent a subset of the survey items, representing approximately two-thirds of the survey. The subset was used to reduce testing burden on any single hospital and to allow for in-depth discussion of some of the practices (versus a superficial review of all). All hospitals received the patient safety culture portion of the survey, and we divided the remaining sections of the survey among the four hospitals.

Cognitive-testing findings. Overall, the survey was received well by the four hospitals. Some individuals expressed concern regarding having yet another survey to fill out, citing the large number of reporting requirements they face and highlighting the length of the Leapfrog survey. However, almost all of them recognized the value of having a "national barometer" of hospital patient safety practice. Further, most stated that it was relatively easy to complete these survey questions, and they estimated that it took approximately two hours to complete the subset of items they received. This time was substantially shorter than their estimated time-to-complete the Leapfrog survey, which several said takes days for a full-time-equivalent staff person.

All the hospital representatives underscored that the survey would need to be divided up and filled out by different individuals in the hospital (i.e., no one person was capable of filling it out in its entirety). As such, it needs to be in a format that can be easily distributed (i.e., clear section headings), and readily transferable (e.g., a printable pdf file or emailed document). Most had a strong preference for a paper version, because they prefer to report their responses on a paper document. Some indicated that they would be willing to enter their responses from a paper version into an online system, but they noted that an online-entry process would be for the convenience of the surveyors—not the hospitals.

As to the items, most requested greater specificity and more definitions of terms used in both questions and related answer choices, to ensure clarity and consistent interpretation. RAND responded by adding definitions for terms that the respondents identified as confusing throughout the survey.

A second key point that was frequently raised was the need for a "partial yes" response in many cases, as is allowed in the Leapfrog survey. Many felt that a simple yes/no response was sometimes inadequate, because it did not accurately reflect where a hospital was in adopting a safe practice. In subsequent survey revisions, we added expanded yes/no scales when appropriate and did not compromise the intended goals of our survey.

In addition to these central points that were consistently made across the four test sites, individuals participating in the testing provided detailed comments on specific items. After the interviews were completed, we discussed these comments with the participants of the testing interviews, as well as among our survey team and internal experts. We responded by making changes to individual items as deemed appropriate through this consensus process.

Validation

After completing the cognitive testing and resulting survey revisions, we validated the survey items using data collected in the roundtable discussions with the 15 hospitals during site visits conducted for our community study. The goals of this validation step were to (1) assess how well the survey questions "fit" how hospitals actually implement and use each practice, and (2) solicit specific comments on individual survey items.

Validation methods. As described in Chapter 2, the 15 hospitals that participated in that study were located in Seattle, Washington; Cleveland, Ohio; Greenville, South Carolina; and Indianapolis, Indiana. The roundtable discussions conducted during the site visits focused on how each hospital was implementing the NQF Safe Practices and their experiences in doing so. The types of hospital staff participating in the roundtables varied, depending on the safe practices being addressed at each roundtable. They often included the Patient Safety Officer, chief medical officer, chief nursing officer, risk manager, quality or performance improvement officer, director of pharmacy, and chairs of pertinent committees.

In preparation for the roundtable discussions, we worked with each hospital to select two groups of NQF Safe Practices that the hospital had been implementing, so the hospital staff would be able to tell the "story" about their experiences in using the practices. One practice was selected from the patient safety culture sections (leadership, risks, survey, or teamwork) and the other group was selected from the other practice groups listed above. For example, if a hospital told us it was particularly focused on improving medication safety, we identified medication safety management as a group of practices to discuss with that hospital. The practice groups discussed with the hospitals, by hospital type, are presented in Table 2.3.

We focused each discussion on the hospital's motivation for adopting practices in the group being addressed and the actions they took to implement them. We also explored their progress to date, challenges encountered, and extent of success in making the practices an integral part of their operation. Then we asked them to talk specifically about how the items in the draft RAND survey corresponded to their use of the safe practices. At the end of each roundtable discussion, we also sought feedback on the survey items. From their feedback, we could identify any differences between the survey items and actual practice regarding how hospitals define or categorize specific practices, and to identify any safe practices (or aspects of practices) that may be missing from the survey.

To perform the validation analysis, a researcher on our survey development team reviewed in detail the written notes from the roundtable discussions. This person identified general themes and specific issues regarding implementation of each safe practice and assessed the extent to which the survey questions were consistent with hospitals' actual use of the practice. The researcher conferred with the leader of each roundtable to ensure the accuracy of conclusions reached. Our core survey-development team then reviewed and discussed the validation findings as a group. Our key findings are based on careful scrutiny of the roundtable notes, the feedback on specific survey items, and the observations by our researchers who led the roundtable discussions.

Validation findings. Overall, our validation process revealed that the survey items accurately reflect the ways in which hospitals tend to implement and use the safe practices—that is, the items are consistent with what hospitals are actually doing. These results are summarized in Table 4.2. For six of the seven groupings, only minor adjustments were required to ensure that the content of the associated items reflects the key efforts hospitals are making to adhere to recommended practices. In some instances, these adjustments took the form of deleting items that were not determined to be salient. The only survey items that required substantial revisions to more accurately reflect the scope of the NQF practice and actual hospital use of it were items for the teamwork practice (Element 3 in the Patient Safety Culture Practice, Table 4.2a).

In all instances where we made changes to the survey content, we adhered to our guiding principle of remaining true to the intent and language of each safe practice. As such, we only made revisions to the survey if the hospitals' feedback related to an important aspect of the safe practice that is clearly noted in the NQF source document. Several comments encouraged us to expand the scope of the NQF practice itself, which we did not do, given that our goal was to capture the existing scope of the practices in the survey—not expand them. Additionally, we did not add items related to topics that are not amenable to assessment with a self-report survey, even if such topics are integral to a given safe practice. For example, practice 11, on patient-discharge planning, emphasizes the importance of ensuring that patients and their families understand discharge plans, and hospitals reiterated this point during the roundtable discussions. However, we did not attempt to develop an item on comprehension of the plans, because an organization survey cannot measure this behavioral phenomenon.

Throughout the survey development and revisions, we remained mindful of survey length and response burden. We aimed to capture the core elements of each safe practice amenable to assessment with an organizational survey, recognizing that a long survey would create response burden for the hospitals and could affect response rates. Finally, we focused primarily on structures needed to implement the safe practices or formally established review processes, which indicated that practices are being used (e.g., regular monitoring of a practice and related outcomes). Many of the processes involved in a practice cannot be assessed readily in a survey of this nature, because they involve complex dynamics that are not amenable to survey data collection or they would require numerous questions (and response burden) to document accurately.

Table 4.2a. Validation Findings for the NQF Patient Safety Culture Practices

Patient Safety Culture Practice	Validation Findings	
	Did draft items accurately reflect hospitals' practices?	Comments
Element 1. Leadership	Yes	Hospitals noted the importance of senior leaders engagement with front-line staff (e.g. walk-arounds). However, given the limitations of assessment with an organizational survey and in the interest of minimizing survey burden, we focused on structures and on well-established, formal processes about which concise responses were feasible (e.g., inclusion of a practice in standard quality-management monitoring process). Additionally, having engaged senior leaders is necessary for having an engaged governing board (about which we do ask).
Element 2. Culture Survey	Yes	An explicit answer choice was added to inquire about dissemination of the survey results to all clinical caregivers and other staff, given the importance placed on dissemination in the practice, as well as hospitals' emphasis on the need for sharing this information with front-line staff.
Element 3. Teamwork	No	Draft items for this practice were found to not accurately reflect either the scope of hospitals' actions for teamwork improvement or the full range of training and implementation elements defined in the NQF practice. In response to this feedback, we revised the questions so that they now accurately reflect the intended scope of the teamwork practice and hospitals' actions.
Element 4. Safety Risks	Yes	Hospitals noted that survey items do not assess actions taken as a result of identifying risks. The related safe practice does explicitly address risk-mitigation and performance-improvement activities. However, we elected to focus on the first step (risk identification) in the interest of survey brevity, and also because the implementation of quality-improvement efforts cannot be assessed readily in a survey of this nature.

61

Table 4.2b. Validation Findings for Other NQF Safe Practices, by Groupings Established for the Survey

Other Safe Practice Groups	Validation Findings	
	Did draft items accurately reflect hospitals' practices?	Comments
Communication with Patients and Families (Practices 3 and 4)	Yes	Hospitals noted the importance of ensuring that patients and their families understand discharge plans, which is explicitly stated in the practice. However, we did not include an item on this issue given that it cannot be evaluated with an organization survey (follow-up is required with patients and families).
Transparency Across Continuum of Care (Practices 10, 11, 13)	Yes	Hospitals noted the importance of electronic medical records (EMRs) for transparency. However, we did not include any items on this topic, given that it is not mentioned directly in the NQF practice, and adherence to transparency should not depend on the type of records system used (e.g., paper medical records versus EMR).
Surgery Procedures (Practices 25 and 26)	Yes	Hospitals noted the importance of assessing how well safe surgical practices, such as time-outs, are implemented. However, an organization survey is not an optimal method, given that it requires self-report of actions or behaviors, often involving social desirability and other issues that need to be managed carefully to encourage accurate self-report by respondents.
Medical Evaluation and Prevention (Practices 23, 27, 28, 29, 30)	Yes	Hospitals noted additional steps they have taken to ensure safety (e.g., *requiring* all staff to receive the influenza vaccine; establishing task forces on specific safety topics). However, we did not include questions capturing this level of detail, because these actions go beyond the scope of the practice.
Medication Safety Management (Practices 12, 14, 15, 16, 17, 18	Yes	Hospitals noted issues that were not addressed by survey items (e.g., alert fatigue; bar-coding overrides). We did not add questions on these issues because they either go beyond the scope of the related practices or would have resulted in increased response burden with limited commensurate benefit from additional information.
Workforce (Practices 5, 6, 7)	Yes	Hospitals noted the importance of ongoing safety training for staff, and underscored that the quality of training may vary significantly. We did not add questions on this topic, because the NQF practice focused on workforce planning and did not explicitly address training (although training is implicit in some of the language of the practice).

Most individual survey items were understandable to the hospitals participating in the roundtable discussions. We modified survey items according to their feedback, including addition of definitions of terms and some clarifications of the instructions for completing the survey. The following are examples of the types of changes made:

- A number of questions in the survey relate to the frequency of monitoring for a given practice. Feedback from the hospitals revealed their confusion about how to report the frequency if the hospital monitors different aspects of the practice at different intervals. To address this issue, we clarified throughout the survey that when a question asks "how often," hospitals should respond with the most frequent interval that they monitor. For example, if a hospital reviews the effectiveness of its medication management process more often for high-alert drugs than for other types of drugs, it is instructed to report the interval for the high-alert drugs.

- The term "review" (such as in the draft question "How often does this hospital review adherence to its standardized medication labeling and packaging practices?) was not always understood. We changed the wording to clarify that the question refers to a formal, comprehensive review, not a casual, less-rigorous check.

- Hospitals were unsure how to respond to the survey if their hospital was part of a larger health system. The use of the term "organization" instead of "hospital" in some instances contributed to this confusion. In our revisions, we added instructions that a hospital should answer for itself only (not the larger system). We also changed the term *organization* to *hospital* throughout the survey to be more precise.

- We changed some response scales to allow for the fact that some hospitals may have reached a maintenance phase in their implementation of a given action. Prior to making this change, hospitals could only indicate that they had "fully implemented," were "in the process of implementing" or "had not implemented"—none of which was an accurate reflection of a hospital that had fully implemented an action but viewed itself as being in an active, phase of maintaining the practice improvements they had achieved.

The final draft survey questionnaire, which consists of 93 questions that address 22 of the NQF Safe Practices, is provided in Appendix E. Appendix F is an accompanying document that provides the rationale for the choices of questions and how they are worded. As any future work is performed on updating or refining the questionnaire, it will be important to refer to this rationale document, because it highlights lessons learned in feedback from hospitals in our cognitive testing and validation processes.

CONSIDERATIONS FOR FIELDING THE FUTURE SURVEY

Sampling

Given the concerns expressed by hospitals about response burden, we considered two possible sampling strategies to reduce that burden while maintaining a nationally representative sample. In both approaches, the sample of hospitals would be divided into groups, and survey items for subsets of practices would be fielded with each group. We envisioned that the items for the Patient Safety Culture practice (all four elements) would be included in the survey for all hospitals, given the importance of culture for effective patient safety. Therefore, these two approaches would differ in how the survey items for the remaining safe practices are included in the survey.

In the first scenario, all hospitals would receive survey items for (1) the patient safety culture practice, and (2) a portion of the remaining six groups of practices. For example, half the hospitals would receive items for practice groups 1 through 3, and the other half would receive items for the remaining three groups. The advantages of this approach are that only two versions of the survey would need to be created, which would entail relatively small survey-administration burden. The key disadvantage is that practice implementation relationships could be examined only for the practices within each half of the survey—i.e., relationships for practices in different halves could not be examined.

In the second scenario, all hospitals would receive survey items for (1) the entire Patient Safety Culture practice, and (2) an overlapping portion of some combination of the remaining six practice groups. For example, the six non–Patient Safety Culture groups could be divided into thirds, and each survey version could contain items for two-thirds of the groups. As such, three versions of the survey would be created (one with the first two groups; another with the first and third groups, and the last with the second and third groups). Other variations on this overlapping approach are also possible, such as giving every hospital a survey with items for the culture practice and three other groups (of the remaining six) but rotating which three are included.

Using any type of overlapping approach, compared to the first approach outlined above, has the main advantage of making it possible to examine the relationships among all safe practice groups in the survey. The disadvantages include reduced power to examine relationships among the different groups; increased survey-administration burden (e.g., creation of three or more different survey versions, ensuring that the correct version is sent to the correct hospital, balancing versions within sampling strata, and rotating versions each year so that hospitals do not receive the same version each fielding); and increased analysis burden (e.g., more-complex data entry and management given subsamples, potential for diverse response rates for each survey version).

In considering the sampling options, we note that it is always possible to reduce response burden more, but the reduction will come at the cost of increased survey-administration and analysis burden, due to the increasing number of survey versions required. Additionally, each time the survey is cut in half, the sample must be doubled to maintain the same power for the overall estimates of items not represented in all versions. By employing the overlapping strategy discussed, the additional sample required can be reduced, but the total sample still would be larger than if the entire survey were fielded with each hospital.

Feedback from hospitals reported that it was not burdensome to complete the survey sections they were given. Although this suggests that the full survey might not be overly burdensome, we estimated that response times to complete the full survey would be 2 to 4 hours (based on information from the cognitive testing). This is substantially shorter than the time required to complete the Leapfrog survey, but it still involves considerable time for busy hospital staff. (According to hospitals participating in our cognitive testing, it took them several days to weeks to complete the Leapfrog survey.)

Considering the disadvantages discussed above of using a modular approach, we recommend fielding the complete 93-item survey with all hospitals, which permits the most analytic flexibility. This flexibility is particularly important in the early fielding of this survey, given the novelty of these data, and the fact that the full extent of potentially important research questions is not known in advance, which makes it difficult to pre-specify sample-size requirements to address potentially important, narrow research questions. Additionally, we recommend taking a stratified, random-sampling approach to ensure that the sample is nationally representative with regard to key hospital attributes, such as ownership type, bed size, and Joint Commission accreditation status.

We base our recommendation in part on the lessons learned when we fielded the AHRQ Adverse Events Reporting System (AERS) survey. The AERS survey also is an organization survey, which is designed to gather information from a sample of hospitals about the nature of their internal adverse event reporting systems and how they use the data on occurrences reported into their systems to improve the safety of the care they provide. We first fielded the AERS survey with a national sample of hospitals in 2005 (Farley et al., 2008a), and a second wave of AERS survey data is being collected in 2009.

The AERS survey is similar to the NQF Safe Practices adoption survey in that hospitals received no compensation for completing the survey and there were no other external motivating factors for responding (e.g., public reporting, as is done with the Leapfrog survey data). We obtained an 81-percent response rate on the 2005 AERS survey, using a combination of mail survey followed by a telephone survey for those who did not complete the mail version. Hospitals apparently saw the value in responding to the survey, and they were willing to take the time to complete it.

We note, however, that the NQF Safe Practices survey is much longer than the AERS survey, which could lower its response rates. Although response burden is not to be taken lightly, the hospitals with which we have conducted testing have recognized the importance of tracking adoption of the NQF Safe Practices, leading us to conclude that it is worth attempting to field the entire survey. Of course, if the pilot test reveals that the survey burden is greater than determined by the validation study, such that the response rate will be affected significantly, consideration should be given to one of the modular approaches outlined above (or a variant thereof).

Mode of Administration

The following survey modes were considered for this survey, each of which has advantages and disadvantages (discussed below):

- self-administered, scannable hard-copy mail survey
- self-administered Web survey
- self-administered emailed survey
- interviewer-administered telephone survey.

Historically, surveys of organizations (organization surveys) have lower response rates than other types of list-based survey samples of individuals (e.g. patients). Lower response rates also are an issue with any type of self-administered organization survey (e.g., mail, Web, or email), compared with interviewer-administered surveys. Self-administered mail surveys present particularly unique challenges. Conversion of refusals to completions (refusal conversion), if needed, is more difficult with a self-administered survey, regardless of mode of administration. With a paper or mailed survey, there is the possibility of respondent error, given that respondents have to navigate skip instructions to identify the appropriate questions to answer (versus in a Web survey in which skip patterns would be programmed in advance). However, a mail survey is relatively inexpensive, and the survey could be completed at times convenient for the respondent, which is attractive in view of the length of this survey and the population to be surveyed (busy hospital staff). Further, given that hospital staff likely would break this survey questionnaire into different sections, for completion by different individuals, a mail survey is a reasonable consideration.

A self-administered Web survey would not require data entry of responses and is less prone to respondent error than a mail survey, since the skip patterns would already be programmed into the survey instrument. A Web survey could also be completed at a time convenient for the respondent. However, during the cognitive testing, several hospitals indicated that an online survey would be for the convenience of those administering the survey—not theirs. If the survey were online, they likely would complete it on paper, involving multiple people in the process, and then one person would take the additional (duplicative) step of entering the data online. An alternative would be to program the Web survey to allow data entry of survey sections by multiple staff, which would involve additional programming requirements.

A phone survey would not burden respondents with skip patterns, and tends to yield higher response rates as noted. However, given that multiple hospital staff need to complete different sections of the survey, a lengthy phone survey with multiple respondents is not practical financially and might not be feasible in practice.

Given the advantages and disadvantages outlined, we recommend a self-administered, scannable, mail survey that can also be transmitted electronically (i.e., an emailed PDF file) to respondents. Such a format would make it easy for the primary point of contact at each hospital to circulate the survey to appropriate staff within the hospital. This point of contact could then compile responses and return one completed survey on behalf of the hospital.

Suggestions for Pilot Test

Given the complexities of the survey-administration process, we strongly suggest that the safe practices survey be pilot-tested to explore how best to manage the various identified administrative issues. Specifically, a pilot test should aim to answer the following questions:

- Who is the appropriate person to receive the survey and how can this person be identified?
- Do the survey procedures designed for the pilot elicit the response levels desired?
- Does the survey elicit the desired information?
- How costly and how burdensome would the survey be?

In all organization surveys, determination of the most appropriate respondent is a major design issue. Our conversations with hospitals underscored that there is not a single individual who will possess or have access to all the information or knowledge required to complete the survey. As such, the survey will need to be completed in consultation with multiple individuals. Nonetheless, one person at each hospital needs to be designated as the "target respondent" for the survey, who will be responsible for the survey-completion process, including distributing survey sections to other staff. The pilot test should test procedures to identify this target respondent. The most likely candidate for target respondent is the hospital's Patient Safety Officer; however, Patient Safety Officers at different hospitals have different functions and titles, and some hospitals may not have one. A pilot study could help better define who should be the primary contact for the survey, and identify alternate, equivalent titles or positions for hospitals that do not have a Patient Safety Officer.

A pilot study can also help to refine the process used to identify appropriate respondents and contact procedures, as well as the associated response rates using those procedures. We anticipate that the survey administration would require the conduct of a preliminary screening telephone call to identify the target respondent, or the hospital's Patient Safety Officer by name (based on job title or functional role within the hospital). If no Patient Safety Officer exists, it will be necessary to determine an appropriate alternate title or position.

We recommend using a similar screening-call process as used for the AERS survey to identify the respondents. We propose the following screening and mailing procedures:

1. Request the name, address, telephone number, and email address of the Patient Safety Officer of interest from the hospital switchboard operator, and the name of the chief executive officer.

2. Send the Patient Safety Officer a cover letter, survey, and postage-paid envelope to return completed surveys by mail. Also send by mail a copy to the CEO, as a notification. If the Patient Safety Officer requests a soft-copy version, send a PDF of the survey via email.

3. Send a reminder postcard and email to the Patient Safety Officer two weeks later.

4. Send a re-mail letter and survey by mail two weeks later.

5. Send another reminder postcard.

In the AERS survey, we did not find it necessary to seek permission from the hospital CEO prior to survey administration. In some instances, respondents discussed the survey with their administrative authority before completing the survey and were given permission to participate. We do not anticipate a problem securing CEO approval for this survey either.

Our findings from the cognitive interviews and validation process suggest that, in general, respondents understood the questions and that the questions obtained the desired information about the hospital's patient-safety activities. Nevertheless, as discussed above, the findings also pointed to several areas of the survey for which some respondents had trouble answering questions. We recommend that the pilot test be used to further examine interpretation of key phrases, definitions, and item intent (e.g., Do terms and phrases have consistent meaning across respondents? Do respondents have uniform understanding of item content?).

Hospitals are frequently asked to complete surveys, and in our discussions with them, many expressed significant resistance to completing yet another survey. Through the testing we conducted, we found that completion of the entire survey requires approximately 2 to 4 hours. However, this preliminary estimate was extrapolated from hospitals' completion of only parts of the survey, not the survey in its entirety. We recommend that the pilot study also test overall hospital and individual respondent burden to complete the survey in its entirety, and determine the hospital cost per completed survey.

DISCUSSION

The survey we have developed is a tool that AHRQ can use to document the extent to which U.S. hospitals are adopting 22 of the safe practices specified by the NQF in its *Safe Practices 2006* document (NQF, 2007). As described in this chapter, our approach to the survey was to develop questions that can gather data on key aspects of the structure or well-established processes that are involved in implementing each of the practices included in the survey. Among the processes included are questions on whether hospitals are tracking their own performance in using practices and the frequency of their performance monitoring. The survey does not focus on outcomes, nor does it judge the actual practice performance of hospitals.

Despite best efforts at developing valid items, this survey has an inherent limitation: it cannot capture the more subtle aspects of practice-adoption status and related actions by hospitals. It shares this limitation with any closed-ended survey that attempts to gather data on health care practices or processes that are difficult to quantify. We believe, however, that it is essential for AHRQ to have the capability to estimate national rates of practice adoption by U.S. hospitals, which can be provided only by survey data. Such rate estimates not only allow AHRQ to document progress being made but also to identify areas in which providers may need additional support or reinforcement to achieve desired progress. Given this limitation, it is useful and valuable to supplement survey results periodically with qualitative analyses that can explore the dynamics of providers' implementation processes. Through such investigations, the richness of the experiences of hospitals can be documented and shared with others to help their implementation efforts. The value of such qualitative information is shown in the results of our community study, from which emerged a number of useful insights that could not have been captured using closed-ended survey methods.

The items in this survey address the majority of the safe practices adopted by NQF in its *2006 Update*, but we determined that it would not be feasible to collect data on the remaining 8 practices using a survey method. Therefore, another limitations of the survey is its inability to monitor progress in adoption of those 8 practices. In addition, the contents of the survey are now somewhat dated by the recent release of the 2009 update of the NQF Safe Practices document (NQF, 2009), although NQF retained many of the practices in the 2006 set of safe practices in the 2009 set.

As updates to the safe practices are periodically made by the NQF, careful consideration will need to be given to revising the current survey version. Although ensuring that the survey reflects up-to-date evidence and recommendations is important, any proposed changes will need to be weighed against the ability to estimate trends in the data, given the importance of being able to conduct longitudinal analyses.

CHAPTER 5.
TRENDS FOR PATIENT SAFETY OUTCOMES

SPECIFIC AIMS

1. Continue much of the outcome trend analysis performed during the third and fourth years of the patient safety evaluation, adding data for the years 2004 and 2005 to the trends. Any effects of the patient safety initiative on outcomes might begin to be seen in these two years.

2. Perform additional geographic analyses to identify possible patterns of outcome differences or changes in relation to possible patterns of diffusion of safe practices in the health care system (e.g., in multihospital systems).

Our work in evaluating patient safety outcomes followed two tracks during the two-year assessment focusing on practice diffusion. First, we continued to estimate trends on several patient-outcomes measures based on encounter or reporting-system data. We present here updated trends using the AHRQ Patient Safety Indicator (PSI) measures and some measures from the Utah-Missouri (UT-MO) studies, as well as measures publicly reported by other organizations. For the first time in our outcome analyses, this year we also sought to identify changes in the trend lines for the measures used, because we had two years of post-baseline data to examine. We have used 2003 as the end of the baseline period (the earliest time at which we estimate that the patient safety activities across the country might begin to show effects on patient outcomes).

Second, we pursued several analytic projects on patient safety outcomes, including an investigation of patterns by which changes in outcomes might diffuse across organizations in the health care system. Examination of diffusion patterns for outcomes measures offers an opportunity to test several different hypotheses about mechanisms for diffusion of patient safety performance, looking across institutions and on a broad geographic scale.

These analyses for patient safety outcomes address one category of effects of initiatives to improve patient safety—effects on patients. Under the CIPP evaluation model, patients comprise one of several stakeholder groups that are likely to be affected by such initiatives (see Chapter 1). Thus, these analyses contribute to an overall product evaluation process, to which other analyses of changes in uses of safe practices and event reporting activities, or of effects on other stakeholder groups also contribute. As such, this chapter sits alongside Chapters 2 through 4 in this report, comprising the work we have done to examine several dimensions of effects.

AHRQ began its patient safety initiative in FY 2000, as other organizations across the country also embarked on patient safety activities. Because we did not expect results of those activities to have observable nationwide effects until at least 2003, and perhaps longer, most of our product-evaluation analytic work has been exploratory. We have focused on estimating baseline trends for selected patient-outcome measures and on doing diagnostic work to develop effective methods for later use to estimate effects of the patient safety initiative. With this report, we look for the first time for changes in patient-outcome trends in the years following 2003.

In concluding our work for the Patient Safety Evaluation Center, one of our aims is to provide suggestions to AHRQ regarding the structure and processes it might use for ongoing monitoring of patient safety outcomes, either doing the work itself or through an external contractor. In *Evaluation Reports III* and *IV*, we offered a number of observations about methodological challenges associated with monitoring safety outcomes, and we continued this inquiry in the two subsequent years (Farley et al., 2007b; Farley et al., 2008b). Our suggestions to AHRQ for continued monitoring methods are presented in Chapter 6.

OVERVIEW

Much of our work on patient-safety outcomes has focused on tracking trends in *clinical outcomes measures*, which directly capture the occurrence of adverse events in health care. Although limited in their coverage, and subject to a variety of methodological criticisms, clinical outcomes measures nevertheless offer the most immediate window onto the safety status of the U.S health care system for consumers.

To date, our findings regarding national trends in outcome measures have been mixed. We have observed that baseline trends in clinical safety outcomes appear to have improved on some measures, deteriorated on other measures, and remained stable on still others. In this chapter, we extend our trends on clinical outcomes with the newest years of available data. These trend lines now include data for the baseline years plus two years—2004 and 2005.

In several of our reports, we presented other analytic methods and results that might serve as models for AHRQ's use in future outcomes trending, and (ultimately) in evaluating the effects of its own safety programs. Examples include the following investigations:

- Impacts of truncated numbers of the *International Classification of Diseases*, Ninth Edition (ICD-9) diagnostic codes in the Healthcare Cost and Utilization Project (HCUP) and the Medicare Current Beneficiary Survey (MCBS) claims datasets on observed PSI rates (from *Evaluation Report III*) (NCHS, 2008)

- Effects of periodic revisions to the PSI definitions and algorithms on observed trends in outcomes (from *Evaluation Report IV*)

- Exploration of methods to examine possible effects of the AHRQ patient safety initiative on outcomes, by combining HCUP data with geographic coding for AHRQ's patient safety investments (also from *Evaluation Report IV*).

Also notable was a modified Delphi consensus process that we conducted in 2006, through which a panel of patient-safety experts used a ranking process to identify the most important safety measures for national monitoring across a large number of candidate measures developed by a variety of sources (Farley et al., 2007; Farley et al., 2008b).[9] We refer the reader to these analyses and reports, as well as to Chapter 6 in this report, for guidance on future assessment activities, techniques, and considerations that might be useful to AHRQ.

In this chapter, we update the baseline trends in patient-safety outcomes that we reported on in *Evaluation Report IV* (final report) to include the new data that have become available in the two subsequent years. We then present an illustrative analysis involving trajectory modeling, by which we show a method for investigating and distinguishing among groups of hospitals that

---

[9] The modified Delphi process was a three-step, structured process in which the panel participants identified candidate measures, rated each measure on importance, and then rated surviving measures on validity. The individuals invited to participate included the leads of all the AHRQ-funded patient safety projects, as well as other individuals they suggested, of whom 47 participated through the step of rating measure importance.

have different time trends for selected outcomes measures. Finally, we present a set of analyses looking at diffusion effects connected with patient-safety outcomes—a model for potential use by AHRQ to analyze patterns of safety outcomes in the future.

OUTCOME TRENDS FROM EXISTING REPORTING SOURCES

To the extent that data on patient outcomes and effects on other stakeholders are currently available, valid, and usable, we have endeavored to establish methods and trend data for measuring changes in those outcomes. Our primary focus has been on outcomes in hospital-based care, for the simple reason that most patient-safety work to date has focused on this setting; consequently outcomes data are most readily available concerning safety in hospitals. We also present updated outcomes trends for several patient safety measures in long-term care.

We start with measures drawn from summary statistics published by other organizations, including Minimum Data Set (MDS) measures for long-term care, Joint Commission sentinel events, and the MedMARx Reporting System for Medication Errors (CMS, 2008b; Joint Commission, 2007; U.S. Pharmacopeia, 2004, 2008). Then we report the results of our own trend analyses for selected measures from the PSIs and Utah-Missouri set of administrative safety measures (AHRQ, 2007a; Utah Department of Health, 2008). The UT-MO measures were developed by an AHRQ-funded demonstration grant on event reporting, using hospital encounter data in the states of Utah and Missouri.

Patient Safety Outcomes in the National Health Quality Report

In 2003, AHRQ began annual publication of the *National Healthcare Quality Report* (NHQR), a resource that provides trend information on outcome measures for multiple aspects of health care quality in the United States, including patient safety (AHRQ, 2008a). The NHQR draws on several data resources and measure sets to provide summary statistics, including the PSIs, the National Nosocomial Infections Surveillance System (NCCID, 2009), the Medical Expenditure Panel Survey (AHRQ, 2009), and the Medicare Patient Safety Monitoring System (CMS, 2009).

Each of the NHQRs has supplementary data tables on almost three dozen patient safety measures (made available through the Internet).[10] However, the printed NHQR limits its focus to only six safety measures, which changed in 2006 and 2007 from those that were highlighted in previous years. The safety measures in the 2007 report included a "postoperative care composite" (including cases of pneumonia, urinary tract infection (UTI), and venous thromboembolic events); appropriate timing of antibiotic administration in surgical patients; adverse events associated with central venous catheters; deaths following complications of care; occurrence of adverse drug events within hospitals; and inappropriate use of medications by the elderly.

Because the National Healthcare Quality Report is freely available through AHRQ (and can be obtained via the Internet), we do not recap summary data here for the patient safety measures included in it. We do, however, reiterate some of our observations about the NHQR from *Evaluation Report IV* (Farley et al., 2008b). In particular, the print version of the NHQR

---

[10] For the 2007 NHQR, see the AHRQ Web site, Appendix page, "Detailed Data Tables," March 2008, at <http://www.ahrq.gov/qual/nhqr07/#Safety>.

tends to provide only minimal background information about the data sources and measures that it summarizes, with the effect of obscuring limitations in the sampling, data, and computational methodology for those measures. The NHQR does include a methods chapter that describes new measures and techniques that have been adopted. However, it does not include a historical summary explaining how the NHQR inventory of safety measures has changed over time or describing the relationship between the measures highlighted in the print report and the larger pool of source measures that are available via Internet appendixes.

Future annual NHQRs could be made more helpful by adding a historical summary, explaining which patient-safety measures are included in the print version (versus online), providing more technical background on the sampling, data, and discussions of methodological issues that affect reported measures. Much of this supplementary material could be added via the Internet and incorporated by reference in the latest print version of the NHQR.

MDS Measures for Nursing Home Care

We have tracked trends for two patient safety measures relevant to long-term care— patient falls and the prevalence of pressure ulcers for nursing home residents. Both measures reflect injuries that residents might experience as a result of inadequate vigilance or attention in care. CMS requires all nursing home facilities certified by Medicare or Medicaid to report health-related data on their residents using the MDS form and data elements. CMS uses these data to generate quarterly reports summarizing trends in MDS measures nationally and by state, which are published on the CMS Web site. In Figure 5.1, trends in resident falls and pressure ulcers are presented, updated with new MDS 2.0 public quality indicators data through the most recent available quarter, ending December 2007 (CMS, 2008a).

As reflected in Figure 5.1, the national rate of falls among nursing home residents has remained stable since 2001, fluctuating between 12 and 13 percent of residents in each quarter. With regard to pressure ulcers, the observed trend is a bit more complex. The overall MDS rate of pressure ulcers was also basically stable between 2001 and early 2005, fluctuating between 10 and 11 percent of residents per quarter. In March 2005, however, CMS modified its data collection and reporting on pressure ulcers, so that the agency stopped tracking *overall* prevalence of pressure ulcers among nursing home residents. Instead, as of June 2005, CMS has reported separately on pressure-ulcer prevalence among *high-risk* residents, and among *low-risk* residents. We show both of those trend lines beginning in mid-2005. Notably, the most recent years of data appear to show some downward drift in the prevalence of pressure ulcers among residents at high risk, dropping from approximately 15.6 percent (mid-2005) to 13.4 percent (end of 2007).

The MDS offers some useful patient-safety data for nursing home settings, as well as a unique infrastructure for collecting that data. In 2007, there are still only a limited number of patient safety measures available that specifically cover long-term care settings; consequently, there is a need to expand the capability for patient-safety measurement in these settings. We continue to believe that the potential for capturing additional patient-safety measures through MDS warrants further exploration, particularly through more detailed assessment of technical issues affecting MDS data validity and reliability.

Another source of measures is the set of Nursing Home Quality Measures (NHQMs), which was endorsed by the NQF in 2003 (NQF, 2004). These measures were the product of earlier CMS-funded work to develop and validate measures for sub-acute, post-acute and long-term care settings. The NHQMs were specified using data available from the MDS dataset, and the measures have been subjected to an empirical validation effort connected with their development. About six or seven of the NHQM measures address patient-safety outcomes, including such measures as uncontrolled pain and inappropriate weight loss. CMS provides quarterly national summary statistics on several of these measures on its Web site, and these could readily be adapted to track additional trends in safety outcomes in the long-term care setting.

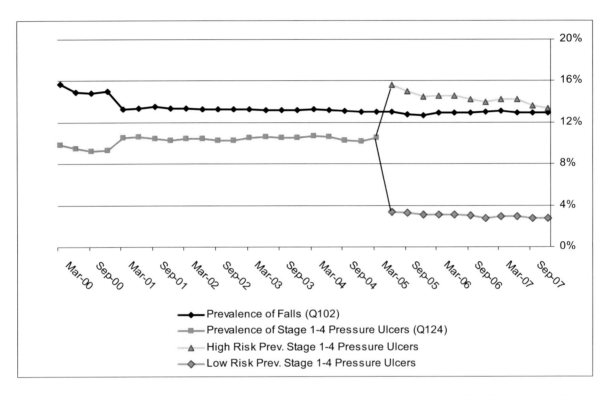

Figure 5.1 National Rates of Falls and Pressure Ulcers Among Nursing Home Residents, MDS Data, 2000–2007

Joint Commission Sentinel Events

The Joint Commission has a long-established accreditation policy regarding reporting of serious adverse events, called *sentinel events*. The Joint Commission defines a sentinel event as an unexpected occurrence involving death or serious physical or psychological injury, or the risk thereof, which requires immediate investigation and response by an affected health care facility. The Joint Commission has promulgated a set of sentinel-event guidelines, which individual facilities are expected to use to develop their own definitions for sentinel events, and to establish local mechanisms for identifying and managing them, and reporting them to the Joint Commission (Joint Commission, 2007). Using information on reported sentinel events, the Joint Commission publishes annual summary statistics on occurrences.

We examined the background and trends for sentinel events because they are well-known, national-level measures. Due to incomplete reporting, however, incidence statistics for the Joint Commission's sentinel events are known to be underestimates of actual rates of serious adverse events. This limitation is experienced by any system for external reporting of events. In addition, because health care facilities establish their own definitions for sentinel events, there is likely to be some inconsistency in how events are classified. Given these limitations, care must be taken in how—or if—data on sentinel events can be used for tracking national trends for the most serious reported adverse events.

We present here trends in the occurrence of selected categories of Joint Commission sentinel events, updating them to incorporate published data for 2006 and 2007, the most recent years available. As reflected in Figure 5.2, the Joint Commission recorded 743 Sentinel Events in 2007, sharply higher than the 526 events reported in the preceding year. The frequency of reported sentinel events has generally risen over the decade that the Joint Commission's sentinel event policy has been in effect. It is not known what factors have contributed to increases in reported events—both increased completeness of facility-based reporting, and changes in the actual frequency of sentinel events, could be involved.

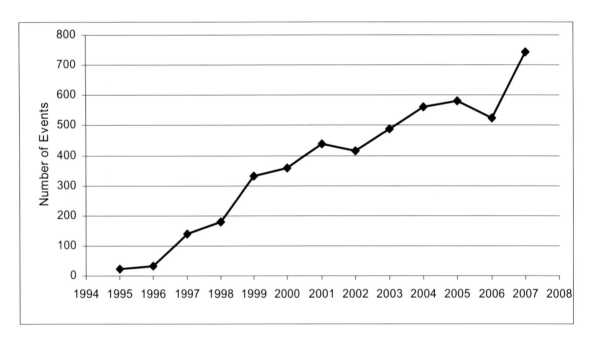

Figure 5.2 Numbers of Sentinel Events Reported to Joint Commission, All Types, 1995–2007

The Joint Commission also publishes a more detailed breakdown of sentinel events data by type of event. Figure 5.3 shows trends in the occurrence of the four most frequent categories of sentinel events, collectively comprising almost 50 percent of all events reported. These categories include patient suicides in hospital settings, operative or post-operative complications, wrong-site surgeries, and medication errors.[11] In 2007, the frequency of reported sentinel events

---

[11] Operative complications and medication errors are limited by Joint Commission guidelines to cases involving "unanticipated death or major permanent loss of function, not related to the natural course of the patient's illness."

increased across all four categories, following a dip for three of the four categories in the preceding year (i.e., post-op complications, wrong-site surgeries, medication errors).

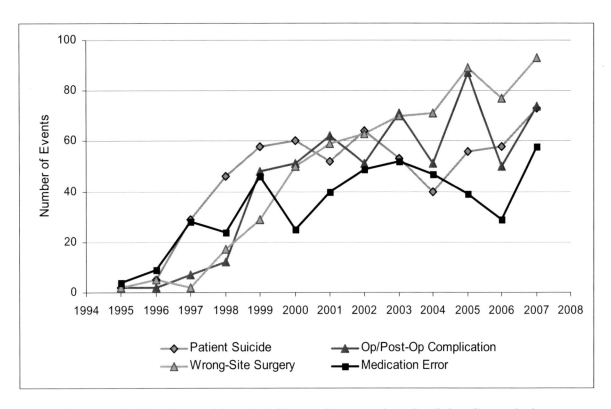

Figure 5.3 Numbers of Sentinel Events Reported to the Joint Commission, for Top Four Types of Events, 1995–2007

The MEDMARx Reporting System for Medication Errors

MEDMARx is a voluntary reporting system for adverse medication events that is operated by the United States Pharmacopeia (USP) through its Center for the Advancement of Patient Safety. It is a subscription-based system in which health care facilities pay a membership fee for the reporting software and for trend analysis of their own reported data (U.S. Pharmacopeia, 2004, 2008). The USP publishes annual reports with descriptive statistics on the aggregated MEDMARx data.[12]

We examined the MedMARx medication event reporting data because, as with the Joint Commission sentinel events, they are well-known, national-level measures. However, they suffer from the same limitations experienced by all reporting systems, including underreporting

---

[12] The annual MedMARx reports include both summary descriptive statistics and supplementary analyses that focus on specific topics of interest that vary from year to year. In 2004, the annual MedMARx report provided a general summary on five-year data trends from 1999 through 2003; in 2005, 2006, and 2007, the annual reports were more narrowly focused on error reporting in ICUs, cardiac catheterization labs, radiological settings, and peri-operative settings, and on adverse events related to medication naming conventions.

and the absence of a representative sample of reporting organizations. Again, care must be taken in how—or if—MedMARx data on medication events can be used for tracking national trends for the most serious reported adverse events.

The MEDMARx reporting system originally became available in August 1998, and the number of participating facilities increased steadily from 56 in 1999 to 570 in 2003 (the number of facilities participating in 2004 was not published in the USP report for that year). More recently, the number of participating facilities reportedly plateaued at 590 in 2005, and then declined to 519 in 2006. The MEDMARx participating facilities are not a representative sample of health care institutions in the United States, and it is not clear whether the characteristics of participating facilities (which include a range of hospitals and ambulatory care centers) may have shifted over time.

Medication events captured by MEDMARx are classified based on the Index for Categorizing Medication Errors, a taxonomy developed by the National Coordinating Council for Medication Error Reporting and Prevention (NCC-MERP). This classification system uses a set of categories for medication events ranging from "circumstances that have the capacity to cause error" (i.e., potential errors) to actual errors that cause varying levels of patient harm. NCC-MERP also captures data on a number of other dimensions, including the type of adverse event, the point in the system where the event occurred, the causes of the event, and contributing factors to the event, as well patient age and consequences to the patient. MEDMARx stresses that the non-harm events provide important information for establishing patterns of medication errors in a medical facility, and for targeting interventions to prevent them.

Figure 5.4 shows the trend in the average number of adverse events and potential events captured by MEDMARx on a per-facility basis, including the two newest years of available data from 2005 and 2006.[13] The trend suggests that the rate of MEDMARx events hit a plateau around 2002 and 2003, following a number of years in which the average frequency of events per facility had climbed rapidly. Since 2003, the per-facility rate of MEDMARx adverse events has been in decline.

Perhaps more strikingly, Figure 5.5 shows the trend in the average per-facility rate of MEDMARx events involving harm to patients, again for the interval between 1999 and 2006. Here, the trend suggests that the rate of harmful medication events has actually been in decline since 2000.

As with other safety measures collected from reporting systems data, the MEDMARx trends are subject to multiple interpretations. Changes over time may reflect some combination of changes in reporting practices, together with changes in the objective frequency of adverse events. Taken at face value, the trends shown here suggest either reduced fidelity in reporting practices over recent years (which seems improbable) or some degree of actual improvement in the occurrence of medication errors in MEDMARx participating facilities. Note, however, that the trends might also be influenced by changes in the makeup of the MEDMARx cohort of

---

[13] Note that the annual MEDMARx report from 2004 did not include information on the number of facilities that participated in MEDMARx during that year. Figures 5.4 and 5.5, therefore, include a missing data point for 2004, and the depicted trends are therefore shown with an interpolated line for the period between 2003 and 2005.

facilities over time—a possibility that would require much more detailed analyses of MEDMARx data to explore.

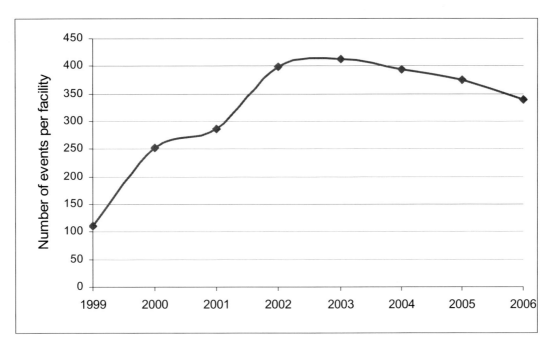

Figure 5.4 Average Frequency per Facility of MEDMARx-Reported Events

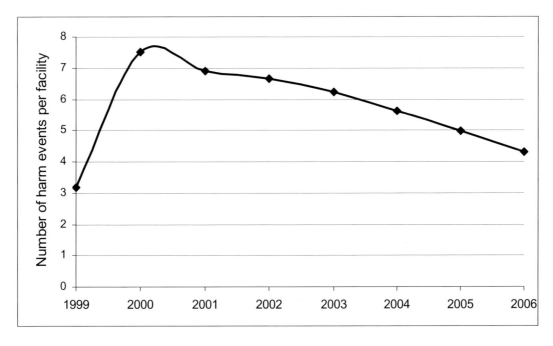

Figure 5.5 Average Frequency per Facility of MEDMARx-Reported Events Involving Harm to Patients

ANALYZING TRENDS IN ENCOUNTER-BASED OUTCOME MEASURES

We have used inpatient encounter-based measures in our analyses of trends in patient safety outcomes. Our goal in selecting a limited number of measures was to identify those that most strongly represent important patient safety issues. We have worked with several of the AHRQ Patient Safety Indicators, which were developed using hospital inpatient discharge data from the HCUP National Inpatient Sample (NIS) (AHRQ, 2007a), and also with several measures developed by a project that AHRQ funded as part of its patient safety initiative. That project was a demonstration grant on event reporting, which was performed using hospital encounter data in the states of Utah and Missouri (the UT-MO study) (Utah Department of Health, 2008). The measures were selected using information obtained from a review of the existing literature, as well as judgments of importance and clinical relevance by several physicians who are researchers at RAND and experienced in patient safety.

In this year's report, we extended the outcomes trends by adding newly available data from the HCUP NIS dataset (for 2004 and 2005). In addition, we added several more PSIs to our trending analysis, based on recommendations from the patient safety experts who participated in the Delphi process to identify important patient safety outcome measures (Farley et al., 2008c), and on our own analysis to identify canary measures among the PSIs that are correlated with several of the other measures (Yu et al., 2009). Table 5.1 lists the 11 specific PSIs for which we estimated updated national trends.

The Delphi panel experts recommended *none* of the UT-MO measures as high priorities for national monitoring. Because of the Delphi panel recommendations, together with changes to the structure of the HCUP NIS dataset in 2003 that made it impossible to calculate many of the UT-MO measures, we dropped those measures from the trends covered in this report.[14]

Table 5.1 AHRQ PSIs Used in This Analysis

PSI Measure	Analyzed in Previous Reports	Recommended by Delphi Experts	Identified as Canary Measure
Death in low-mortality DRGs	X	X	
Postoperative PE or DVT	X	X	
Failure to rescue	X	X	
Postoperative hip fracture	X		
Postoperative hemorrhage or hematoma	X		
Foreign body left during procedures		X	
Postoperative sepsis		X	
Obstetric trauma–vaginal delivery with instrument		X	
Obstetric trauma–Cesarean delivery		X	
Birth trauma–injury to neonate		X	
Selected infection due to medical care			X

NOTES: DRG=Diagnosis-Related Group; DVT=deep vein thrombosis; PR = pulmonary embolism.

---

[14] In *Evaluation Report IV* (Farley, et al., 2008b), we described the structural changes to e-coding in the HCUP NIS, which had the effect of undermining the calculation of the UT-MO measures.

In addition to updating the PSI outcome trends by adding new years of data, we re-analyzed the HCUP NIS dataset from 1994–2005 using an updated revision of the PSI definitions and software, Version 3.1 (AHRQ, 2007a). The reanalysis was done to ensure that our estimated trends were based on the same method across all years to calculate the measures, given that AHRQ typically revises its PSI definitions and algorithms each year or so.[15] Shifting coding practices and annual revisions to the PSI definitions make it important to re-examine trends on a regular basis, using the most current set of PSI definitions.

Figures 5.6 through 5.9 show the updated trends in outcomes, with separate trend lines for each PSI. Four different patterns exist in the figures:

1. National rates for some PSIs have been fairly stable for many years (e.g., "Postoperative Hip Fracture," "Death in Low Mortality DRGs," "Obstetric Trauma–Cesarean Delivery," and "Foreign Body Left During Procedures").

2. Rates for one PSI ("Postoperative Hemorrhage or Hematoma") appear to have declined modestly in 2004 – 2005, following a slight increase in 2003.

3. Rates for several PSIs have followed a sustained downward trend ("Failure to Rescue," "Obstetric Trauma–Vaginal with Instrument," and "Birth Trauma–Injury to New Neonate").

4. Rates for several other PSIs have consistently trended upwards or downwards, but with apparent slowing in 2005 (e.g., "Postoperative PE or DVT," "Postoperative Sepsis," and "Selected Infection Due to Medical Care").

Collectively, these figures suggest that the PSIs are capturing different aspects of safety outcomes. There is no clear overall national trend across indicators, toward either improved outcomes or deteriorating outcomes.

Furthermore, we could not confirm changes in rates from the baseline trend lines for any of the PSI measures for which we have estimated trends. Rates for Obstetric Trauma–Vaginal with Instrument, Postoperative PE or DVT, Postoperative Sepsis, and Selected Infection Due to Medical Care may have started to decline in 2004 or 2005. However, given the small size of change and limited number of years of post-baseline data, differences in post-baseline rates from projected baseline trends are not statistically significant.

---

[15] Revisions to the PSI definitions and algorithms are undertaken, in part, to incorporate annual updates to the ICD-9 diagnostic codes and DRG codes (which define key data elements used in calculating PSI rates).

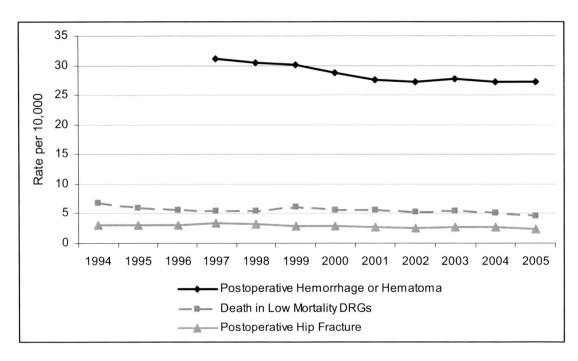

Figure 5.6 Trends for Selected PSI Measures, 1994–2004 (I)

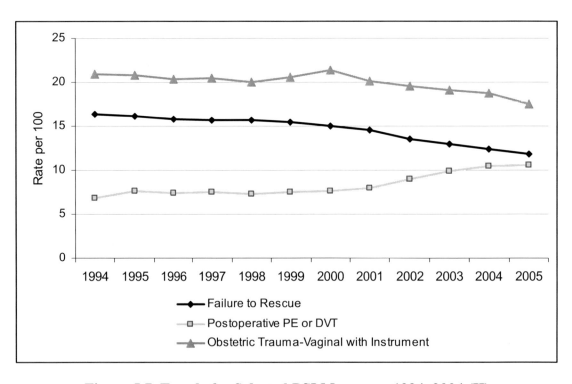

Figure 5.7 Trends for Selected PSI Measures, 1994–2004 (II)

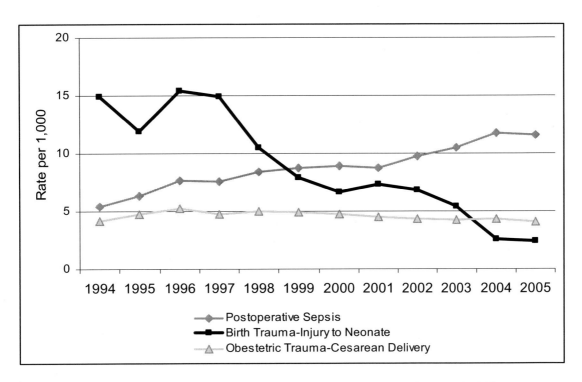

Figure 5.8 Trends for Selected PSI Measures, 1994–2004 (III)

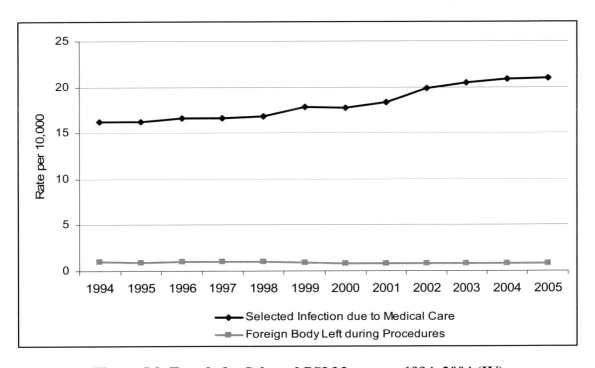

Figure 5.9 Trends for Selected PSI Measures, 1994–2004 (IV)

TRAJECTORY MODELING OF CLINICAL SAFETY OUTCOMES

Looking at national trends in patient safety outcomes across states and hospitals offers a useful national perspective, but it also can mask more-dynamic processes embedded in the

81

underlying encounter data. For example, although the *average* national trend in outcomes for a single PSI may show improvement, the trend may conceal that important underlying groups of hospitals have actually experienced stable or deteriorating outcomes on the same measure.

One of our aims in investigating outcomes has been to explore different techniques for analyzing encounter data, in ways that might be useful to AHRQ for monitoring patient safety effects in the future. We illustrate here a method for drawing on encounter data and the PSIs to identify discrete groups of hospitals that follow different trajectories in safety outcomes. We include two examples, applying trajectory modeling techniques to safety outcomes data.

Methods for Group-Based Trajectory Modeling

The group-based trajectory modeling technique (Nagin, 2005) takes advantage of longitudinal data, here encounter data for individual hospitals, to determine whether *groups* of hospitals appear to follow distinct trends in safety outcomes. Trajectory modeling supports both an estimate for the number and size of distinct groups (or clusters) of hospitals implied by the data, as well as an estimate for the actual trajectory in outcomes for each group. As a result, groups of hospitals with stable rates of outcomes can be distinguished from those with either increasing or decreasing rates.

Trajectory modeling estimates the appropriate number of groups to be compared, based on a combination of statistical scoring, direct observation of trajectory plots, and application of subject-matter knowledge (i.e., regarding safety outcomes in hospitals). The trajectory methodology is based on maximum likelihood estimation (MLE). A statistical score, called the Bayesian Information Criterion (BIC) score, is derived from the maximized likelihood score and is recommended as one device for helping to select the appropriate number of groups to use in trajectory models (Nagin, 2005).[16]

Once the number of groups and the trajectories for those groups are estimated in a trajectory model, each hospital then has an estimated probability of being assigned to each group. For example, if trajectory modeling suggests that the data contain two groups, then each hospital will have some probability of being assigned to each group, and many hospitals will have a much higher probability of being in one group than the other. Based on a hospital's observed rate of adverse safety outcomes over time, the model may assign that hospital a strong likelihood of being in the group associated with a low, stable rate of adverse outcomes, and a much lesser likelihood of being in the group associated with a high and increasing rate of adverse outcomes.

In principle, the assignment of group-membership probabilities for each hospital can enable descriptive characterization of the different groups, using hospital-level characteristics. Although we have not attempted to do this kind of characterization in the examples that follow, AHRQ could potentially do so in the future to link best-practice adoption (and other institutional attributes) to different trajectories in outcomes.

---

[16] The number of groups that yields the largest BIC score is one estimate for the number of groups supported by the data. However, adding more groups to improve the BIC score may not improve understanding of the patterns of patient safety in the data.

Illustrative Findings

To demonstrate the group-based trajectories approach, we present two analyses that apply trajectory modeling to rates of "Failure to Rescue" (PSI 4) and "Decubitus Ulcer" (PSI 3) among California hospitals over the period 1997–2006. For these analyses, we applied AHRQ's Patient Safety Indicator Software to the HCUP State Inpatient Dataset for California: a comprehensive data repository for all hospital discharges within the state. We used Version 3.1 of the AHRQ (2007a) PSI software, and consistent with those algorithms, we incorporated the use of "present on admission" indicators in the California data in computing rates for the PSIs. This addition allows the analysis to distinguish between a problem that already existed at admission from one that was acquired during hospitalization. We focused on general, acute care hospitals, and computed a risk-adjusted, smoothed patient safety rate for each hospital in each year.[17]

For each instance of "Failure to Rescue" and "Decubitis Ulcer," we tested several trajectory models with different numbers of groups. After comparing the BIC scores and plots, we decided that the best model for "Failure to Rescue" included three groups, and the best model for "Decubitis Ulcer" included four groups. For "Failure to Rescue," the three-group solution had the highest BIC score of any trajectory model. For "Decubitus Ulcer," some trajectory models with more than four groups had higher BIC scores than did the four-group solution, but our review of the trajectory plots suggested that including more than four groups in the model yielded little additional information or insight.

Figure 5.10 depicts the three-group trajectory model for "Failure to Rescue" in California hospitals during 1997–2006. Over the same period, the average national and California trends for all hospitals on "Failure to Rescue" were decreasing (see also Figure 5.7). By contrast, the group-based trajectories approach suggests that the majority of hospitals in California actually had stable rates for "Failure to Rescue" during this period.

The dashed lines in Figure 5.10 represent the estimated trajectories for each group; the solid lines represent the observed average rates. The observed rates for two groups appear to have declined modestly, but there is no statistical difference between those observed rates and the (constant) estimated trajectories for those groups. Thus, two large groups of California hospitals appear to have had unchanging rates of "Failure to Rescue" in the 1997–2006 period: a low prevalence group and a middle prevalence group. By contrast, a third group started with a high rate of "Failure to Rescue" in 1997, then experienced a brief period of worsening rates followed by a long period of improvement (approaching the performance of the other group by 2006). In sum, the decreasing overall trend in "Failure to Rescue" in California observed in the overall "Failure to Rescue" trend was driven primarily by the roughly one-quarter of hospitals in the group that started with relatively high rates. The overall trend masks the fact that most California hospitals experienced no change in rates of "Failure to Rescue" at all.

---

[17] The AHRQ PSI algorithms include a formal protocol for smoothing the computation of the indicators from claims data, to limit the influence of observations from smaller hospitals, which can be subject to high year-to-year variations in adverse safety-event rates). Because such variations might affect the results from trajectory modeling, we applied smoothing to the computation of PSI rates. We used PROC Traj (Jones, Nagin, and Roeder, 2001) in SAS Version 9.1 to generate our model estimates and our plots of the trajectories.

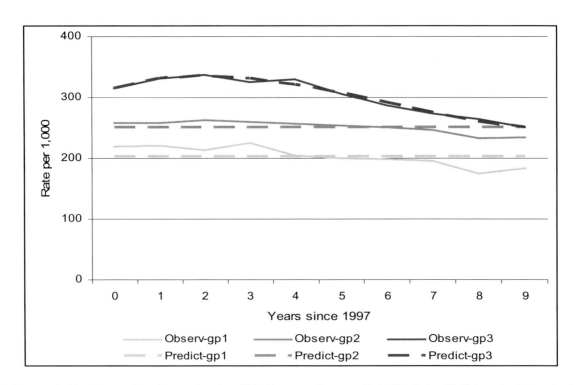

Figure 5.10 Three Trajectories for "Failure to Rescue" (PSI 4) in California Hospitals

Figure 5.11 illustrates a very different story with regard to safety outcomes on "Decubitis Ulcer" during the same period. Across all groups, the average trend for California hospitals on "Decubitis Ulcer" was a constant or slightly increasing rate of about 2 to 2.5 per 1,000 discharges. However, Figure 5.11 shows that, whereas most California hospitals are on one of two stable trajectories of "Decubitis Ulcer" outcomes, a little over 6 percent of hospitals experienced a more dynamic trajectory in "Decubitis Ulcer" outcomes. Among the 6 percent of hospitals that did not have stable outcomes on "Decubitis Ulcer," group 4 started with high rates that subsequently improved to about the same level as Group 3. Group 2 started at a somewhat lower rate, but then got steadily worse until 2004, when it began to improve.

In this case, California's state average "Decubitus Ulcer" rate is relatively low and constant, and it represents the apparent rate for most hospitals in California. Nevertheless, the average state trend also masks three small, but possibly important, alternative trajectories—one group of hospitals that seemed to have a constant but higher rate than the state average throughout the period, and two other groups of hospitals that experienced significant changes in their rates of "Decubitis Ulcer" over time. A closer examination of the hospitals with increasing or decreasing rates of "Decubitis Ulcer" might reveal important hospital characteristics associated with different trajectories over the period.

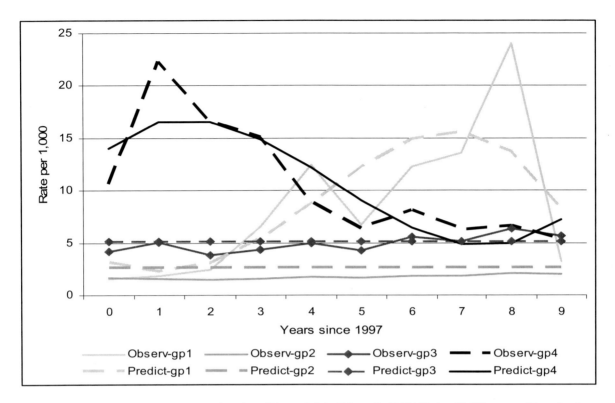

Figure 5.11 Four Trajectories for "Decubitis Ulcer" (PSI 3) in California Hospitals

Discussion

For two reasons, we believe that the group-based trajectories technique is potentially important for examining trends in patient safety outcomes. First, it seems intuitive that aggregated national or state-level trends may conceal multiple different institutional trajectories for patient safety outcomes, across the population of hospitals. Identifying different trajectories in outcomes, and examining important groups of hospitals more closely, may lead to a better understanding of why safety outcomes appear to improve or worsen over time, and which institutions, characteristics, and practices are best associated with different trends.

Second, a tendency in some quality-improvement initiatives is to try to focus attention primarily on outcomes among top-performing hospitals. However, as the examples above make clear, very large groups of hospitals may sometimes experience differing rates of adverse events. Thus, while it may technically be possible to identify a top percentage of hospitals based on annual patient safety performance, this endeavor may be less useful than identifying low-performing hospitals or hospitals that are most in need of improvement, when a large proportion of hospitals is doing very nearly as well as the top performers.

DIFFUSION MODELING OF CLINICAL SAFETY OUTCOMES

One of our major analytic activities in the final year of the evaluation has been to investigate patterns of diffusion in safety outcomes. Modeling of diffusion in safety outcomes is based on the idea that good performance in one hospital can spread to others, through any of several possible channels of transmission. For example, superior safety performance might spread among local market competitors or within hospital ownership networks. Diffusion analysis as applied to *safety practices* has the advantage of focusing directly on something that can be exported or shared from one facility to another (e.g., hand-washing techniques, medication bar-coding technology). Diffusion analysis as applied to *patient safety outcomes* has a different advantage of directly tracking the ultimate clinical outcomes of interest, in terms of direct effects on patients.

For this report, we have undertaken a set of diffusion analyses using the PSIs and California encounter data for 1997–2006. We offer these analyses, in part, as a template that AHRQ could follow in the future, to explore patterns in the spread of safety outcomes over time. We also use these analyses to observe whether there is any evidence for diffusion in safety outcomes to date and, if so, to identify the mode of transmission. In sum, we found evidence to suggest that network membership has been important to diffusion of safety outcomes among hospitals, for at least two PSIs. However, we also found that recent changes in the PSI definitions (from Version 2.1 to Version 3.1) caused our findings to change, raising significant questions about the usefulness of the PSIs for this sort of epidemiological research.

Data and Methods

Using California hospital inpatient data (from the HCUP State Inpatient Database [SID]) for 1997 through 2006, we calculated annual hospital-level PSI rates, adjusted for patient mix. We then consolidated annual rates into three periods: early (1997–1999), middle (2000–2002), and late (2003–2006). We did this partly to obtain more-stable rates for rare PSIs (and small hospitals) than would otherwise obtain; and also because we felt that these three periods were meaningful in capturing different levels of patient safety activity and awareness throughout the nation.

For each of several of the PSIs, we then constructed multiple regression models, in which we predicted hospital-level PSI rates during the middle or late period, by using a set of earlier-period variables corresponding to different mechanisms for diffusion (lagged effects). Those variables included *network membership* (i.e., whether a hospital was part of a proprietary chain of three or more hospitals), *network environment* (i.e., the actual average performance by the hospital's network on the designated PSI), *network seed* (i.e., for a designated hospital, whether any of the hospitals within its network fell in the best decile of performance on the designated PSI), *market environment*[18] (i.e., for a designated hospital, the average performance by all hospitals deemed to be its economic competitors on the designated PSI), *market seed* (i.e., for a designated hospital, whether any of its economic competitors fell in the best decile of performance on the designated PSI), and *for-profit status* (i.e., whether the designated hospital was a for-profit facility).[19]

We present here results from our models focusing on middle-period outcomes, as predicted from early-period variables.[20] Moreover, to explore possible variation in results

---

[18] We constructed the *market environment* and *market seed* variables by using the methods described by Zwanziger and Melnick (1988).

[19] In all of our regression models, we also included a variable to account for each hospital's own prior performance as a predictor of subsequent performance on the designated PSI. For our purposes, we were interested in looking for diffusion effects that occur even after hospital prior performance has been taken into account.

[20] We also calculated models that predicted *late* period outcomes from *early* and *middle* period variables— these models produced similar but more-complicated findings.

associated with periodic updates to the PSI definitions, we computed two separate sets of diffusion models using Versions 2.1 and 3.1 of the PSI algorithms. Because of limitations in the California data that were available to us, and problems we encountered in computing rates for some of the PSIs, we restricted our analyses here to PSI 3 ("Decubitis Ulcer"), PSI 4 ("Failure to Rescue"), PSI 7 ("Selected Infections Due to Care"), PSI 9 ("Postop Hemorrhage or Hematoma"), and PSI 12 ("Postop Pulmonary Embolism or Deep Vein Thrombosis").

Results Regarding Practice Diffusion

Table 5.2 shows results from several of our diffusion models, particularly reflecting whether there were effects on hospital safety performance based on *network membership* and *network environment*.[21]

For two of the PSIs, "Selected Infections Due to Care" and "Postop Pulmonary Embolism or Deep Vein Thrombosis," *the results suggest that significant diffusion effects were associated with these outcomes*. Simply being a member of a hospital-network during the early period predicted improved safety performance by a hospital during the subsequent middle period, on both indicators. Likewise, the early-period network average performance was also predictive for member hospitals' individual performance in the subsequent middle period (e.g., lower average event rates within the network predict lower rates for individual member hospitals in the next period). Notably, these diffusion results were robust across two different specifications of the PSIs (Version 2.1 and Version 3.1).

**Table 5.2 Predicted Effects of Early-Period Network Characteristics
on Middle-Period Outcomes for Hospitals**

		Regression Coefficients [a]			
		Network Membership		Network Environment	
PSI No.	Patient Safety Indicator	PSI V. 2.1	PSI V. 3.1	PSI V. 2.1	PSI V. 3.1
3	Decubitis Ulcer	−4.05*	−0.71	5.28**	0.42
4	Failure to Rescue	57.75**	−37.76	−39.44**	24.94
7	Selected Infections Due to Care	−1.89**	−0.80*	2.35**	0.57**
9	Postop Hemorrhage or Hematoma	1.01*	−0.80**	−0.55*	0.57**
12	Postop Pulmonary Embolism or DVT	−2.25**	−1.62**	2.50**	0.80**

* $p < 0.05$;   ** $p < 0.01$

a Difference in rates of events per 1,000 eligible discharges (for hospitals in networks versus other hospitals)

By contrast, for the other three PSIs we studied ("Decubitis Ulcer," "Failure to Rescue," and "Postop Hemorrhage or Hematoma"), we did not see the same kind of consistent diffusion effects. These results may suggest that diffusion of safety outcomes across hospitals does not

---

[21] Across a number of specifications of our diffusion models, we generally found that neither *network seed*, *for-profit status*, *market environment*, nor *market seed* variables were consistently significant as predictors of subsequent hospital safety outcomes. Consequently, we do not summarize findings on those predictor variables in Table 5.2.

work in the same way for all PSIs, and that some types of safety outcomes may be more susceptible to diffusion effects than others.

A striking finding from Table 5.2 is that the diffusion-modeling results for "Decubitis Ulcer," "Failure to Rescue" and "Postop Hemorrhage or Hematoma" were *not* consistent across two specifications of the PSI measures: Version 2.1 of the PSIs produced different results from Version 3.1, when applied to the same California encounter data. We observed similar inconsistencies in our findings for these three measures with regard to other diffusion models (not summarized in Table 5.2) in predicting safety outcomes for the late period. Significant diffusion effects sometimes appear when using Version 2.1 of the PSIs that disappear when using Version 3.1 of the PSIs, and vice versa.

That significant diffusion effects can appear or disappear from the data, depending on the PSI specification used, is disconcerting. To our knowledge, the update in the PSIs from Version 2.1 to Version 3.1 involved two major definitional changes (and many other minor changes[22]): the use of "present-on-admission" flags in defining the indicators, and the exclusion of children from the at-risk populations for many of the indicators (AHRQ, 2008b). It is not clear why either of those definitional changes should have any effect on the apparent diffusion of safety outcomes over time.

As discussed above, we have previously commented on several other ways in which periodic revisions to the PSI specifications, or changes to the structure of HCUP encounter data, have made it difficult to compute or interpret time trends for outcomes. Our current diffusion-analysis results, however, illustrate a more serious problem. Ordinarily, we would not expect complete instability in analytic results in connection with revisions to the PSIs, at least if we assume that the measures themselves are retaining their basic continuity and meaning over time. Given that the diffusion results do shift from PSI Version 2.1 to 3.1, however, we are left uncertain as to which effects are "real" and which ones are measurement artifacts.

One plausible interpretation of the inconsistencies might be that the newer specifications of the PSIs (Version 3.1) are superior, simply because they reflect a more recent set of revisions implemented by AHRQ. We are not convinced, however, that this is necessarily so, and we do not have any independent basis for validation that would lead us to prefer one specification of the PSIs over another. In consequence, we are able only to conclude that recent revisions to the PSI definitions have made it difficult to undertake diffusion analyses or potentially any epidemiological modeling, and that many of the results from our own diffusion analyses are now ambiguous.

Discussion

We continue to believe that diffusion of safety outcomes is an important area of investigation and monitoring for AHRQ to undertake in the future. From our own work, we see at least some evidence to suggest that diffusion is occurring through proprietary hospital networks, rather than through market competition, for two specific types of safety outcomes ("Selected Infections" and "Postop PE or DVT"). This being said, the more important finding

---

[22] One example of a "minor" change in the PSIs involved AHRQ revisions to the algorithms for carrying out patient-mix adjustments for the indicators. Conceivably, this sort of change could significantly affect the computation of the PSIs.

from our analyses is that recent updates to the PSIs have had major effects on the safety outcomes estimated from encounter data, and in observed patterns of diffusion over time. One might argue that those effects simply follow from the fact that the newer version of the PSIs is better, and the older version is worse, and that we should ignore the latter in favor of the former.

Absent independent validation of Version 3.1 of the PSIs, our results lead us to another conclusion: that periodic PSI updates have made it very difficult to interpret analyses using different versions of the indicators, or to know how truly comparable the PSIs are from one version to another. We recommend again that AHRQ pursue more analytic effort in connection with its updates to the PSIs, in documenting the effects of updates on observed outcomes and trends, and in explaining the reasoning for the changes. We also reiterate our recommendation that independent validation of the PSIs against chart review could be a key step in establishing the usefulness and meaning of the indicators, for purposes of national epidemiological monitoring.

CONCLUSIONS

Results of our most recent trend analyses for PSI patient outcome measures, which now include two years immediately following 2003 (the last year in the baseline period), offer some hope for potentially being able to observe, within a few years, statistically significant reductions in rates for some of the PSIs we have tracked. As discussed above, we observed slight downward changes in national rates for four of the PSIs, relative to their baseline trends. However, because of the small sizes of changes and limited number of years of post-baseline data, it is too early to tell if those changes are real. Another few years of data will be needed to be able to test possible changes analytically.

The updated outcomes trends we present in this chapter suggest that different measures of clinical outcomes are trending in different directions, and that there is no single, national patient safety story that emerges across measures. Some of the PSIs have shown improved outcomes, some have shown deteriorating outcomes, and some have remained roughly stable.

One of the lessons from our assessments is the importance of carefully considering which outcomes measures should be used for assessing effects. This is highlighted by the large differences in trends that we observed for both the reported events (e.g., sentinel events, MedMARx) and the measures that are rates (PSIs). For example, if only measures with upward trends were chosen for monitoring, the interpretation of effects would be quite different than if other measures with downward trends were used. The results of the Delphi process we conducted can guide these choices, because they represent expert consensus on which measures are most important.

Continued national monitoring and analysis of clinical safety outcomes should be a priority to any future patient safety initiatives undertaken by AHRQ. Monitoring of patient outcomes can help the agency to track the safety of the healthcare system from the patient perspective, to identify aspects of the system in which safety is either improving or deteriorating, and to help target future safety investments to where they are needed most. The NHQRs reflect one context where AHRQ is already committed to doing this sort of monitoring into the future. More detailed safety monitoring and analytic efforts, drawing on a broader pool of clinical outcomes measures, could be helpful both to AHRQ and to others, in assessing the national status of safety throughout the U.S. health care system.

The preferred types of measures for monitoring changes in outcomes over time are those for which objective data are available on a national level. Such data can yield estimates that are robust in completeness, validity, and reliability, both in any given year and in trends over time. Measures expressed as rates best fulfill these criteria, because they control for changes in the size of the denominators over time, or for differences in denominators across subsets of the population within any time period. However, as discussed above, these types of measures are vulnerable to other measurement challenges that must be considered.

A consistent theme in our evaluation work has been that coding and definitional issues connected with administrative measures, such as the PSIs, can exert significant effects on the computation of those measures, and consequently, on observed trends in outcomes. Annual revisions to the PSI definitions to some degree reflect changes in underlying ICD-9 and DRG coding schemes and, it is hoped, serve to maintain the continuity of the indicators over time, or else to improve them (as in the case of recent revisions to incorporate the use of "present on admission" flags in encounter data). Notwithstanding the valid reasons for periodic updating to the PSIs, our analyses over the years have suggested that differing versions of the indicators have sometimes generated very different values for the measures, when applied retrospectively to the same years of data. This kind of finding highlights the importance of providing background details on methods and specifications used in generating PSI trends, whenever these are reported out in national monitoring efforts.

However, incomplete reporting of events by health care providers into external reporting systems precludes use of such events to monitor trends in outcomes, because of the downward bias in occurrence frequencies (e.g., Joint Commission sentinel events). Further, it usually cannot be determined which factors are affecting frequencies of reported events and, therefore, how accurately they represent underlying safety issues. Increases in reported events may reflect improved patient-safety vigilance and reporting practices, which is positive for safety improvement, because the events must be identified before providers can act on them. Alternatively, an increase may reflect real increases in events, which is undesired, or it simply could be the result of improved completeness of reporting to external systems (of events already known internally). Reported events remain important contributors to the vigilance aspect of monitoring, however, because observable changes in the frequency of events being reported could signal an emerging patient-safety problem.

Results of our analyses lead us to conclude that, to be effective, the monitoring process for AHRQ's patient safety initiative should track trends in both patient outcome measures and the implementation of safe practices that are supported by scientific evidence as being effective in reducing harm to patients. As the adoption of evidence-based safe practices grows over time, it may be inferred that these practices are leading to improved patient outcomes, many of which may not be detectable in the outcome measures selected for national monitoring.

In addition to the trend analyses, other analyses we have performed over the course of the evaluation might serve as models for AHRQ in future outcomes trending, and (ultimately) in evaluating the effects of its own safety programs. Indeed, results of two of those analyses (trajectory modeling and diffusion analyses) are presented in this chapter. We suggest that AHRQ explore ways to use these methodologies as tools in its future patient-safety monitoring activities and assessments of effects of patient safety initiatives on outcomes in practice.

Some important opportunities remain for future action by AHRQ. Ambulatory and long-term care settings continue to be a high priority for measure-development efforts. State-level reporting systems also present a priority for refining and harmonizing adverse-event measures, ultimately in support of the ability to aggregate reported data on a regional or national basis. Inconsistency in coding of administrative data, and lack of continuity in measurement definitions for the PSIs, remain serious concerns in ongoing efforts to use these data.

CHAPTER 6.
SUGGESTED APPROACH FOR MONITORING EFFECTS OF THE PATIENT SAFETY INITIATIVE

SPECIFIC AIM

1. To provide suggestions to AHRQ regarding the structure and processes for a program of ongoing monitoring of patient safety outcomes, performed either by itself or through an external contractor, after the work of the Patient Safety Evaluation Center is completed.

Over the course of our work on the patient safety evaluation, we have developed a framework for examining the effects of nationwide patient safety activities, including those of the AHRQ patient safety initiative. We also have identified some measures to assess these effects, and we have performed analyses for these measures. This work has been our product-evaluation component of the CIPP program evaluation model (see Chapter 1).

Our product evaluation focused, in large part, on examining trends in patient outcome measures for inpatient hospital care. We took this focus simply because we could not examine other types of effects due to lack of appropriate, validated measures; lack of national-level data to use in analyzing trends in those measures; and a lack of tools to collect that data.

SETTING THE STAGE FOR ONGOING MONITORING BY AHRQ

As the AHRQ patient safety initiative moved through its first five years, we worked with the available outcome measures and data to estimate trends in those measures and to diagnose the issues involved in affecting the validity and reliability of the estimates. We also explored methods to assess other aspects of tracking changes in outcome measures. In addition, we began to explore how effects of national patient safety activities on other stakeholders might be measured and analyzed. The results of this work were reported in the evaluation reports. The most recent (and final) results are presented in Chapter 5 of this report.

Even after five years of activities, the funded studies in the AHRQ patient safety initiative have only recently been generating the information needed to assemble and disseminate new evidence on safe practices to health care providers. Further, as we learned in our most recent community studies (presented in this report), the health care community is still building momentum in implementing the changes needed to make health care practices safer for patients. Therefore, it still is too early to expect to detect significant effects on patient outcomes at the national level. However, we have begun to see changes in patient safety practices by health care providers and should be able to document effects on them and other stakeholders.

We anticipate that AHRQ will continue its own monitoring efforts after our evaluation effort ends. In this chapter, we pull together what we have learned methodologically through our product-evaluation analyses, and we present a suggested approach that AHRQ can use for continued monitoring. Such national monitoring would provide policymakers and the public with transparency regarding the status of patient safety in the U.S. health care system. It also would enable AHRQ to assess effects of its own investments in patient safety and refine its understanding of which initiatives are most effective in promoting patient safety.

COMPONENTS OF A SUGGESTED MONITORING PROGRAM

As a result of our work on the product evaluation, one of our key conclusions was that, to be effective, the monitoring process for AHRQ's patient safety initiative should track trends in

- Implementation of safe practices
- Patient outcome measures
- Effects on other stakeholders.

Although the difficulty in identifying and measuring appropriate patient outcomes is an obvious reason for pursuing other effects, we believe it is a secondary reason. An effective monitoring program, at a minimum, should examine how the nation's patient safety activities are affecting the range of stakeholders involved. If it does not, it risks missing important effects that merit attention. Further, by tracking trends in adoption of key patient safety practices, it is possible to infer that progress is being made in the right direction that, eventually, should be manifested in improved patient outcomes (if the practices are evidence-based).

The safe practices of interest are those that are supported by scientific evidence as being effective in reducing patients harm. As growth in the adoption of evidence-based safe practices is observed over time, it may be inferred that these practices are leading to improved patient outcomes, many of which may not be detectable in the outcome measures selected for national monitoring.

The monitoring program we are suggesting consists of four components: tracking trends in patient safety practice adoption, tracking trends in relevant patient outcomes, assessing effects on other stakeholders, and assessing how the AHRQ patient safety initiative has been contributing to these three types of effects.

Trends in Adoption of Patient Safety Practices

Data on safe practice adoption could be used not only to infer the extent to which progress may be being made toward improving outcomes, but also for feedback to the patient safety initiative to guide focus on practices or issues requiring more reinforcement or refinement. Despite the importance of such data, national-level data on adoption of safe practices by health care providers does not exist, in large part due to data and measurement issues.

As described in Chapter 2, in our practice diffusion work in 2007 and 2008, we addressed these constraints by developing a questionnaire for use in a national survey of hospitals regarding their status in safe-practice adoption. This questionnaire addresses the majority of safe practices endorsed by the National Quality Forum. Although other organizations (e.g., the Leapfrog Group, Joint Commission) collect data on some or all of the NQF practices, their data-collection processes serve very different purposes and do not generate national estimates of practice adoption. After the questionnaire is field-tested (which we did not do because of budget constraints), AHRQ can used it to establish data on current adoption status, which can serve as a baseline for comparison with data from additional follow-up administrations of the survey.

More development work remains to be done in this area, however, because of the limited progress thus far in implementing patient safety practices in other health care settings. In particular, our community studies (see Chapter 3) highlight the limited patient safety activities under way in ambulatory care and long-term care. As more attention is focused on activities in those settings, AHRQ has the opportunity to establish data and trends on adoption patterns for these settings as well, through development of similar surveys.

Trends in Patient Outcomes Related to Safety

The preferred types of measures for monitoring trends in patient outcomes are those for which objective data are available on a national level, and which can yield estimates that are complete, valid, and reliable, both in any given year and in trends over time. Measures expressed as rates best fulfill these criteria, because they control for changes in the size of the relevant patient populations (denominators) over time, or for differences in sizes of subgroups of a population being compared within any period. The other type of measure is counts of adverse events (or other negative safety outcomes) that are generated by reporting systems. Because it is difficult to impossible to define accurate denominators for reported events, valid trends cannot be developed for them and they cannot be compared across providers or geographic areas.

Currently, the only data source for calculating rate measures that comes close to providing objective data on a national level is the HCUP data. Alternative sources would be data from surveys on the measures of interest (e.g., AHRQ's adverse-event reporting system survey, or other surveys fielded by federal agencies).

State-level adverse-event reporting systems are key sources of data on reported patient safety events. Their effectiveness has been limited, however, by the lack of a common event taxonomy, widely varying definitions for adverse outcomes, inconsistent compliance by medical providers and facilities with reporting requirements, and limited feedback mechanisms with regard to reported data.

Effects on Other Stakeholders

To have confidence that the full effects of practice changes are indeed being captured in any monitoring program, assessments of effects of patient safety activities on other involved or affected stakeholder groups, as well as patients, should be important program components. Such stakeholders include health-care practitioners, hospitals, other providers, credentialing or accreditation bodies, federal or state agencies, and other involved organizations. With insufficient knowledge about effects on various stakeholders, actions by AHRQ could influence stakeholders to act in ways that inappropriately affect intended safety outcomes. The measurement challenges are perhaps greatest for this work, because the needed data cannot be collected using standard national surveys, analysis of administrative data, or chart data. For example, effects on health-care practitioners and providers are localized and vary widely, and data on those effects require in-depth study of particular implementation processes.

As an example, we examined some effects for stakeholders in the last year of the patient safety evaluation by focusing specifically on the experiences of a subset of the original patient safety grantees (those funded in FY 2000 and FY 2001). Through interviews with the leads for those projects, we obtained their estimates of how various groups of health care personnel were affected by the safe-practice interventions implemented in their projects. We identified a list of stakeholder groups and asked them to identify which of the stakeholders had been affected by the intervention they implemented, and the direction and severity of effect (negative or positive). We recognized that these subjective estimates were vulnerable to positive bias (overestimating positive effects), but they offered preliminary insights into the dynamics of the implementation processes of these projects (Farley et al., 2008b).

The goal of this component of a monitoring program would be to develop a toolkit of methods that were rigorous enough to gather valid and reliable information. These methods could be applied to collect data on stakeholder effects of AHRQ-funded projects, for use in developing estimates of the effects of AHRQ's investments in this work. They also could be applied to assess stakeholder effects of other patient safety initiatives sponsored by other organizations.

Attributing Effects to the AHRQ Patient Safety Initiative

An evaluation question that interested parties can be expected to ask is, Can any observed changes in patient safety practices or outcomes be attributed to AHRQ's patient safety initiative? Although an appropriate question from a policy perspective, it is extremely difficult to answer with any confidence, for at least the following key reasons:

- It would be necessary to observe actual improvements in practices or outcomes. No improvements on the national level have been observed yet, in large part because it is still too soon for the relatively recent momentum of practice improvements to become sufficiently large to have detectable effects on outcomes.
- An effective method would have to be developed for measuring the intensity of the patient safety initiative (dosage of intervention).
- It would be necessary to disentangle the contributions of the initiative from those of other independent factors that also are affecting any observed safety improvements.

While recognizing these considerable measurement challenges, we felt that the evaluation center had an obligation to explore the feasibility of developing a method to assess the effects of AHRQ's investment in its patient safety initiative. We tested one such method by identifying geographic regions in selected states that we characterized either by high or low levels of AHRQ investment, and then comparing trends in outcomes across the two sets of regions. We do not have reportable results from this diagnostic work, in part because we had worked with baseline data and in part because of the measurement uncertainties involved.

We encourage AHRQ to explore other approaches for assessing how, specifically, its patient safety initiative has contributed to changes in practice adoption, patient outcomes, or effects on other stakeholders. For assessing patient outcome effects, and to test such analyses on a national basis, AHRQ might want to explore further the methodological approach we developed. The methodological lessons gained from our analysis, which are presented in *Evaluation Report IV* (Farley et al., 2008b), could provide a foundation for any future methodological development efforts.

CAPABILITIES NEEDED FOR AN EFFECTIVE MONITORING SYSTEM

Through our exploratory analyses of effects of national patient safety activities on relevant outcomes, we identified a number of issues that are barriers to achieving valid and reliable measures that can be monitored with confidence. Our discussion here of needed monitoring-system capabilities examines these issues and possible ways to address them.

Establishing Appropriate Patient Outcome Measures

Measures for other settings. The majority of available clinical safety outcome measures are for hospital-based outcomes, and relatively few are available for outcomes in ambulatory and long-term care settings. This situation reflects in part the fact that hospitals are locations in which intensive treatment is delivered and adverse events that harm patients are more likely to occur. By contrast, adverse events in other settings (such as ambulatory care) may involve a qualitatively different set of safety concerns (e.g., more focus on events of omission than of commission) and different time frames (e.g., adverse "events" that are of longer duration). Adverse events involving hand-offs between different settings of care have also been less of a focus for research and tracking, and again may involve a qualitatively different set of safety concerns from hospital-based acute care.

AHRQ is in an ideal position to lead and influence the development of new measures for other settings, as a natural extension of the measure-development work it already has done. The modified Delphi process we conducted in 2006 made a start on measure identification for ambulatory care and long-term care settings, the results of which could be a starting point for additional work by AHRQ (Farley et al., 2008c). Given the limited patient safety work in these settings thus far, this development process also will require establishment of effective data sources that can be used to calculate values and trends for the newly established measures.

Measures from event reporting systems. For measures based on reported events, the incomplete reporting of events by health care providers into any external reporting system is a serious limitation, resulting in downward bias in reported event frequencies. Further, the factors affecting frequencies of reported events usually cannot be determined and, therefore, neither can their accuracy in representing underlying safety issues.

Because of these issues, and also because lack of denominators precludes rate calculations, measures based on reported events are not good candidates for monitoring changes in outcomes over time. Event reports should play an important role, however, as part of the vigilance aspect of monitoring—to detect and act on new safety issues that become observable through changing frequencies of reported events.

It also would be useful for AHRQ to explore ways to encourage reporting systems to capture meaningful information about denominators from the organizations reporting events to them (i.e., appropriate at-risk populations), which could be a substantial contribution to improving the utility of those measures. With the implementation of the Patient Safety Organization program under the Patient Safety and Quality Improvement Act of 2005, AHRQ has a ready mechanism through which it could pursue such improvements. The Act authorizes AHRQ to establish data networks to receive data from the PSOs designated under the Act, including establishment of standards for measures and data to enable comparisons across data sources (Public Law 109-41, 2005).

Measures of patient and family safety experiences. Despite extensive measurement work under way for patient safety outcomes and effects, almost all existing measures are based on data from health care providers. Few instruments are available to collect data from patients and families on the patient safety issues they encountered as they used the health care system. Self-reports from consumers are potentially important sources of patient safety information, and if changes in the problems they report are observed over time, such information would contribute to evidence regarding effects of safety-improvement activities occurring in the health care system. In particular, patients and families can identify errors or events that may never be detected by providers as underlying causes of adverse events, or that are inherently important but may not lead to severe outcomes.

To obtain usable consumer-reported data at the national level, it will be necessary to establish a valid set of survey questions on patient safety that can be included in surveys administered across the country. One set of instruments that could be used is the AHRQ Consumer Assessment of Healthcare Providers and Systems (CAHPS®) surveys. Patient safety questions could be added to the CAHPS surveys for ambulatory care, hospital services, long-term care, and other services. Sets of supplemental patient-safety items could be developed and made available for users of the CAHPS surveys.

Measures of practice adoption. Substantial work is waiting to be done on collection of valid data regarding the adoption of safe practices and related tools by health care organizations. The Hospital Safe Practice Survey we developed is only a starting point (Appendix E). The next steps for AHRQ would be to have the survey questionnaire field-tested and then use it to conduct national surveys of hospitals. By repeating the survey every two or three years, AHRQ could develop useful information on trends in the use of the practices addressed in the survey. Ideally, AHRQ then would be able to build on the capability to collect data on U.S. hospitals' adoption of safe practice, to expand the measurement activity in other health care settings. In addition, AHRQ may want to expand the set of safe practices for which data are collected, as the evidence base grows and other important practices are identified.

Establishing Valid Measures

Validating patient-outcome rate measures. AHRQ should undertake an ongoing effort to validate encounter-based measures against medical-chart data. All analyses of encounter-based patient safety outcome measures are open to competing interpretations regarding changes in billing and coding practices over time or regarding fundamental changes in patient safety outcomes. This kind of ongoing validation could contribute additional credibility to future analyses of trends in encounter-based measures.

Validating event-report measures. Trends in many measures of reported safety events are influenced by shifting patterns in reporting practices over time, in addition to actual changes in clinical outcomes. This kind of criticism can be applied to national reporting systems, such as the Joint Commission Sentinel Event mechanism and the MEDMARx medication-error tracking system, as well as to the various state-level systems for institutional reporting of adverse events. Here again, cross-validation studies involving reporting systems and other measures of safety outcomes (e.g., based on chart review) could help to build confidence in the robustness of reporting-system measures while also contributing to the interpretability of outcomes trends for the same measures.

Consistent Definitions and Calculation of Measures

Defining a patient-safety event. There are fundamental scholarly disagreements about the definitions related to a patient safety "event," and therefore, what ought to be captured in measures of clinical safety outcomes. In talking with leading safety researchers, we rehashed now-seminal distinctions between adverse events and errors, between events of commission and events of omission, between near misses and harm events, and between sentinel events (i.e., the most serious events involving patient harm) and other sorts of adverse safety events. There is no simple resolution of all these conceptual distinctions, and they capture different elements of outcomes that may be important in different contexts, or in different ways. For example, near misses may be more helpful for quality-improvement efforts than epidemiological tracking, and the definition of "error" may depend on local legal notions of culpability.

For future AHRQ monitoring, these conceptual issues can be used as a framing device so that users can better understand the challenges involved in doing safety measurement. These issues should also remain squarely on the table for future development work on new patient safety measures, designed to expand available safety measurement capabilities to capture new contexts and health care settings.

Coding issues for the PSIs. PSIs based on e-codes present some data and reliability problems. The ICD-9 e-codes, which are coded separately from the main ICD-9 codes, are used to denote external causes of injury. First, we understand from our own conversations and interviews that some experts view PSIs based on e-codes as more susceptible to bias, because of the fact that ICD-9 coding of e-codes is inconsistent in many facilities, and these codes are not specifically required for billing practices. Meanwhile, the way that e-codes are incorporated into the architecture of datasets, such as the HCUP NIS, has changed over time, making the calculation of some safety measures impossible. For example, recent dataset architecture changes to the HCUP NIS have added "present on admission" flags (see below) for ordinary diagnosis codes, but not for e-codes. As a result, the handful of PSIs based on e-codes has become more problematic to calculate compared to the rest of the PSIs.

"Present on admission" (POA) flags, which identify whether each diagnosis listed on a record was present when the patient was admitted to the hospital, provide important data that can help identify which diagnosis codes represent effects resulting from inpatient care. These POA flags also should be dealt with in a consistent way across all HCUP datasets (and other encounter datasets, as well). The newest version of the PSIs recognizes that some encounter datasets do include POA flags and other datasets do not. As a result, the newest version of the PSIs allows the defining algorithms for individual indicators to shift, depending on whether those POA flags are available. This brings confusion to the PSI definitions, with the possible result that two different attempts to calculate the same PSI using the same algorithms using different datasets may produce noncomparable results.

We suggest that AHRQ work with e-codes in a consistent way across all HCUP datasets; collaborating with or encouraging other government entities (for example, CMS) to pursue a common course in dealing with e-codes and POA flags in encounter data. All necessary steps should be taken to add the same POA flags to HCUP NIS e-code data that are now available for diagnosis code data. We also suggest that systematic validation and bias studies be performed of e-coding in encounter data, to better understand the limitations of safety measures based on e-codes. Finally, we would suggest that e-coding would be more useful for epidemiological purposes if hospitals were required to apply e-codes to their records with reasonable fidelity: something that could potentially be mandated either at state or federal levels.

Developing additional needed data sources. AHRQ should work with organizations in the field to initiate measurement capabilities for tracking safety effects for which data sources do not yet exist. A growing number of national-level organizations are assuming leadership roles in stimulating patient-safety improvements in the areas for which they are responsible (e.g., the American Hospital Association [AHA], medical-specialty societies). These organizations are also in positions to stimulate measurement of progress in these areas of jurisdiction, and many of them already are doing so. By collaborating with such organizations in the development of measurement processes, AHRQ can leverage its finite resources while also building the infrastructure necessary for maintaining measurement and monitoring on a regular basis.

Consistency across state event-reporting systems. State-level public patient-safety reporting systems are highly varied in the measures they collect and in other aspects of data architecture. Although state-level safety data could be an important resource for tracking of national progress, they will not be until the data become directly comparable. AHRQ should continue to track the progress of the states in harmonizing their reporting requirements and data systems, and should provide assistance and encouragement to them in moving toward a more uniform reporting standard. Eventually, AHRQ should be able to include state reporting-system data in its national patient safety monitoring program.

At least two activities have the potential to reinforce standardization of event-reporting data. With the passage of the Patient Safety and Quality Improvement Act in 2005, AHRQ has an important opportunity for promoting common standards in adverse-event reporting and better measurement of patient safety outcomes—one that AHRQ currently is pursuing. In addition, many of the individuals who were trained through the Patient Safety Improvement Corps, one of the patient safety projects sponsored by AHRQ, are working to refine their existing state-level reporting systems or to create such systems if they do not currently exist.

Appropriate Trending Methods for the PSIs

As discussed in Chapter 5, consistency in data definitions and specifications is essential to developing valid trend data for patient safety measures. We suggest that AHRQ take the following related steps to achieve reliable estimates for outcome trends for the PSIs:

- Any publication of updated PSI definitions or algorithms should include not only a full version history, describing all updates and changes, but also the rationale behind those changes.

- Any longitudinal tracking effort (e.g., NHQR) should state explicitly which version of the indicators is being used, and the effects of any minor updates to the indicators should be examined and published as well.

- When major revisions are made to the PSIs, retrospective analyses may be needed to see what the effects of new definitions are on old years of data—major measurement changes may make old years of published summary statistics noncomparable to more recent years of data.

One example of the specification issues involved is the issue discussed above about the new use of POA indicators in the updated PSI definitions. This change offers a more refined way of capturing true patient-safety events in hospitals. However, it also represents a major shift in the PSI definitions, and one that presumably could have a retroactive effect on calculations for PSI rates in older years of data. Indeed, results of some of our trend analyses for PSI outcome measures have shifted in connection with recent updates to the PSI measures.

Finally, and on a related note, in the periodic updates to the PSIs, AHRQ has not typically addressed the question of whether the newest version of the measures is feasible to apply to old sets of encounter data. Better AHRQ documentation on this point could be helpful to future attempts to build state and national time trends using the PSIs.

Transparency in Public Reporting of Trends

AHRQ has performed public reporting on health care quality for a number of years through its annual *National Healthcare Quality Reports*, which also include some measures on patient safety outcomes. However, recent NHQRs have moved away from providing explanations of how its small set of reported measures have been drawn from the many available measures. In addition, for the patient-safety outcome measures it covers, the NHQR has not discussed the methods used and limitations for sampling, data, or measure computation.

For the most recent years of the printed NHQR (2006 and 2007), the report has focused on a set of six core patient-safety measures, without including a listing of the full set of patient safety outcomes from which those measures were drawn. Earlier years of the NHQR focused on different "core" measures, and none of the annual reports has explained in any detail how the core measures were selected for inclusion. In the 2006 and 2007 NHQRs, trends on most safety measures were limited to only two or three years of data—a practice that makes it impossible to interpret trends with any confidence.

As a result of these issues, the NHQR has lost some of its usefulness to policymakers, researchers, and health care providers. Future NHQRs could be made more helpful simply by providing a clearer explanation of which patient safety measures are included in the print version versus online, together with more technical background information on the sampling, data, and methodological issues that qualify the interpretation of trends in patient safety outcomes. It also is important to present more than a few years of data on each measure, to give a more-accurate perspective regarding patterns of safety outcomes over time. Changes in underlying definitions and data collection mechanisms can be denoted through footnotes.

DISCUSSION

AHRQ showed great foresight in providing for this two-year analysis on the diffusion of safe-practice adoption at the end of the Patient Safety Evaluation Center contract. It recognized the importance of starting to assess how safe practices were being used in the field, and to examine effects of patient safety activities and practice adoption on the various types of stakeholders involved. Our work in this two-year analysis, the results of which are presented in this report, has been a good "first step" in this assessment process, but much remains to be done.

Although AHRQ needs to attempt specifically to measure effects of its own initiative on patient safety activities and outcomes in the U.S. health care system, it will be extremely difficult to do so, for several reasons. One key issue is that AHRQ's funding has been small relative to the magnitude of the problem, so AHRQ is not likely to have a large effect on outcomes measured at the national level. In addition, AHRQ is one of numerous players working on patient safety across the country, and it has taken a collaborative approach of working in partnership with many other organizations to effect change. AHRQ has chosen well in taking this approach, with the intent of building synergy across multiple participants, but as a result, it will be nearly impossible to isolate effects that can be attributed specifically to AHRQ's work within the larger picture. Attribution likely will be most feasible when examining the effects of the AHRQ-funded projects on safe-practice adoption or other outcomes; if AHRQ had not funded them, many of these projects would not have happened.

Moving forward on future monitoring activities, we encourage AHRQ to use the product-evaluation model to guide its work on tracking practice-adoption activities and their effects on various stakeholder groups. This model guided our suggestions regarding the monitoring program and needed capabilities described here. Over time, AHRQ can use it to ensure that its own assessments have considered all the key system components and stakeholder groups.

APPENDIX A.
BOUNDARY SPANNERS INTERVIEWED IN THE COMMUNITY STUDY

Stakeholder Group	Indianapolis, IN	Seattle, WA	Cleveland, OH	Greenville, SC
Health care organizations [1]	14	5	8	7
Local health coalitions [2]	2	3	2	
Government agencies [3]	1	2	2	2
Insurers	1	2	2	1
Purchasers	2	1	1	1
Consumers			1	1
Professional & industry associations		2	3	1
Health policy & improvement organizations	2	1	5	1
Total	22	16	24	14

[1] Includes health care leaders responsible for inpatient, ambulatory, and long-term care services.

[2] Includes representatives of coalitions focused specifically on patient safety, as well as those with a broader scope of quality activities.

[3] Includes state and local public officials.

APPENDIX B.
CASE STUDIES FROM THE COMMUNITY STUDY

Indianapolis, Indiana

CONTEXT AND HISTORY

Market Composition and Competition

The highly competitive environment in Indianapolis has been feeding expansion activity in the four private hospital systems, which have all been expanding their facilities both within Indianapolis and into the surrounding suburbs. Clarian Health Partners led the charge into the suburbs, followed by Community Health Network, St. Vincent's Health System, and St. Francis Hospitals & Health Centers. Wishard Health Services, a county-owned hospital and network of community clinics is the main safety net provider. An increased number of uninsured patients has caused Wishard to implement cost-cutting measures, such as increased copayments, staff reduction, and more aggressive bill collection from third-party payers.

As the insurer for several large Indianapolis-based companies, Anthem BlueCross BlueShield is the dominant health insurer in the market. Meanwhile, national insurers United Healthcare, Aetna, and Humana have been gaining membership at the expense of provider-owned local insurers, such as M-Plan and Advantage Health Solutions.

Economic Environment in Indianapolis

The large employers in the Indianapolis region include Eli Lilly, General Motors, Marsh Supermarkets, and St. Vincent's Health. They have struggled with containment of health care costs and are now shifting costs toward employees and focusing on developing tiered provider networks. The concern is that health care costs seen in Indianapolis and the state are higher than those in other regions in neighboring states, which may affect future business development.

In the following sections, we describe patient safety activities in the hospital, ambulatory and long-term care sectors, characterize the views of local stakeholders, and then conclude with key lessons learned from the Indianapolis experience.

CURRENT COMMUNITY COLLABORATIONS

Indianapolis Coalition for Patient Safety

The key patient safety initiative in Indianapolis is the Indianapolis Coalition for Patient Safety (ICPS), which operates within the hospital sector. Begun in 2003, the ICPS brings together the six major hospital systems in the metropolitan Indianapolis area. The systems are Clarian Health, Community Health Network, Richard L. Roudebush VA Medical Center, St. Francis Hospitals & Health Centers, St. Vincent Health, and Wishard Health Services. What grew into the ICPS began in 2001 as discussions between the chief executive officers (CEOs) of the major health systems. The CEOs were motivated by *To Err Is Human*, the Institute of Medicine (IOM) report. The ICPS currently is considering expansion to include the hospital systems in the suburban ring around Indianapolis.

Major overarching goals of the ICPS include making Indianapolis the "safest city (for patients) in the country," "not to compete on safety," and to bring a high degree of standardization to practices across all participating health systems. The last goal was crucial, given that a large number of patients receive care in multiple systems and a large number of providers cross systems as well. The initial goals of working together were very broad and largely educational in scope. However, within a short time, and with the assistance of an outside facilitator, the group decided to initiate specific collaborative patient safety improvement activities across the six member hospital systems. The choice of initiatives was highly influenced by external organizations, among them the Joint Commission, Centers for Medicare and Medicaid Services (CMS), and the Institute for Healthcare Improvement (IHI) 100,000 Lives and 5 Million Lives campaigns.

The initial set of ICPS initiatives has occupied the member hospitals since the inception of the coalition. It includes a standard practice for surgical-site markings and surgical timeouts, improving patient safety related to high-alert medications, such as anticoagulants and insulin, and the implementation of a standard policy for "do not use" abbreviations. Patient safety initiatives that are in early stages or on the horizon include medication reconciliation and standardized patient-identification practices.

Having set the tone for cooperation and collaboration, the six CEOs also brought their high level administrators (chief medical officers, chief nursing officers, and directors of patient safety and pharmacy) into the coalition as active participants. These individuals play a critical role in setting priorities for the coalition, implementing specific initiatives, and engaging their hospital staff to participate and make the necessary behavior changes. The success of specific initiatives is also aided in many cases by physician and nurse champions at the individual hospitals who interact with and motivate front-line staff.

The stakeholders interviewed identified several factors that contributed to ICPS's success. One early key factor was the financial and in-kind support provided by Eli Lilly, whose headquarters are in Indianapolis. Lilly's support included devoting staff time to coordinating meetings, hosting meetings and providing office space—providing "neutral ground" for the coalition members to meet and support for coordination activities.

Lilly involvement with the ICPS has declined in recent years, but it still is involved in patient safety initiatives. For instance, Lilly has provided grants to hospitals to work on specific patient safety initiatives and also offered the assistance of several LEAN/Six Sigma Black Belts to work with hospitals on various projects. One example is a project at Wishard Health Services in which they analyzed the insulin-delivery and -administration process "from the receiving dock to the patient's bedside." Along the way, safety risks and process-improvement steps were identified and subsequently implemented.

To accomplish the goals of specific initiatives selected by the ICPS, the members have developed a collaborative model that they feel has greatly contributed to success in changing practices within their individual hospitals. For each initiative selected, each hospital puts forward the high level administrators from their hospitals who are most knowledgeable about the practice area. These six form the cross-system workgroup. That workgroup meets regularly to review relevant empirical evidence on the practice and the experience of others who have implemented it, share information about the current practice at their own individual hospitals, and then determines what the standard of practice should be for all the ICPS hospitals.

Hospital representatives with whom we spoke reported that the role of the workgroup has been critical to the success of these individual initiatives. The workgroup determines the general practice, but each hospital has the flexibility to implement the practice in a way that best fits in its setting. Interviewees believed that to enforce a "cookie-cutter" approach (that forces the member hospitals to have identical policies and procedures) would impede the hospitals from being able to successfully implement the necessary changes, given their unique characteristics (such as hospital size, staffing, patient population, and location).

Indiana Patient Safety Center

Another patient safety coalition active in the community is the statewide Indiana Patient Safety Center (IPSC). The IPSC was formed on July 1, 2006, with the mission to facilitate "the development of safe and reliable health care systems that prevent harm to patients across Indiana." Housed at the Indiana Hospital and Health Association's offices, the IPSC is funded by a portion of hospitals' association membership dues and is staffed by the hospital association. It is pursuing designation as a Patient Safety Organization (PSO). Members of the center include the state's medical schools, the Quality Improvement Organization (QIO), the medical associations, and research institutes, including Purdue University Regenstrief Center for Healthcare Engineering.

The work of the IPSC spans the state and the range of health care settings. For example, in the first year of the center's operation, the staff worked on coordinating statewide efforts to improve the safety of healthcare delivery systems, conducted assessments of clinicians' perceptions of patient safety culture in their organization, and fostered participation in the IHI 5 Million Lives Campaign. An upcoming focus will be to work on a pressure ulcer-prevention initiative involving long-term care settings, along with the state health department and QIO. Additionally, the center is working toward developing, or enabling the development of, regional patient safety coalitions through the state.

HOSPITAL ACTIVITIES

In Indianapolis, patient safety quickly became a top priority for the six large hospital systems that dominate the market. Hospital systems are clearly the dominant player in patient safety in Indianapolis. The six hospitals involved in the ICPS have agreed that, while they compete for market share in other ways, they will not compete on safety. Since ICPS's inception, the members have completed, or are well on their way to completing, several patient safety initiatives and have put systems in place to monitor the improvements and ensure that the improvements are sustained. In other words, the initiatives will never completely end but will continue to be monitored and will evolve into new activities.

Hospitals in the ICPS have experienced many benefits from their participation, including pooled resources and economies of scale by bringing together staff from all the organizations to collaborate on common issues and goals, and highly valued ICPS support to the members when an error occurs. For instance, one of the member hospitals experienced a tragic error when several newborns died from being given an adult dose of heparin. All the ICPS hospitals "rallied around" the hospital where the error occurred and provided public support for the individual health care providers involved, while they also highlighted the need to look at patient safety as a systems and culture issue. When ICPS participants spoke specifically about the heparin incident, they talked about how it could have happened at any of their facilities. For development of the coalition, this incident was not a tipping point for getting the hospitals to *begin* work on patient safety, but was reported to be an *accelerator* for work that was already under way. It motivated them to work faster and more intensely.

Another major benefit voiced by several participants is that the coalition offers health care professionals a safe forum to share experiences and best practices. Before the coalition, patient safety work involved a very siloed approach within institutions, and if information was exchanged between organizations, it was in an informal way. The collaborative structure offered a significantly different method and opportunity for sharing information.

A wide variety of facilitators and barriers to progress are at play in the Indianapolis community, and a facilitator in some situations can act as a barrier in other situations. For example, a mandatory state reporting system can create awareness of patient safety issues, but it can also create tension with health care providers because responding to reporting demands take time away from patient safety improvement efforts and can be considered a punitive approach to reducing medical errors. A somewhat unique facilitator present in Indianapolis is the degree of health information technology being used by health care organizations, along with the development of the Indiana Health Information Exchange, which is supporting the sharing of patient information across organizations and health care settings.

In spite of their success at creating a coalition and getting initiatives under way in a collaborative fashion, members of the ICPS experienced challenges as they worked to improve patient safety within their own hospitals. As in most process-improvement efforts, the coalition members reported that they struggled to free up sufficient financial resources, struggled to find sufficient staff time to devote to coalition activities, and experienced provider resistance to making the behavior changes necessary to change practice. Additionally, while valuing reporting as necessary to improving patient safety, members of the coalition felt burdened by pressures from multiple external organizations that have different reporting requirements, definitions that vary, and measures that are not aligned. Fulfilling the requirements of these external organizations is a "drain" on the hospitals and creates competition between external and internal priorities.

The hospitals highlighted two major issues that are critical to maintaining the improvements they have accomplished through their work. One of those issues is the need for constant vigilance and monitoring of process changes *after* the implementation period is completed. In other words, the initiatives and related changes are not "one-time fixes." One way hospitals are monitoring the maintenance of improvements is including measures on their "dashboards" that are reviewed regularly by the Patient Safety Committee, or subcommittee of the Board of Directors.

Another major concern of the hospitals was that there needs to be better integration of patient safety practices into medical education—in both the physician and nursing fields. This issue was acutely felt in teaching hospitals because medical students and residents spend brief periods of time at different hospital systems around the city. If the standardized patient safety practices that the hospitals are developing were integrated into the medical and nursing school curricula, students would arrive at each of the six hospitals already trained in best practices in patient safety. In the view of these stakeholders, by incorporating patient safety practices in medical education, and reducing variability among the hospitals, patient-safety risks would be substantially minimized.

In addition to their activities with the ICPS, hospitals reported working on other patient safety initiatives on their own, including

- Fall prevention
- Medication reconciliation
- Patient handoffs
- Teamwork and communication
- Implementing rapid-response teams
- Insulin-administration safety
- Patient safety walk-arounds (executive and non-executive versions)

AMBULATORY CARE ACTIVITIES

Relative to hospitals in Indianapolis, less patient safety activity has occurred in ambulatory care settings. Hospital systems that also provide ambulatory care have initiated some interaction between their inpatient and ambulatory practices related to safety, but these interactions have been primarily educational. Stakeholders believe that patient safety work in the ambulatory setting is on the horizon, although they admit it will be extremely challenging, given that there are fewer pre-packaged patient-safety interventions available from outside sources than is true for hospital care and the difficulty of standardizing practices outside the hospital environment. Where there is activity in ambulatory care, it has been primarily focused on medication reconciliation. For stand-alone ambulatory practices (i.e., those not affiliated with a particular hospital system), it is less clear that patient safety is currently a priority or focus.

One advantage that Indianapolis has in ambulatory care is the existence of the Indiana Health Information Exchange (IHIE). IHIE was formed in 2004, by the Regenstrief Institute, Inc., private hospitals, local and state health departments, BioCrossroads, and other Indiana organizations. It was this collaboration on the IHIE that created the platform for the development of the ICPS, and ICPS is housed by the IHIE. The overarching goal of IHIE is to improve transparency, efficiency, and quality at the point of care. One way the IHIE is enabling patient safety in the ambulatory setting is through supporting greater adoption of electronic medical records (EMRs) and the ability to exchange information seamlessly among health care providers. Exchanging accurate information in a timely manner is key to medication reconciliation and to reducing the risk of medication errors. The stakeholders with whom we spoke admitted that progress has been slow within ambulatory care; however, they believe that patient safety is likely to be an area of growth over the next couple years.

LONG-TERM CARE ACTIVITIES

According to stakeholders within long-term care systems, patient safety always has been a priority, although it was not always referred to as "patient safety." Among the major safety issues stakeholders reported were fall prevention, pressure ulcer prevention, reducing the use of restraints, and improving medication reconciliation.

In Indianapolis, the major partners working with long-term care facilities are the state's QIO (Health Care Excel, Inc.), the Indiana State Department of Health, and a national initiative called Advancing Excellence in Nursing Home Care. The state's QIO provides technical assistance to nursing homes and attempts to bring nursing homes and state regulators together to work on patient safety issues (e.g., use of restraints). The Indiana State Department of Health sponsors statewide conferences on patient safety issues twice a year. Thus far, they have covered fall prevention and pressure ulcers, and the next two conferences will focus on reduced use of restraints and emergency preparedness. Attendance has increased over time, perhaps indicating an awakening of interest in patient safety issues. The conferences are funded through a civil-penalties fund (nursing-home fines). Funds were also used to purchase one sophisticated bed designed to prevent pressure ulcers for each nursing home in the state.

Advancing Excellence in Nursing Home Care, begun in 2005, is a national, voluntary, coalition-based initiative working to improve the quality of nursing home care. Participating nursing homes in Indianapolis track their progress on four clinical goals (reducing pressure ulcers, reducing the daily use of restraints, and improving pain management for long-stay and short-stay residents) and four process goals (targets for clinical quality improvement, measuring satisfaction and using satisfaction data in quality-improvement activities, measuring and reducing staff turnover, and adopting consistent assignment of certified nursing assistants to residents). While not insignificant, none of these activities resembles the kind of active, collaborative change that is being pursued in hospital settings in Indianapolis.

A potential barrier to successful collaboration between government (the state health department) and long-term care facilities is the fact that the state health department is the regulatory agency for nursing homes. Further complicating the situation is the trend toward more resident autonomy in long-term care settings The culture in long-term care settings is shifting toward allowing residents to make more of their own decisions. It is anticipated that this trend will strengthen as the baby-boomer generation ages. This autonomy must be balanced with the needs of staff and regulators to ensure patient safety

Financial resources have historically been a major challenge for long-term care facilities and are likely to continue to be a barrier to patient safety initiatives. For example, the use of health information technology in long-term care is lagging far behind that in other health care settings and, without an infusion of resources, is not likely to change. Few, if any, health IT applications have been designed for long-term care settings, and those that exist are not easily adapted for long-term care. Additionally, the explicit use of evidence-based practices has been limited in the past in long term care settings, although that may be changing.

VARIATIONS IN STAKEHOLDERS' PERSPECTIVES

There is general consensus in Indianapolis that the major hospital systems are leading the way in patient safety, particularly the systems that are participating in the ICPS.

Provider views. Hospital providers generally view themselves as playing the most important role in improving patient safety. No institutions within the coalition were viewed as playing a lesser role than the others.

Purchaser views. At this point, purchasers (employers) have not been much of a force in patient safety although their attention is increasing with the growing belief that they are the ones "footing most of the bill" for medical errors. As yet, employers have not tried taking a punitive approach (such as refusing to pay for care related to medical errors). They encourage hospitals to participate in Leapfrog, and many of them do. As pay-for-performance grows in popularity, some stakeholders anticipate that employers may begin rewarding hospitals for patient safety improvements.

Consumer views. We were unable to identify any consumers to interview as stakeholders, either from our Web search or from talking to other local stakeholders. At present, consumers are not viewed by health care providers as partners in moving the patient safety agenda. Consumers exhibit some increasing awareness of patient safety issues, but they are not demanding changes. The media are playing a role in increasing that awareness; however, the majority of the time, stories about patient safety issues tend to be highly dramatized and focused on errors, rather than disseminating information about existing initiatives or progress in improving the safety of health care. The ICPS has invited representatives of the media to press conferences and meetings, but doing so has not increased public understanding of patient safety.

Insurer views. To some degree, there is a perception among these stakeholders that their perspectives are not seen as having much influence on the actions of hospitals and other providers.

Public health and government views. Stakeholders outside hospitals point to the state's governor as being a progressive leader and making patient safety a bigger priority. On the governor's second day in office, he issued an Executive Order requiring the Indiana State Department of Health to develop and implement a medical error-reporting system. The system began collecting data on January 1, 2006.

INFLUENCES OF EXTERNAL ORGANIZATIONS OR ACTIVITIES

Several external organizations are playing a very influential role in what hospitals are doing to improve patient safety. The most influential are IHI, through its 100,000 Lives and 5 Million Lives Campaigns, and the Joint Commission, through its accreditation requirements. The benefit these organizations provide to hospitals is that they give the hospitals a strategy (or roadmap) for patient safety, whereby the initiatives provide direction and assistance with priority-setting, as well as linking hospitals to tools and resources that assist them in making process changes.

On the negative side, hospitals noted that many organizations, including IHI and the Joint Commission, as well as CMS, Leapfrog, and the states' reporting system for quality and errors, are placing burdens on hospitals as a result of disparate voluntary and mandatory data collection and reporting programs. The volume of data collection and reporting is one concern. Another concern is the challenge posed by these measurement activities when the measures are not aligned. Hospitals want to participate in these activities, but the lack of alignment results in wasted expenditures of limited resources. Additionally, the hospitals experience competing priorities when they must balance meeting the requirements of external organizations and responding to their own internally recognized priorities.

A common sentiment among health care providers is the desire for one organization at the national level to step forward and take the lead in aligning all the various measurement initiatives of other organizations and bringing them together under one entity to which health care organizations could report data. There is general consensus among hospitals in Indianapolis that the Agency for Healthcare Research and Quality (AHRQ) should be that lead organization. AHRQ is viewed as having the credibility, balance, and neutrality that would be critical to an endeavor like this.

KEY TAKE-HOME MESSAGES AND ISSUES

The following key issues emerged from interviews with Indianapolis leaders:

- Providers can compete for market share while also collaborating to make meaningful changes that improve safety for patients. Safety is not an either/or proposition.

- Patient safety can be "evolutionary" as well as "revolutionary" in nature. It does not always have to be a high-profile error that brings a hospital to the point of recognition that change needs to happen. And even after change is begun, a high-profile error can serve to increase motivation to continue making improvements.

- The media could be a powerful facilitator in increasing awareness of patient safety issues and in enabling consumers to become more educated and actively encourage their providers to make process improvements that will improve their safety. By contrast, the media also can be an adversary. Hospitals may need assistance (e.g., toolkits, training) to work effectively with the media.

- Barriers to making leaps in patient safety are time, money, culture change, and—specifically with physicians—behavior change.

- A high priority should be integrating current knowledge and best practice on patient safety into medical and nursing school curricula.

- Greater standardization of practices across hospitals within a local community (rather than having different versions of a practice implemented within each individual hospital) holds promise for making substantial improvements in patient safety in communities in which patients use multiple providers and physicians routinely work in more than one health care institution.

- Perhaps most important, the current state of measurement initiatives by national and state organizations cannot go on. It is placing an immense burden on hospitals and other health care providers. Providers are increasingly committed to transparency and recognize the value in having performance data, but organizations need to coalesce around measures, definitions, and goals for measurement and reporting activities. A lead organization is needed to fill the role of bringing the organizations together, as well as potentially developing a national data repository for patient safety data. Stakeholders in Indianapolis believe that AHRQ should take on that critical role.

Seattle, Washington

CONTEXT AND HISTORY

Market Composition and Competition

The major hospital systems in the Seattle area include Swedish Medical Center, Virginia Mason Medical Center, University of Washington Medical Center, Overlake Hospital, and Harborview Medical Center (the main trauma and safety-net provider, affiliated with University of Washington). Hospitals in the Seattle area have been expanding both in the core urban Seattle area and also in the surrounding suburbs. Physicians have been gravitating toward profitable services (e.g., ambulatory surgery centers, sleep centers, vein clinics, laser surgery), partly to cope with financial pressure resulting from increasing operating costs and relatively low reimbursement levels from health plans and public programs. Financial pressures are also encouraging physicians in smaller practices to join larger groups or seek hospital employment. Safety-net providers are struggling to meet demand as the number of uninsured rises.

Premara Blue Cross is one of the largest insurers in Washington state. Others include Aetna, Regence Blue Shield, and Group Health Cooperative (a staff/group model health maintenance organization [HMO] whose direct services focus on ambulatory care). Under pressure from employers to contain costs, health plans are paying closer attention to measuring provider-network performance. Accordingly, health plan products in Seattle are shifting toward tiered networks with preferential cost sharing for consumers who choose providers in the high-quality/low-cost tier.

Past Activities and Experiences

Seattle has a diverse and competitive group of health care providers, although the competition tends to be less "head-to-head" and more segmented—either by service (e.g., medical specialties and "centers of excellence") or by geography (e.g., urban versus suburban). Despite the competition, the Seattle health care community has a long history of collaboration and health care coalitions evidenced in past community public-health and quality-improvement initiatives (the latter particularly through IHI and regional learning collaboratives). This "culture of collaboration" has been partially attributed to a pervasive "voluntary" ethos (hospitals are nonprofit) and strong relationships among senior leaders across providers, payers, and government agencies (many of whom trained together locally).

CURRENT COMMUNITY COLLABORATIONS

Six currently operating Seattle-area collaborative programs were identified.

Washington Patient Safety Coalition

The main collaboration, the Washington Patient Safety Coalition (WPSC), was founded in 2002 after leaders from the State Department of Health and the Health Care Authority (public healthcare purchaser) attended an AHRQ-sponsored safety conference. The two organizations approached the Foundation for Healthcare Quality in Seattle as a trusted neutral home for the initiative to bring together multiple interests and stakeholders. The focus of the WPSC has been on supporting safety improvement among health care providers and sharing of best practices. The coalition was initially formed around hospital-based Patient Safety Officers, but also has enlisted a range of participants, including government agencies, insurers, and employers. It has been focused primarily on safety in inpatient care, but recently has explored initiatives directed outside of hospital settings, such as consumer education and outpatient care.

Puget Sound Health Alliance

The other major health collaboration in the Seattle area is the Puget Sound Health Alliance (PSHA). It similarly represents a coalition of multiple community stakeholders, but was formed through the impetus of local county leadership to address health care quality and cost as a public imperative. The PHSA has focused on ambulatory care and, as an Aligning Forces for Quality site, has embarked on an ambitious community-wide data-sharing and public-reporting project of quality indicators in medical practices. More recently, the coalition has attracted participants with a stronger patient-safety interest.

Washington State Hospital Association safety program

The Washington State Hospital Association has pursued an active patient-safety agenda since 2004. Although primarily limited to the interests of its hospital membership, its activities have ranged from sponsoring specific improvement initiatives (e.g., rapid-response teams, hand hygiene, medication safety), advocacy and policy work on safety-related issues (e.g., public transparency requirements, the state's voluntary infection rate-reporting bill), and encouraging members to participate in other patient safety initiatives (e.g., ensuring Washington state's high rates of participation in Hospital Compare, and the IHI's 100,000 Lives Campaign—the latter having reached 100 percent).

Other Foundation for Healthcare Quality programs

In addition to the WPSC, the Foundation for Healthcare Quality also sponsors other quality- and safety-related improvement initiatives, such as the Surgical Care and Outcomes Assessment Program (SCOAP) and the Clinical Outcomes Assessment Program (COAP), which although focused on hospital settings, are more physician-driven than WPSC initiatives, which tend to be driven by safety and quality officers.

Ambulatory care initiatives

Relatively smaller collaborative initiatives related to patient safety that involve local providers include a recent program by the Community Health Plan (an insurer servicing low-income consumers) focusing on major safety issues in ambulatory community health clinics, such as diagnosis delays and health literacy, and the Washington State Department of Health's chronic care collaboratives for pediatric and family medical practices, which occasionally touch on patient safety, such as asthma medication safety.

HOSPITAL ACTIVITIES

As described above, local hospitals have participated in a number of collaborative initiatives based at the regional, state, and national levels. For most all the major hospitals and systems with inpatient facilities, these activities have been part and parcel of substantial internal safety and quality initiatives that have developed beginning, in some cases, six or more years ago. An early response by leading hospitals in the community of full public disclosure of serious adverse events helped to raise the bar for transparency and public communication around safety and quality. Many hospitals in the Seattle area have adopted the IHI's Plan-Do-Study-Act (PDSA) rapid cycle change methodology as their main approach to implementing safety and quality improvements. A few have been early and highly visible adopters of the Toyota Production System, or LEAN approach to quality, sending staff to Japan for direct exposure to the approach and viewing it not simply as a quality program but as a fundamental management system. There has been some attention among other hospitals to the principles of the Baldrige National Quality Award as a framework for organizing quality and safety activities, although achieving Baldrige recognition was mentioned as a further-off objective. Patient centered care and its connection to patient safety has also found strong adherents in the Seattle hospital community, both in viewing better-designed patient-oriented facilities as ultimately safer and in involving patient representatives directly in internal safety committees and discussions.

Hospitals have also put substantial effort into developing information technology (IT) that can support patient safety goals. Several major hospitals in the area were early implementers of computerized physician order entry (CPOE), and the rest are in the midst of advanced planning or implementation of CPOE systems. Several hospitals and integrated systems have implemented EMR, but are at early stages of data exchange between inpatient and other settings of care. More generally, there is a sense that hospitals have yet to fully realize the potential of data collection and IT systems to improve safety.

AMBULATORY CARE ACTIVITIES

Ambulatory care settings tend to consider themselves as focused on "quality" (e.g., Healthcare Effectiveness Data and Information Set (HEDIS)measures) and less likely to identify patient safety explicitly as part of their quality agenda. Those ambulatory providers that did expressly pay attention to safety emphasized that certain issues are more salient in the outpatient context, such as problems in health literacy and errors due to delays in diagnosis, although some issues are shared with inpatient settings, such as medication reconciliation. Within integrated hospital and health systems, quality and patient safety support are typically based in the inpatient setting, with variable reach into ambulatory units. The PSHA's Aligning Forces for Quality initiative involves all types of ambulatory providers (whether groups within integrated systems, independent medical practices, or safety net community health centers); although it focuses primarily on quality measures per se, it does consider itself to have safety implications.

LONG-TERM CARE ACTIVITIES

Patient safety has tended to be a high priority among long-term care (LTC) organizations throughout Washington state, driven in large part by regulatory oversight and a desire to avoid citations stemming from incident reports and inspections. As a result, attention to safety issues in the LTC sector has appeared more reactive than proactive. Those facilities that are part of larger health care systems, however, have been inclined toward more-active safety programs coordinated at the corporate level. Even so, most facilities, whether independent or part of a larger system, have patient safety committees and do staff rounds. And the state provides each facility with a quality assurance nurse who visits quarterly to give technical assistance on such topics as pressure ulcers or fall-prevention protocols. The QIO for the state in particular has played a leading role in quality and safety improvement for LTC providers, having offered voluntary programs on such issues as pain management, pressure ulcers, and restraints. Facilities that have worked with the QIO were also noted to be more likely to use general improvement methodologies, such as root cause analysis. One of the biggest safety concerns for LTC facilities is falls. Site-safety committees have looked at the physical environment within facilities, as well as technologies (e.g., hipsters, landing strips) to reduce the number of falls and injuries from falls. Prevention also has branched out into other areas, such as nutrition (i.e., to keep strength to prevent falling). A major underlying factor contributing to poor safety is high staff turnover, which makes sustaining any type of improvement difficult. Similar to patient-centered care in inpatient settings, the movement toward resident-centered programs among LTC facilities is also considered to enhance safety, because residents tend to feel more comfortable in homelike settings, and designs of facilities based on these principles are sensitive to safety and ergonomics.

VARIATIONS IN STAKEHOLDERS' PERSPECTIVES

Provider views. Providers across the spectrum felt that collaborative efforts have been worthwhile and that individual institutions have made notable progress toward nationally recognized patient safety goals. However, there was widespread frustration with the increasing number of measures to report ("seems like a different set every week") and entities producing these measures (e.g., CMS, Leapfrog, NQF, Joint Commission, and AHRQ). There was also concern over public reporting of data and how best to achieve transparency. Although hospitals have come to recognize the value of public reporting for stimulating patient safety efforts within their own organization, providers tend to be skeptical of the validity of many measures, their actual effect on driving patient safety, and the willingness and ability of consumers and purchasers to pay attention to them. Hospitals have recently resisted public reporting of adverse events by the state, prompting a harsh reaction by the public, which to some indicated that consumers are interested in having access to this information, even if they do not use or do not know how to use it. Another frequent concern about the increasing demands for reporting is that it diverts limited resources that could be better spent on implementation of improvements. In general, providers complained of a lack of resources for patient safety efforts and, in particular, IT, even when safety goals are given high priority. Providers also pointed to the difficulty of implementing patient safety across the interface with ambulatory and other settings of care, even within integrated systems. Greater standardization of measures and protocols across these settings (as CMS is doing) would be helpful, as well as equivalent emphasis on safety (e.g., a relative lack of attention to patient safety in physician-owned freestanding surgery centers).

Purchaser views. Employers in the Seattle area, led primarily by Boeing Corporation, have been highly active in promoting patient safety—in particular, by bringing pressure to bear on hospitals to join Leapfrog and major insurers to institute incentives for inpatient providers who meet Leapfrog standards. Employers have held meetings with individual hospitals to discuss progress on patient safety goals, and they have supported other local safety and quality initiatives, including WPSC and PSHA. To date employers have not put much pressure on ambulatory care providers to pursue patient safety. Companies with younger workforces have been reluctant to become involved in such patient safety efforts. In these efforts, large employers have as much or more leverage with health-care providers than small employers.

Consumer views. There was general consensus that consumers still tend to be passive recipients of care, and that education is needed to raise awareness on the variability of care receive by consumers and how to ensure they are getting good-quality care. Work in this vein often fell under the rubric of "health literacy" to provide health information to consumers through various venues (e.g., libraries, clinics, pharmacies) as well as to equip physicians to converse with patients about managing their own care. There was also a sense that health plans, in addition to providers, could play a useful role in informing and activating consumers around quality and safety issues.

Insurer views. For their part, insurers have implemented modest payment incentives for providers and retain formal membership in coalitions, such as the WPSC and PSHA, but are unsure of the effectiveness of the incentives and what kind of meaningful role they can play as active partners in such collaborations. Nonprofit health plans appeared more greatly concerned about patient safety in inpatient settings and work more closely with hospitals to improve safety. For-profit plans serving the Seattle region put greater emphasis on cost efficiency and quality indicators per se. Although these insurers considered safety to be an important issue, it was generally considered to be best addressed by other entities. Previous attempts by commercial plans to institute their own data collection and incentives for safety and quality measures were met with strong resistance by providers and the American Medical Association (AMA), causing them to curtail their own reporting systems and instead support initiatives more accepted by providers, such as the PSHA's Aligning Forces for Quality. Some insurers also voiced skepticism of hospital claims about lack of resources and sufficient payment for reporting and implementing safe practices, given the large capital project spending by many hospitals in recent years and the relatively modest proportion of revenue that these efforts constitute, especially compared with what other industries spend on data systems and safety.

Public health and government views. Government agencies at the state and local levels have been highly involved in patient safety issues, helping to establish, among other things, the WPSC and PSHA, respectively. Thus state and county officials tend to be well aware of safety efforts within hospitals in particular. However, access (e.g., getting medication in the first place, before worrying about the likelihood of getting the wrong medication) still tends to be the overriding concern of public officials, especially for safety net populations.

INFLUENCES OF EXTERNAL ORGANIZATIONS OR ACTIVITIES

The following general points emerged from the interview information on influences of external organizations:

- National initiatives can take a long time to make an impact. Local and regional initiatives have the potential to speed progress.

- Each of the national initiatives has made complementary contributions, but there is also a great degree of overlap. Without stronger consolidation in the number of measures and entities making requirements, providers are prone to confusion, implementation fatigue, and weak adoption of practices merely to conform.

- The multiplicity of standards and requirements also has led to squandering resources on low-value issues and inconsistency in priorities among hospitals and other providers.

- Not all required measures address underlying issues. Some harmonizing and testing of indicators and standards have occurred, but much more needs to be done.

Joint Commission. The Joint Commission's core measures were consistently rated as the highest priority indicators for hospitals, both because of their consequence for certification and because of confidence in their usefulness for tracking safety and implementing improvement. A number of hospitals also praised the shift in Joint Commission accreditation in the past few years to a more process-oriented approach that follows patients through the continuum of care.

CMS. Hospitals and other providers were attuned to CMS' list of "never events" and its potential consequences for reimbursement rates. However, there was acknowledgment of CMS' accountability to taxpayers and little voiced opposition to the policy. CMS was also credited with helping to drive change across a range of health care delivery settings, including inpatient, ambulatory, and long-term care.

AHRQ. Most hospitals reported utilizing various resources and tools produced by AHRQ, including the patient safety culture survey, the Patient Safety Improvement Corps (PSIC) and TeamSTEPP (teamwork) training, the Patient Safety Indicators, and its patient safety Web resources for both providers and consumers. Once prompted to think about AHRQ's activities, a variety of stakeholders also expressed appreciation for the agency's important but more indirect role in building the scientific understanding of safety issues, advocating for patient safety within the health care community, and generating dialogues on the issues that stimulate action (e.g., the conference that was the impetus for the WPSC). However, there were a number of suggestions for AHRQ to enhance its role in advancing patient safety. Although hospitals are aware of AHRQ and its resources, the agency does not have the same reach within local physician communities. Similarly, AHRQ provides a wealth of information on its Web site, but this tends to be in a "narrow band" (e.g., best practices for ambulatory settings are not as available as those for hospitals). There were also calls for AHRQ to both expand its scientific research agenda and invest more in supporting actual implementation of safe practices. Finally, there were numerous calls, particularly among hospitals, for AHRQ to play a more forceful role in consolidating and harmonizing standards, measures, and reporting—considered a traditional strength of the agency that has waned in recent years.

Leapfrog Group. With the strong support from Boeing and other employers in the Seattle area, most hospitals in the area now participate in Leapfrog. While the roll-out was generally viewed by hospitals as heavy-handed (and contrary to the local cooperative culture), it admittedly has spurred change within their organizations. However, hospitals voiced concerns over the accuracy and validity of the measures, as well as the relative usefulness and burden of the survey.

Government agencies. As discussed, state and local agencies have been very involved in patient safety initiatives touching on providers in the Seattle area. The Washington State Department of Health and Health Care Authority were prime founders of the WPSC, and both support a variety of safety programs and collaborations. Likewise, the local county government was instrumental in forming the PSHA. More recently, Washington state has begun a program of voluntary reporting of sentinel events.

KEY TAKE-HOME MESSAGES AND ISSUES

The following key issues emerged from interviews with Seattle leaders:

- Broad multistakeholder coalitions can help achieve consensus on patient safety goals and progress in the community, but require time to enlist participants and produce effects.

- It may be especially difficult to figure out how to obtain active involvement in such coalitions by stakeholders who are not providers (e.g., insurers, consumers).

- Even with available public reporting and emphasis on transparency by local providers, consumers remain poorly informed and poorly activated around patient safety issues, and questions remain about the use of publicly reported data by consumers.

- Multiple systems and programs for reporting of patient safety data consume limited resources and make prioritizing safety activities difficult.

- National patient safety goals and measures are not always relevant to local needs and priorities, especially for institutions serving different types of populations.

- National leadership is required to help rationalize reporting systems and measures, a role that AHRQ has historically played but would fulfill more forcefully now.

Cleveland, Ohio

CONTEXT AND HISTORY

Market Composition and Competition

Health care market consolidation in Cleveland began in the late 1990s, leading to 36 independent hospitals being consolidated into three major health systems plus a small number of remaining independent hospitals. The three large systems established are University Hospitals, Cleveland Clinic, and the MetroHealth System. This consolidation included acquisition of physician practices by the health systems, as well as alignment with related health plans, such that nearly 50 percent of the primary care providers are employed by one of the systems, Kaiser, or the Veterans Administration Health System. One positive effect of consolidation was the early adoption of electronic medical records (EMRs) in Cleveland, with leadership by the three systems but also extending beyond medical practices within the systems to reach other practices.

The presence of Cleveland Clinic and University Hospitals, in particular, makes Cleveland a distinct market. Both systems are large and have highly specialized services, and they define the nation (and sometimes the international market) as their markets for many of these services. By contrast, the MetroHealth System grew from a safety-net hospital and tends to serve more patients with public health benefits (Medicaid and Medicare) than the other systems.

Marketing is an important activity for all the major health systems. In particular, there is a high degree of competition between Cleveland Clinic and University Hospitals. The public hospital (MetroHealth) is trying to compete with the private systems to gain more insured patients, to help subsidize low public reimbursement.

Economic Environment in Cleveland

The health care sector is a dominant source of employment in Cleveland, with Cleveland Clinic being the largest employer in the area. Other, traditional "rust belt" jobs are fading away. There are few other large employers that might drive employer-based initiatives for health care issues.

Cleveland has a nursing shortage, and nurses have become a more organized labor force. Although many nursing schools are in the area, the schools have been able to supply only part of the demand for nurses. All three major health care systems are Magnet-certified by the American Nurses' Credentialing Center, a status that leads to significant process-improvement activity within the hospitals.

Past Activities and Experiences

The Cleveland Health Quality Choice (CHQC), which began in 1990 with strong involvement by the local business community, focused on collecting and public reporting of hospital data for a variety of quality measures. CHQC ended in 1999, when the Cleveland Clinic withdrew its participation. A variety of financial and political factors caused many participants (hospitals and employers) to have negative experiences with the CHQC, which had lasting effects on levels of inter-organizational trust. As a result, many organizations have been reluctant to participate in larger initiatives.

The Benjamin Rose Institute was a nursing home coalition, which all nonprofit nursing homes (26 facilities) participated in and supported financially. The coalition used the Minimum Data Set (MDS) data to look at key outcomes (e.g. falls, pressure ulcers, weight loss, inactivity), to provide quality-improvement support through peer-to-peer shared learning. An outside company benchmarked these data on a quarterly basis, with participants receiving blinded reports. The coalition was discontinued because nursing homes experienced financial pressures related to declining Medicaid reimbursement rates.

CURRENT COMMUNITY COLLABORATIONS

Community-based collaborations are in limited use in Cleveland, due in part to the dominance of the two large health care systems in the community. When coalitions have been used, their focus has been on quality in general and not specifically on patient safety.

Development of Aligning Forces for Quality (AF4Q) project

This project is part of a national project funded by the Robert Wood Johnson Foundation. The safety net providers (MetroHealth and community health centers [CHCs]) took the initiative to pursue it, to address quality improvement in ambulatory care. There has been broad community involvement in AF4Q, including all three major health systems, health plans, Kaiser, and the VA. The VA's participation is noteworthy because the VA is typically not included in community collaboration initiatives.

AF4Q is focusing on improvements in discharge planning, readmissions, chronic care, and patient education. As characterized by interviewed participants, it is using a "raise all boats" approach to help improve care across the health care continuum, using public reporting and consumer activism, supported by data from EMRs, registries, and health plan claims. Participating health plans and businesses see this project as an opportunity to exchange valuable health data. Challenges include balancing interests of multiple stakeholders, sustainability of funding, and consumer activism. Leadership by the safety-net providers has helped to create trust for collaborative work.

Health Information Exchange Database

The goal of this initiative is health information exchange among Cleveland hospitals. The Center for Health Affairs (the Cleveland hospital association) houses a database of health data (e.g. utilization data, length of stay) into which most of its member hospitals report. Only hospitals that report into the database can access the data, which are reported in a blinded format. The Center for Health Affairs convenes a data-users group that decides what data should be reported each quarter or year. The hospitals use these data for planning and marketing purposes.

Safety-Net Strategic Alliance

This initiative developed as a forum for Cleveland's community health centers and other safety-net clinics to share best practices and to advocate for their needs with a unified voice. The Alliance has sub-committees that deal with a variety of issues—for example, one subcommittee is dedicated to diabetes and examines ways to improve diabetes care for the safety net's population. Its main challenge has been adequacy of resources to sustain its work.

Linking electronic information systems

The chief information officers of the three major health systems in Cleveland are working to create health information-sharing linkages between their systems. This effort is currently in the very early stages.

HOSPITAL ACTIVITIES

Most of the patient safety activity in Cleveland is occurring in the hospital setting. Community collaboration in this work has been lacking, with each of the individual systems working within its own organization to implement safety improvements. In general, hospitals have been focusing first on Joint Commission core measures, although they also have addressed issues involved in other major initiatives (e.g., Leapfrog Group) as they emerged. Much of the major attention to patient safety has emerged within the past 2 or 3 years. Although some efforts preceded that time, they were less cohesive than the more recent activities. Some hospitals took action in anticipation of public reporting requirements. Changes often were stimulated by new system leaders who made patient safety a priority for both boards and staff. Typically, when patient safety became a priority, it was part of a larger quality initiative, which included reorganization of the quality/safety activities to make them more central in the organization, reporting to executive management and often run by physicians. Some systems tie financial incentives for management to meet quality/safety goals. Even with systemwide initiatives in place, the systems often reported that safety activities varied across their individual hospitals.

The large health care systems are focusing on benchmarking performance at the national level to achieve and sustain national-level recognition and market competitiveness. The safety-net hospital does not see itself as having any quality disadvantages as a result of caring for an indigent population.

Examples of patient safety activities undertaken are Magnet status (nursing), which requires ongoing process-improvement activities; participation in national initiatives (e.g., NQF, IHI); executive walk-arounds in hospital units and departments; and teaching safety techniques to residents and staff physicians. Some specific patient safety practices that have been implemented include medication reconciliation, management of anti-coagulation medication, hand washing at all sites of care, and regular incident reporting. Care-coordination practices that have been implemented include hand-offs at shift changes and transfers using the community-wide transfer form, and use of electronic information systems for inter-organizational sharing of patient information.

The greatest challenges identified by the systems have been getting physicians on board with safety priorities and actions, establishing a patient safety culture that is safe for reporting, resource limitations, work overload due to "initiative creep," and need for continuous training of new personnel due to staff turnover (especially residents and students).

The following needs were identified consistently by representatives of the hospitals we interviewed:

- A clear business case needs to be made for quality and patient safety, to guide strategies within their financial constraints.

- Duplicative and conflicting requirements by multiple authorities (e.g., Joint Commission, Medicare, Leapfrog) for reporting on quality and safety performance need to be replaced by one consolidated set of requirements, to eliminate inefficiencies that dilute providers' resources to take needed actions. Although standards are becoming more consistent, reporting formats and schedules still differ across authorities.

- The hospitals would like to have more ways to share and learn locally about patient safety, rather than having to go to national conferences to obtain needed information.

- The hospitals wanted to develop better data and monitoring capability to track clinical outcomes, to move beyond the current focus on monitoring process measures.

AMBULATORY CARE ACTIVITIES

The patient safety activity in the ambulatory care sector appears to be affected by whether medical practices are part of the major health systems or are independent practices. Almost half the physicians in the Cleveland area are in practices owned by one of the three major hospital systems. Practices that are part of a system tended to be included in systemwide patient-safety initiatives, but they usually were secondary targets for actions, with most of the focus being on the hospitals. Only recently have systems begun focusing on safety in their ambulatory care services. The EMRs established by the large systems have provided communication and coordination-of-care capabilities. Although some systems extend their EMR systems to independent practices that send patients to the systems for care, not all such practices have access to EMRs.

The systems identified the lack of patient safety literature and tools specific to outpatient care services as one of the deterrents to patient safety progress in this setting. Some standards are now being developed for ambulatory settings, but resources are still very limited. Some systems have tried to adapt inpatient practices to ambulatory care, but some practices do not adapt well to this setting.

The patient safety goals in ambulatory care differ between the safety-net providers (the CHCs) and other private practices. Ambulatory care practices in large systems follow the larger goals of the system, which tend to be driven by hospital priorities. Other private practices do not appear to be pursuing focused goals for safety improvements. By contrast, one of the CHCs has set a goal to be ready for Joint Commission accreditation by preparing for review on quality and safety standards. All CHCs previously had an accreditation-driven process before discontinuing accreditation, which some CHCs feel will return in the near future. They report being constrained by the absence of electronic data systems and limited resources.

LONG-TERM CARE ACTIVITIES

Similar to the ambulatory care practices, the patient safety activities of long-term care (LTC) organizations appear to have been influenced by whether they are part of larger health care systems, part of larger LTC organizations, or freestanding entities. Those that are part of larger health care systems have been included to some extent in the systems' patient safety activities and have received quality/patient safety directives from the corporate level. Activities of other LTC organizations have been more limited thus far, with little diffusion of ideas from the inpatient or ambulatory care settings.

Larger, not-for-profit LTC organizations tend to be collaborative and do some informal sharing across organizations. However, there is little formal sharing, which may be due, in part, to competitive positioning, in which nursing homes see quality as their "bread and butter" and tend not to share practices with other nursing homes.

For the most part, the long-term care organizations have not yet set clear patient safety goals. Long-term care tends to focus on measures that are required to be reported, and the activities of such organizations often are driven by the survey process, including issues of patient autonomy, quality of life, transfer methods, fall prevention, pressure ulcers, and clinical caregiver safety. LTC organizations tend to focus more on physical safety of workers and patients, compared with hospitals, which often focus more on high-risk clinical procedures. Further, home care faces different challenges from nursing homes or acute long-term care, including consideration of the way the patient lives, placement of furniture and rugs, and the condition of housing.

Challenges identified included high rates of nursing-home buyouts and closures, which create unstable environments, low reimbursement, a shift toward home care away from nursing homes, and problems with coordination between hospital emergency care and the nursing homes for patients transfers. There also is limited patient safety literature related specifically to long-term care, which long-term care facilities need to support their work. In particular, they identified the need to build a business case for practices that improve safety.

VARIATIONS IN STAKEHOLDERS' PERSPECTIVES

All interviewed stakeholder groups in Cleveland considered patient safety to be an integral part of quality. They had more divergent views, however, about progress being made in improving safety and the need for information about safety status and trends.

Provider views. State associations had a more positive view of collaborative activities for quality and patient safety than the providers at the more local, "ground" level. Litigiousness of the health care culture and the medical education system were seen as barriers to advancement, especially in the large, academic systems. Insufficient leadership commitment also was identified as a barrier to progress. Providers also had differing opinions regarding the role of consumers in patient safety initiatives. Little consumer involvement has occurred in local patient safety activities, although some providers felt the priority on safety was being driven by patients. Most of this involvement, however, has been by consumer advocates, rather than by the average patient. Some providers believed that consumers do not understand quality and safety, and that consumers care more about price than quality or safety.

Purchaser views. The regional employer group, Health Action Council, thinks of itself as having brought patient safety to the forefront for the community. It is credited with raising awareness of patient safety through the Leapfrog initiative, and hospital representatives recognized its importance in the community. In general, employers are supportive of approaching patient safety from a business/risk-management perspective.

Purchasers tended to view the health system consolidation as being harmful, because it masks variability among hospitals in the large systems, and the consolidated systems appear to have increased marketing activities rather than pursuing genuine quality or safety improvements. The consolidation also has given the systems market power, with the result that health plans are less able to "shop" among individual providers within the systems to drive market share toward high performing hospitals. Some purchasers view patient safety efforts by health plans as being marginally effective, because they affect only a portion of health-plan membership (e.g., all GM employees in Ohio).

Consumer views. Consumers have not been able to see what hospitals are doing to improve patient safety and quality, although they are aware that safety is a priority for hospitals. Some believe that individual hospitals are doing more than the systems that own them. At major academic institutions, in particular, consumers view making change as difficult because everything is in silos. User-friendly public reporting is seen as having value, but only for those who will read the reports because they have a strong interest in the issue.

Insurer views. The insurers report that they have focused on measuring and reporting provider safety performance, using existing measures from a variety of sources. They are moving toward electronic information sharing, and they are working to tie payments to quality performance. They think that provider-behavior changes likely will be the result of many different activities, rather than just one initiative by health plans. They believe that hospitals initially viewed safety improvement as a resource-intensive undertaking, but they now see that it is not necessarily expensive and can yield efficiencies. Insurers view hospitals as being very resource-thin.

Public health and government views. These groups are not interfaced strongly with the hospitals in Cleveland, so they tend to be outside observers of providers' patient safety activities. They tend to think that little is going on in patient safety: that no leaders have emerged from the health systems, and employers have not pushed for quality. The large systems in town are so large that they can take initiative on their own and do not need to collaborate. Some see the need for greater alignment of different organizational-improvement efforts to gain synergy.

INFLUENCES OF EXTERNAL ORGANIZATIONS OR ACTIVITIES

The following key points emerged from our analysis of interview information about the influences of external organizations:

- The health care organizations reported that they adapt as much patient safety information, products, and guidance as they can from other organizations, for use within their own organizations.

- Health care organizations set their patient safety priorities based first on what they are required to do, so the patient safety goals and accreditation standards of the Joint Commission are high priorities for them.

- Another strong driver has been the new Medicare policy of not paying for hospital-acquired events or conditions, to which providers are responding actively.

- Hospitals face multiple measurement and reporting requirements from various entities (e.g., Medicare, Joint Commission, Leapfrog), requiring substantial time for fulfilling the requirements that could be spent on improving safety performance.

- They also have found conflicts between some of the standards and measures with which they are expected to comply, making them have to choose which of the conflicting standards they should use and which they should ignore. Such conflicting requirements may be harming safety, rather than improving it.

- Even with some of these frustrations, the health care organizations tend to use each reporting process constructively, as an opportunity to learn and improve.

- AHRQ appears to be both a direct and indirect resource for local health care organizations. The interviewees usually did not identify AHRQ spontaneously as they thought about patient safety resources, but with prompting on specific products or activities, they generally recognized its importance as a resource. They also reported that they used a variety of AHRQ products and tools.

- Although numerous state-level activities are under way, the interviewees generally thought these initiatives are not having much effect in Cleveland. The reason for this lack of effect is not clear, but it may be the unique nature of the two very large health systems in Cleveland, which have substantial resources of their own and may be less inclined to participate in coalitions than smaller organizations.

Joint Commission Influences. The Joint Commission was reported to have strong effects on both hospitals and community health centers, with accreditation requirements affecting how hospitals and CHCs set priorities. One of the only instances of data sharing among the Cleveland hospitals is around the Joint Commission core measures. For the community health centers, Joint Commission certification is being used to prepare for the return of a CMS-mandated review process, and the Joint Commission's standards are a useful tool for improving quality.

AHRQ as a Resource. AHRQ was viewed as an important resource, both as a source of knowledge on patient safety and for the specific tools it develops. People reported that they were using several AHRQ products, including the Patient Safety Indicators (used by both the Ohio Hospital Association and the State of Ohio), the patient safety culture survey, and the Patient Safety Net (PSNet) Web site. Hospitals reported that the culture survey was valuable, providing guidelines and bringing staff attention to patient safety. AHRQ also has been an important information resource regarding the direction of the country and current national initiatives, and it has been a source of scientific literature on patient safety.

Leapfrog Group. Mixed views were expressed about the Leapfrog survey and process. Hospitals reported that they participate because it is the "right thing to do," but the long survey has been burdensome for them. They have concerns about lack of validation of the survey data, and some expressed doubt that consumers are actually using the Leapfrog information to make decisions. The business community saw value in participating in a larger national initiative with potentially more staying power than solely local efforts, and there was recognition by providers that the Leapfrog Group was not going away.

KEY TAKE-HOME MESSAGES AND ISSUES

The following key issues emerged from interviews with Cleveland leaders:

- Although the 2000 IOM report brought attention to patient safety and sparked discussion across the Cleveland community, providers and health plans in the area took several years to implement actions in response to the issues the report raised.

- The presence of two large, competitive health care systems in Cleveland has a strong effect community-wide, including barriers to collaboration across systems for quality or patient safety, as well as resistance to efforts by others (e.g. purchasers, insurers) to influence their actions.

- The focus of providers on practices and measures required by accreditation bodies or payer-led initiatives (especially with national visibility) highlights the importance of these organizations in stimulating safety improvements.

- With limited first-hand knowledge of what the health care systems are doing in patient safety, other stakeholders tend to perceive that these systems are focusing on marketing rather than taking substantive actions to improve safety.

- A significant evidence base on safety practices and tools needs to be available for each health care setting, to support providers' safety-improvement actions; this resource is not yet available for ambulatory care and long-term care settings.

- Both providers and purchasers are looking for well-documented business cases for safe practices in all settings—in particular, for ambulatory care and long-term care.

Greenville, South Carolina

CONTEXT AND HISTORY

Market Composition and Competition

The Greenville area health care market is dominated by several large hospital systems. The Greenville Metropolitan Area comprises the cities of Greenville, Spartanburg, and Anderson. Within Greenville, the delivery system is dominated by Greenville Hospital System, which has a 70 percent market share, competing mainly with Bon Secours St. Francis, which has a 20 percent market share. Spartanburg and Anderson are home to other hospital systems. Competition is strong in the areas in between these three cities, particularly the area between Greenville and Spartanburg, where the population has been growing rapidly. Specialty service lines are a growing area of competition between the systems. The hospital systems routinely feature patient-safety and quality-of-care information prominently in their marketing campaigns.

The hospital systems are closely aligned with local physician practices, either through employment or contracting. The hospital systems have been moving toward greater integration with physician practices, with some approaching "closed" integrated systems with their employed physicians. Most of the hospital systems also include long-term care providers.

Some patient safety activities are driven at the state, rather than the regional, level. South Carolina is a fairly small state, with 50–60 hospitals. This size is considered conducive to state-level collaboration, since the number of participants is manageable, yet not so small as to allow for competitive behavior that would detract from collaboration on patient safety. A few health insurers offer coverage in the community, but the market is clearly dominated by Blue Cross Blue Shield of South Carolina.

Economic Environment in Greenville

The economy in the Greenville area has been growing rapidly in recent years, creating a tight labor market. Textile industry employment has been replaced by manufacturing, with BMW and Michelin among the largest area employers. Economic growth has been accompanied by rapid population growth, particularly in the area between Greenville and Spartanburg. A large amount of investment has been made in new health care infrastructure accompanying the economic and population growth. The health sector is also a large source of employment.

Past Activities and Experiences

The evolution of patient safety activities in the Greenville area has followed a steady progression over a long period, and has not been punctuated by any defining events with particularly large effects on the agenda. Hospital systems in the Greenville area have been actively pursuing quality-measurement activities for more than ten years. Their agenda has evolved largely in line with the national patient-safety agenda. Although the infection-control community has been active in patient safety for a long time, until recently, no infrastructure was in place that provided opportunities to exchange information and best practices. Patient safety first began to come to the forefront as an issue with the publication of the Institute of Medicine report *To Err Is Human* in 1999. Public awareness of patient safety issues has provided an additional impetus to address patient safety in recent years. Patient safety has become especially prominent in the past 1–2 years, as the emphasis has shifted from reacting to regulation and external requirements to transparency and a culture of safety.

CURRENT COMMUNITY COLLABORATIONS

Community-based collaborations have had limited use in Greenville, due in part to the dominant roles in the market of several consolidated hospital systems. However, several coalitions have played a role in patient safety activities in the local area. We describe three coalitions below. The South Carolina Business Coalition on Health is specific to Greenville, and the other two are active in Greenville but span other parts of the state.

South Carolina Business Coalition on Health

The South Carolina Business Coalition on Health (SCBCH) was originally created with the goal of improving quality and controlling health care costs. As such, one issue they focus on is reducing medical errors, which contribute to high health care costs. The coalition's members include purchasers and providers of health care in the Greenville community and surrounding areas. SCBCH publishes a hospital report card for consumers based on Leapfrog data and National Quality Improvement Goals. In the future, the report cards will include data from the newly implemented statewide hospital infection-reporting system.

Health Sciences South Carolina

Launched in 2004, this initiative brings together three South Carolina hospital systems with three universities—Clemson University and Greenville Hospital System University Medical Center, Palmetto Health and the Medical University of South Carolina, and the University of South Carolina and Spartanburg Regional Healthcare System—in a statewide effort to develop and share information on quality, patient safety, and related areas. It specifically seeks "to conduct collaborative health sciences research to improve health status, education (for health professionals), workforce development (for health care sector), and economic well-being for all South Carolinians." The HSSC has several affiliated Centers of Excellence, including the Center for Clinical Effectiveness and Patient Safety, which operates simulation centers located across the state, one of which is on campus at Greenville Memorial Hospital. Examples of patient safety–related research being conducted by the centers includes training of rapid-response teams, central-line placements, and labor and delivery care. As part of HSSC activities, the research and best practices developed at each simulation center are shared with other centers for wider dissemination.

South Carolina Partnership for HealthCare Quality and Safety

The South Carolina Partnership for HealthCare Quality and Safety is conducting a statewide initiative called Every Patient Counts. The mission of the initiative is to "establish a culture of continuous improvement in safety and quality across all hospitals statewide." Led by an Advisory Council made up of an interdisciplinary team of administrative and clinical leaders from member hospitals, the initiatives provide strategic guidance to the South Carolina Hospital Association on activities to improve quality and safety. One component of the initiative is the development of a voluntary reporting system for hospitals that collects and reports on standardized quality and safety indicators.

HOSPITAL ACTIVITIES

Most of the patient safety activity in the Greenville area is occurring in the hospital setting. In general, each hospital system has pursued its own patient-safety agenda independently. The hospital systems do collaborate informally to share learning on patient safety, despite their competition in the marketplace. Patient safety is generally viewed as a high priority by the Greenville-area hospital systems. The systems are driven to be perceived as "the best" by the community, and quality and patient safety are an important component of their marketing strategies. Public reporting of quality and patient safety information is viewed as particularly important, since it is used for hospitals' competitive advantage in marketing activities.

The hospitals focus first on the Joint Commission Core Measures and the related CMS Hospital Quality Initiative measures as top priorities. The Leapfrog standards are also a priority at the hospitals. Patient safety activities are generally viewed within the context of larger quality initiatives. Leaders at the hospitals have largely been strong proponents of the quality and patient safety agendas within their institutions, and they pay close attention to how their hospital systems are performing on available metrics. The hospital systems attempt to anticipate future public reporting or other requirements from external organizations, taking an increasingly proactive rather than a reactive approach to external requirements.

Infection control has been a particular area of focus among Greenville-area hospitals, in part, because of public reporting of hospital infection rates mandated by the Hospital Infections Disclosure Act, which took effect in 2007. However, infection-control activities had become a priority among Greenville-area hospitals before public reporting was mandated, because recognition of the importance of the problem had grown in the region and nationally. Some infection-control activities have developed out of bioterrorism-preparedness initiatives.

Examples of patient safety activities undertaken are participation in national initiatives (e.g., IHI's 5 Million Lives Campaign); executive walking rounds; and the use of simulation in training. Specific patient-safety practices implemented include the IHI bundles for process improvements (AMI, hand hygiene, surgical infection prevention, etc.); universal medication reconciliation; infection control; computerized physician order entry (CPOE); hand hygiene; and bar coding.

The dominant hospital systems in the Greenville area include multiple hospitals of varying sizes. In some cases, the systems will first roll out patient safety initiatives in the smaller hospitals, in which the implementation hurdles are more manageable than in the larger hospitals.

Physicians in the Greenville area are mostly aligned closely with one of the hospital systems. In some cases, they are employed directly by a hospital system; in other cases, they are contracted. These physician-hospital relationships are viewed by the hospital systems as important factors in giving the physicians "ownership" of the quality and safety of the care provided in the hospitals. The hospital systems also use financial incentives to reward physicians for improving the quality and safety of care they provide.

The greatest challenge identified by the Greenville-area hospital system representatives is their capacity to address a large and growing number of patient safety activities that are introduced by national organizations, such as the Joint Commission, CMS, and the Leapfrog Group. Hospital representatives expressed that, after addressing the priorities of external initiatives, there is little residual capacity for further changes that may have been identified internally. The bottlenecks are mainly in the form of human capital (i.e., having enough staff with appropriate skills), as well as financial resources. "Change fatigue" among front-line workers, particularly nurses, was cited as a main barrier to new patient safety initiatives. Front-line workers are being asked to "do more with less." One hospital system explained that they are attempting to address this issue by creating career ladders for those with an interest in patient safety, giving financial support for education to those who take a leading role in patient safety initiatives.

Many of the hospital representatives expressed a desire for greater coordination between the often-duplicative and often-conflicting requirements of multiple external organizations. One hospital system representative explained that their staff goes through an internal process of analyzing the various national programs, identifying areas of overlap, then assigning teams to address each area. Greater coordination between the external organizations would facilitate this process.

A second challenge identified by Greenville-area hospital systems is creating and maintaining a culture of safety. Patient safety leaders with the hospitals often have difficulty in convincing staff that new initiatives are worthwhile and for the common good. Unless the case was made strongly, staff tend to view new initiatives as yet another burdensome requirement that needs to be met. The case for improving quality was considered easier to make than the case for patient safety. Hospitals have been investing in team-building activities, but they have found that transformation in this area has been slow and challenging.

AMBULATORY CARE ACTIVITIES

Despite the high degree of integration between ambulatory care physicians and the hospital systems, patient safety activities in the ambulatory setting have lagged far behind those in the inpatient setting. Hospital systems have taken some steps to encourage patient safety in affiliated ambulatory care settings. The systems provide education and training for ambulatory care clinicians, and monitor a limited set of quality and safety data. Some hospital systems work with ambulatory settings to develop patient safety plans. In one hospital system, electronic health records covering both ambulatory and inpatient care are used for case management and early identification of potential problems in the patient population. Greenville-area hospitals are also working toward a universal medication-reconciliation system, which would establish a shared database among hospitals, ambulatory physicians, and pharmacies about patients' medications.

Blue Cross Blue Shield of South Carolina, the most prominent insurer for the area, operates several activities aimed at improving ambulatory care quality and safety. They reward physicians for achieving National Committee for Quality Assurance (NCQA) accreditation for diabetes and cardiovascular care. They contract with Active Health, a company that reviews claims data, identifies potential quality gaps in care, and contacts physicians with information addressing the gap, including patient and treatment information, recommended alternative treatments, and the supporting evidence base. Blue Cross Blue Shield also rewards physicians for e-prescribing.

LONG-TERM CARE ACTIVITIES

Some long-term care providers are owned by hospital systems, and these providers benefit from some of the patient safety initiatives undertaken by the systems. Patient safety initiatives in other settings were described as more uneven. South Carolina's Medicaid program was described as not very generous, and many long-term care facilities are resource-poor.

Within the hospital systems, some lessons learned in the hospital settings on subjects such as fall prevention and infection control have been applied in long-term care settings. Some systems are using quality-measurement and quality-improvement techniques across settings, including long-term care. One hospital system is building "cottage"-style long-term care facilities that will be designed to maximize patient safety.

VARIATIONS IN STAKEHOLDERS' PERSPECTIVES

In interviews with various stakeholders, striking differences in perspectives on patient safety emerged. Consumers and employers do not believe that the major hospital systems are doing enough to address patient safety. In contrast, those with closer knowledge of the hospital systems had a more positive view on current activities, although they acknowledged that there is much more progress to be made.

Provider views. Providers generally had a positive view of ongoing patient safety initiatives. They believe that they are committed, and taking the right steps, toward improving patient safety to an appropriate level. While they acknowledge the amount of work left to do, they recognize that the capacity for change is a limiting factor on the time line for improvement.

Purchaser views. Representatives of employers expressed frustration with the difficulty in convincing providers to buy in to new initiatives, such as a recently launched report card on Leapfrog safe practices. In part, this may be due to the highly consolidated nature of the health care market, which makes network selection difficult. However, leaders of large area employers are able to exert direct personal pressure on the leaders of the hospital systems. They also did threaten to exclude nonparticipating providers from their networks.

Consumer views. Patient advocates distrust the local providers and believe that they are not committed to improving patient safety. They believe that hospital employees are deliberately trying to work around requirements such as the proper use of identification badges mandated through state legislation.

Insurer views. Insurers in the Greenville area have largely taken a supporting role in patient safety initiatives, and they have a generally positive assessment of patient safety initiatives undertaken by hospital systems in that area. They view themselves as providing reinforcement for national initiatives, such as the Joint Commission, Leapfrog, and CMS, by providing additional incentives for meeting those targets. They have also taken a role in addressing the ambulatory care sector, an area they perceived as one of the main gaps in initiatives undertaken by the hospital systems.

Public health and government views. The government has focused primarily on infection control. They have mandated public reporting of hospital infection rates. They view positively the steps taken by the Greenville-area hospital systems in addressing infections.

INFLUENCES OF EXTERNAL ORGANIZATIONS OR ACTIVITIES

National initiatives were praised for their role in bringing focus to important issues, allowing for benchmarking, and sharing of best practices. In some cases, national initiatives give support to patient safety champions whose ideas were previously challenged by others in the organization. However, some provider representatives expressed that local-area variables often affect the ability of organizations to actually make changes, and that such variables are very difficult to predict. In some cases, external requirements that have good intentions have different effects in the implementation phase. Some of the requirements, when implemented in the local setting, were criticized as too heavy-handed in relation to the importance of the specific problems they aim to fix (one observer described this as "using a nuclear bomb to kill an ant").

Joint Commission Influences. The Joint Commission is viewed as one of the major, and most long-standing, drivers of the patient safety agenda, through its accreditation process. The Joint Commission Core Measures are also a key part of Greenville-area hospital systems' public-reporting focus.

AHRQ as a Resource. AHRQ is generally viewed positively, although not the first national organization that came to mind for Greenville respondents. When asked, many respondents were familiar with AHRQ tools and resources. Many expressed a desire for AHRQ to take an even more prominent role in promoting the patient safety agenda nationally, and in particular would like AHRQ to help coordinate national initiatives and set priorities.

Leapfrog Group. Reporting on Leapfrog Group standards has become accepted by the Greenville hospital systems, after initial resistance. These standards are viewed as a secondary priority to Joint Commission and CMS measures and requirements, however.

State Initiatives. Two pieces of legislation passed in recent years have had a big impact on ways that hospitals address patient safety. The first piece of legislation, the Lewis Blackman Hospital Patient Safety Act, was passed in 2005. Named after Lewis Blackman, a 15-year-old boy who died as a result of medical errors, the Act sets forth several requirements for hospitals that encompass identification badges. The requirements include specification of the information to be included on the badge, who must wear a badge, and how it is worn; provision of written information to patients that include the name of the physician responsible for the patient's care while in the hospital; and a mechanism for patients and families to be able to request assistance at any time when they have concerns about a patient's medical needs. The components of the Act are closely related to specific factors believed to have contributed to Lewis Blackman's death. The passage of the Act was largely consumer-led. Several stakeholders we spoke to questioned the degree to which the Act is being consistently implemented within hospitals.

Another state initiative is the Hospital Infections Disclosure Act (HIDA), passed in 2006. The Act requires hospitals to regularly report data on hospital-acquired infections to the South Carolina Department of Health and Environmental Control (DHEC) through the CDC's National Healthcare Safety Network reporting system. DHEC makes the data available to the public through regular reports, the first of which was a preliminary report released in February 2008. The implementation of the Act was guided by an advisory council made up of consumers, infection-control professionals, physicians and other stakeholders; yet tensions exist regarding the early public reporting of the data. The conflict is primarily around the issue of releasing data before it has been validated. Some stakeholders view the situation as a rush to report data without regard to its accuracy; other stakeholders view any resistance to publishing the data as resisting transparency. To address the conflict, DHEC and others are making significant efforts to educate the public about the meaning of the data and how to use it.

KEY TAKE-HOME MESSAGES AND ISSUES

The following key issues emerged from interviews with Greenville-area leaders:

- The relatively small size of the market with a high level of concentration in several hospital systems has led to a dynamic whereby competition, not collaboration, has driven patient safety activities.

- The competitive atmosphere has led hospital systems to embrace transparency of quality and patient safety information. As providers have become more comfortable with the transparency of information, they have become more open to collaborating informally in order to understand differences in performance between systems.

- Patient safety activities have been primarily driven by national initiatives, including the Joint Commission, CMS, the IHI, and the Leapfrog Group. As patient safety has become more of a priority, hospital systems are increasingly trying to proactively address the issues raised by these groups, rather than reactively complying with regulations and requirements.

- Providers struggle to address the requirements of multiple external organizations, which are often duplicative or conflicting. Capacity for addressing new patient safety initiatives, especially among front-line staff, is strained. Greater coordination between initiatives is a top priority among Greenville-area leaders.

- The highly integrated organizational structure in the Greenville area has facilitated patient safety activities. Physicians buy in to patient safety initiatives more readily when they are more closely aligned with hospitals, and systems are able to transfer some learning and practices between the hospital, ambulatory care, and long-term care settings. Nevertheless, patient safety activity in ambulatory and long-term care settings lags behind the hospital setting.

- Hospital systems have had success in implementing measurement and public reporting, process improvements, and implementation of technology. Establishing a culture of patient safety has been more challenging—particularly because of staff turnover and the high number of other competing priorities for staff time and attention.

APPENDIX C.

SUMMARY OF RESULTS FROM ROUNDTABLE DISCUSSIONS ON NQF SAFE PRACTICES

Table C.1a Hospital Actions for NQF Patient Safety Culture Practices

	Patient Safety Culture Practices			
	Leadership	Survey	Teamwork	Risks
NQF Practices Addressed	#1A	#1B	#1C	#1D
Number of Roundtables	3	4	4	4
Main Priorities	**High priority area,** including engaging Board and medical staff, clarifying accountability, and creating shared sense of responsibility for safety throughout the organization.	**Generally important.** Main goals focused on identifying particular cultural dimensions or units within the hospital to target for improvement.	**Generally important.** Two aspects were prioritized: committee teamwork, and clinical teamwork (NQF focuses only on the latter).	**High priority area.** Goals included creating a non-punitive reporting climate, ownership and "proactive" mentality for addressing errors, and transparency of information related to risks, events, and corrective actions.
Extent and Type of Implementation	Greater communication to both Board and staff on safety issues, Board and executive walk-arounds, taking proactive approach (e.g., sentinel events, investing resources for safety to prevent events rather than in reaction), engaging medical and other staff in safety through multi-disciplinary teams, training and involvement in decision-making.	Common use of the AHRQ Hospital Culture Survey, some use of other unit specific surveys (e.g., surgery); trending over time and benchmarking to develop organizational goals; analysis and comparison of units to develop department-specific action plans.	Strengthening committee teamwork (communication principles, charter for managing safety initiatives) and clinical teamwork (SBAR, TeamSTEPPS, and TCAB training; measuring team performance; use of care plans; and inclusion of patients/families in care team).	Improving reporting systems and participation (online systems; internal marketing campaigns); Education and training on safety awareness, and risk identification & improvement techniques; Integration of reporting and data systems for identifying and monitoring risks across the organization.

135

Table C.1b Main Challenges Encountered by Hospitals in Implementing Patient Safety Culture Practices

	Patient Safety Culture			
	Leadership	Survey	Teamwork	Risks
Inertia of systems and culture, tendency to "backslide"	X		X	X
Prioritizing limited resources	X			X
Implementing and managing complex technical systems		X		
Managing info/work across disciplines, organizational boundaries, and multiply affiliated staff	X			X
Lack of responsibility/ initiative to act	X	X		
Physician resistance, especially among older clinicians				
General staff resistance and inertia, tendency for workarounds		X		X
"Overload" on staff from increasing safety-related demands, requirements				X
Designing systems to accommodate range of staff, staff turnover				X
Balancing incentive schemes, positive and negative incentives				X

Table C.1c Main Facilitators Experienced by Hospitals in Implementing Patient Safety Culture Practices

Facilitators Identified	Patient Safety Culture			
	Leadership	Survey	Teamwork	Risks
Leadership providing necessary coordination and resources	X			
Communication and feedback to frontline staff			X	X
Systems-oriented, non-personal problem solving approach to safety issues	X			
Flexibility in procedures and inclusion of relevant stakeholders			X	X
Support and involvement of clinical leaders			X	
Empirical evidence for safe practices	X			
Clear responsibility for monitoring and enforcement of practices				
Credibility of systems and leadership			X	
Impetus/motivation of external requirements and publicly reported data	X			

Table C.2a Hospital Actions for Other NQF Patient Safety Practices

	Other Patient Safety Practices				
	Transparency Across the Continuum	Surgery Procedures	Medical Evaluation and Prevention	Medication Safety Management	Workforce
NQF Practices Addressed Number of Roundtables	#10, 11, 13, 14 2	#25, 26 3	#23, 27, 28, 29, 30 3	#12, 15, 16, 17, 18 4	#5, 6, 7 2
Main Priorities	**High priority** area, in particular proper labeling and patient identification (NQF safe practice #10).	**One of the highest priority** areas. Hospitals also focused on issues outside the NQF practices considered equally important, including settings beyond the OR.	**Generally important,** except for NQF practice #30 related to contrast media-induced renal failure (severity potentially high, but incidence low).	**One of the highest priority** areas ("huge concern").	**Generally important.** Specific priorities included ensuring adequate staff recruitment and retention (especially in face of labor shortages), and staff training on core competencies and evidence-based care.
Extent and Type of Implementation	Establishment of multidisciplinary groups responsible for range of initiatives, including effective wristband systems, requiring matches on multiple identifiers, specifying when units "own" a patient, labeling items in real-time, and standardizing labeling processes across the hospital.	Developing tools and auditing for time-outs to ensure conducted properly (not just pro forma); use of pre-op/pre-anesthesia clinics to identify when to administer beta-blockers prophylactically. Attending to other surgery safety issues such as use of blood products, proper positioning, room temperature, and hand-offs	Many of these practices have been worked on since before they were published as NQF standards. Annual flu vaccination programs have expanded from patients to employees, DVT/VTE and pressure ulcer assessments occur at admission and regular intervals, while procedures for anti-coagulant	Establishment of multidisciplinary groups responsible for a range of initiatives, including heavy use of reporting systems to identify adverse medication events, working to implement CPOE, standardizing labeling/packaging (incl. bar codes), identifying "high alert" medications, and integrating pharmacists closer	Varied initiatives to address staffing issues, including annual competency and periodic on-floor skill assessments, support for continuing and peer education, shared governance councils, hiring additional staff (incl. hospitalists), cross-training and certification, succession planning, and retention strategies, such as staff surveys and informing leadership of staffing needs.

	between surgical and ICU staff.	management are the most incomplete and in flux.	to the point of care.

Table C.2b Main Challenges Encountered by Hospitals in Implementing Other Patient Safety Practices

	Patient Safety Practices				
	Transparency Across the Continuum	Surgery Procedures	Medical Evaluation and Prevention	Medication Safety Management	Workforce
Inertia of systems and culture, tendency to "backslide"	X				
Prioritizing limited resources			X	X	X
Implementing and managing complex technical systems	X				
Managing info/work across disciplines, organizational boundaries, and multiply affiliated staff	X		X	X	X
Lack of responsibility/ initiative to act		X			
Physician resistance, especially among older clinicians		X		X	
General staff resistance and inertia, tendency for workarounds	X	X			
"Overload" on staff from increasing safety-related demands, requirements				X	X
Designing systems to accommodate range of staff, staff turnover					X
Balancing incentive schemes, positive and negative incentives			X		

Note: The safe practice grouping on Communication with Patients or Families is not included in these summaries, since we were not able to hold a full roundtable discussion on this topic at the assigned hospital.

Table C.2c Main Facilitators Experienced by Hospitals in Implementing Other Patient Safety Practices

Facilitators Identified	Patient Safety Practices				
	Transparency Across the Continuum	Surgery Procedures	Medical Evaluation and Prevention	Medication Safety Management	Workforce
Leadership providing necessary coordination and resources			X	X	
Communication and feedback to frontline staff	X				
Systems-oriented, non-personal problem solving approach to safety issues	X				
Flexibility in procedures and inclusion of relevant stakeholders	X		X		
Support and involvement of clinical leaders		X			
Empirical evidence for safe practices				X	
Clear responsibility for monitoring and enforcement of practices	X				
Credibility of systems and leadership					
Impetus/motivation of external requirements and publicly reported data		X			

APPENDIX D.
NQF SAFE PRACTICES NOT INCLUDED IN SURVEY

Safe Practice	Reason for Exclusion
Practice 2 (teach back of consent or information delivered to patients)	Use of the teach-back method cannot be evaluated via a survey because the teach-back actions happen in "real time" during patient interactions and are not documented reliably in hospital records. Observation is required to assess whether this safe practice has been implemented appropriately.
Practice 8 (communication/transmittal of care information to patients and families)	This type of communication cannot be evaluated via a survey because the communications take place in "real time" in many locations across the hospital and are not documented in hospital records. Observation is required to assess whether this safe practice has been implemented appropriately.
Practice 9 (read back of verbal or phone orders)	This type of communication cannot be evaluated via a survey because read backs happen at the time orders are given and, although order verification may be documented subsequently in information systems, this does not ensure that verification occurred in the immediate exchange between clinicians. Therefore, observation is required to assess whether this safe practice has been implemented appropriately.
Practice 19 (ventilator bundle intervention practices)	A key component of this safe practice requires physical manipulation of the patient (opening airway) that is not likely to be recorded in the medical chart. Observation is required to assess whether this safe practice has been implemented appropriately.
Practice 20 (prevention of CV catheter-associated blood stream infections)	Key components in the implementation of this safe practice involve washing hands, using barrier protection (e.g., cap, mask, sterile gloves) and the selection of catheter site. Observation is required to assess whether these steps have been properly implemented. While it is possible to inquire in an organizational survey about the use of chlorhexidine by asking if the hospital requires use of a kit with chlorhexidine in it, this practice is only one component of the multi-pronged prevention strategy outlined in this safe practice. As such, RAND concluded that this safe practice could not be assessed through a survey.
Practice 21 (prevention of surgical site infections)	Key components of this safe practice can only be obtained via clinical chart review (e.g., timing of pre- and post-operative antibiotic administration; glucose management). As such, RAND determined that this safe practice could not be assessed via a survey.
Practice 22 (hand washing)	Proper hand washing techniques cannot be evaluated via a survey. Observation is required to assess whether this safe practice has been implemented appropriately.
Practice 24 (provide patients with information on facilities with reduced risk for high-risk elective cardiac procedures)	It seems that this practice is more appropriately carried out in a physician's practice or other setting, when patients are considering which group or hospital to use, rather than in the hospital that will be performing the procedures. This type of communication with patients cannot be assessed via a hospital survey.

Hospital
Safe Practices Survey

August 2008

Thank you for taking part in this Patient Safety Safe Practices survey. The questionnaire takes about one to two hours to complete. It is possible that more than one person within the hospital will need to be involved to provide the information sought by the survey. If you have any questions, please call XXX.

Instructions

Please note the following guidance for responding to some questions:

- "This hospital" in some questions is defined as the hospital that was designated to complete this survey (not a larger organization in which the hospital is a member).

- For questions about whether a practice is fully implemented, use the response "fully implemented and in maintenance" if active adoption work is completed, even if you feel the practice still could improve. Use "in process of implementing" when you still are working on introducing a practice.

- For questions about "how often this hospital conducts a formal review," we understand that sometimes the hospital may be doing continuous monitoring of a practice. We are interested in <u>formal</u> reviews that also may be done on less frequent basis.

- Do not use felt tip pens to complete the survey.

- Mark response boxes with an X.
  CORRECT: [X]

- Make no stray marks on this survey.

- Erase cleanly any marks you wish to change.

- Please try to answer every question (unless you are asked to skip questions because they do not apply to you). If you prefer not to answer a specific question for any reason, leave it blank.

- If you are not sure of the answer, please try to give us your <u>best estimate.</u>

- Please return the completed survey in the enclosed postage-paid envelope addressed to XXX.

PATIENT SAFETY CULTURE

The first several questions are about this hospital's PATIENT SAFETY PROGRAM AND CULTURE.

1   An integrated patient safety program provides hospital-wide oversight and alignment of all activities to monitor and improve patient safety, and to ensure that all individuals working in the hospital are educated and participate in safety and quality initiatives.

Has this hospital established an integrated patient safety program?

> *(Check One)*

☐ 1 Yes, implemented and in maintenance

☐ 2 Yes, in process of implementing

☐ 3 No

2.   Does this hospital have a SINGLE individual – regardless of their job title – who functions as a patient safety officer?

> *(Check One)*

☐ 1 Yes

☐ 2 No

3.   Has this hospital implemented performance improvement interventions (e.g., teamwork skills, reducing falls) to address issues identified from analysis of patient safety performance or events?

> *(Check One)*

☐ 1 Yes, implemented and in maintenance

☐ 2 Yes, in process of implementing

☐ 3 No

4. The following question refers to the governing board of the hospital, which may be called the board of directors or board of trustees. If this hospital does not have a governing board with decision-making authority, but has an advisory board, the question applies to the advisory board.

Which of the following actions does this hospital's governing board perform regularly in its oversight of the hospital's patient safety issues and activities?

(Check One Answer for Each Item a-e)

	Yes	No
a. Review policies or guidelines on patient safety goals, priorities, and strategies	☐₁	☐₂
b. Review reports on risks and hazards identified by hospital management	☐₁	☐₂
c. Review reports from all patient safety culture survey or other culture measures	☐₁	☐₂
d. Review progress in patient safety improvement activities	☐₁	☐₂
e. Review level of participation by patients and families in the hospital's patient safety activities	☐₁	☐₂

5. Does this hospital's governing board (directors, trustees, or advisory), or one of its standing committees, include the review of patient safety issues and improvements in a standing agenda item for every board meeting, either as a separate agenda item on safety or as part of a larger agenda item?

(Check One)

☐₁ Yes, done by the board

☐₂ Yes, done by a standing committee. Please specify: _____

☐₃ No

The next several questions are about this hospital's use of a PATIENT SAFETY CULTURE SURVEY.

6. Has this hospital conducted a standardized survey of its staff to assess its patient safety culture?

(Check One)

☐₁ Yes

☐₂ No ➜ SKIP TO Q.11 ON PAGE 3

146

7. How often does this hospital conduct a patient safety culture survey?

    (Check One)

    ☐₁ Monthly or more often

    ☐₂ Quarterly

    ☐₃ Twice a year

    ☐₄ Yearly

    ☐₅ Less often than once a year

The next questions are about this hospital's MOST RECENT patient safety culture survey.

8   Which patient safety culture survey did this hospital use for its MOST RECENT survey?

    (Check One)

    ☐₁ Hospital Survey on Patient Safety Culture (AHRQ survey)

    ☐₂ Patient Safety Climate in Healthcare Organizations (Sara Singer survey)

    ☐₃ Safety Attitudes Questionnaire (Sexton/Helmriech survey)

    ☐₄ Survey developed by the hospital (i.e., "homegrown")

    ☐₅ Other, specify: _____

9. How many units or departments did the MOST RECENT patient safety culture survey include?

    (Check One)

    ☐₁ All units or departments

    ☐₂ Some units or departments

    ☐₃ None

10. Has this hospital taken any of the following actions based on the results of the MOST RECENT culture survey results?

(Check One Answer for Each Item a-f)

	Yes	No
a. Changed policies and procedures to support patient safety culture	☐₁	☐₂
b. Implemented specific performance improvement interventions	☐₁	☐₂
c. Disseminated survey results to all clinical caregivers and other staff	☐₁	☐₂
d. Held education/training for staff on patient safety principles and practices	☐₁	☐₂
e. Worked with management to create a safe environment for staff	☐₁	☐₂
f. Other, Specify: _____	☐₁	☐₂

The next questions are about this hospital's use of TEAM-BASED CARE.

11. In TEAM-BASED CARE, all clinical caregivers and other staff in a particular clinical area function as a team, with all team members responsible and empowered to work as partners using a shared mental model of care, clear communications, mutual support for prevention of incidents, effective handoffs of patients across shifts and functions, and debriefs of care experiences to further strengthen TEAMWORK.

    Has this hospital taken specific actions to improve teamwork in ANY units or departments?

    (Check One)

    ☐₁ Yes, ALL units or departments

    ☐₂ Yes, SOME units or departments

    ☐₃ No ➜ SKIP TO Q.14 ON PAGE 5

12. For units or departments in which this hospital has taken actions to improve teamwork, which training model was used to help staff develop teamwork and communications skills?

    (Check All That Apply)

    ☐₁ TeamSTEPPS (AHRQ)

    ☐₂ MedTeams

    ☐₃ Flight team training model

    ☐₄ NASCAR training model

    ☐₅ A formal team training program developed by this hospital

    ☐₆ Frontline coaching on team practices during service provision (on-the-job training)

    ☐₇ Other, specify: _____

13. Has this hospital taken actions to improve teamwork in any of the following high-risk units?

    (Check One Answer for Each Item a-g)

	Yes, Implemented And in Maintenance	Yes, In Process of Implementing	No
a. Critical care unit(s)	☐₁	☐₂	☐₃
b. Emergency department	☐₁	☐₂	☐₃
c. Surgical operating room	☐₁	☐₂	☐₃
d. Labor and delivery unit	☐₁	☐₂	☐₃
e. Outpatient procedural care units (e.g., same day surgery, dialysis unit)	☐₁	☐₂	☐₃
f. Other, specify: _____	☐₁	☐₂	☐₃

14. Has this hospital provided basic training on issues and skills related to team-based care for any of the following groups?

        (Check All That Apply)

☐ 1 Executive managers

☐ 2 Governing board members (directors, trustees, or advisory)

☐ 3 Medical staff members

☐ 4 Midlevel managers (e.g., department heads, nursing managers)

☐ 5 Frontline nurses

☐ 6 Other, specify: _____

☐ 7 No basic teamwork training has been provided to any groups

The next questions are about identification and mitigation of patient safety risks and hazards.

15. In the last 2 years, which of the following has the hospital used to RETROSPECTIVELY identify patient safety risks and hazards?

        (Check One Answer for Each Item a-i)

	Yes	No	Not Familiar With Tool
a. Sentinel event reporting and analysis	☐ 1	☐ 2	☐ 3
b. Event reporting	☐ 1	☐ 2	☐ 3
c. Root cause analysis	☐ 1	☐ 2	☐ 3
d. Analysis of closed claims	☐ 1	☐ 2	☐ 3
e. Analysis of hospital-level system failures	☐ 1	☐ 2	☐ 3
f. Monitoring of Patient Safety Indicators (PSI)	☐ 1	☐ 2	☐ 3
g. Tracking retrospective triggers	☐ 1	☐ 2	☐ 3
h. External reporting of adverse events	☐ 1	☐ 2	☐ 3
i. Other, specify: _____	☐ 1	☐ 2	

16. In the last 2 years, which of the following has this hospital used to identify patient safety risks and hazards in REAL TIME OR NEAR REAL TIME?

(Check One Answer for Each Item a-e)

	Yes	No	Not Familiar With Tool
a. Trigger tools, manually or technology enabled	☐1	☐2	☐3
b. Tools for direct observation of processes in high-risk areas	☐1	☐2	☐3
c. Technology tools, such as electronic health records	☐1	☐2	☐3
d. Real time risk identification tools	☐1	☐2	☐3
e. Other, specify: _____	☐1	☐2	

17. In the last 2 years, which of the following has this hospital used to PROSPECTIVELY identify potential patient safety risks and hazards?

(Check One Answer for Each Item a-c)

	Yes	No	Not Familiar With Tool
a. Failure Mode and Effects Analysis (FMEA)	☐1	☐2	☐3
b. Probabilistic Risk Assessment (PRA)	☐1	☐2	☐3
c. Other, specify: _____	☐1	☐2	

18. Hospital-wide risk assessments integrate information -- across service lines and departments -- on patient safety risks, in order to prevent systems failures. Does this hospital use hospital-wide risk assessments to identify system-level patient safety risks and hazards?

(Check One)

☐1 Yes

☐2 No

COMMUNICATION WITH PATIENTS OR FAMILIES

The next questions are about documentation of patients' preferences for life-sustaining treatments.

19. Does this hospital have written policies and procedures, protocols, or other guidelines, for ensuring that written documentation of each patient's preferences for life sustaining treatment is prominently displayed in his or her medical chart?

(Check One)

☐1 Yes

☐2 No ➜ SKIP TO Q.21 ON PAGE 7

20. Does this hospital review its adherence to this policy or guideline as part of its standard performance improvement (quality assurance) program?

(Check One)

☐₁ Yes

☐₂ No

The next questions are about communication to families about serious unanticipated outcomes.

21. Serious unanticipated outcomes include sentinel events, serious reportable events, and other unanticipated outcomes that require provision of substantial additional care. Which of the following actions are part of hospital practice for communication about serious unanticipated outcomes with patients and families?

(Check One Answer for Each Item a-i)

	<u>Yes</u>	<u>No</u>
a. Initiate conversations with the patient and family within 24 hours of the event	☐₁	☐₂
b. Provide an explicit statement of "the facts" about what happened and why the event occurred	☐₁	☐₂
c. Express regret explicitly and empathically that the outcome was not as expected	☐₁	☐₂
d. Make a commitment to investigate the event and take action to prevent future occurrences	☐₁	☐₂
e. Provide detailed feedback of results of the investigation	☐₁	☐₂
f. Provide an apology if the event is found to be the result of error or system failures	☐₁	☐₂
g. Provide emotional support for patient and family by trained clinical caregivers	☐₁	☐₂
h. Provide emotional support for clinical caregivers and other staff involved in the event	☐₁	☐₂
i. Other, specify: _____	☐₁	☐₂

22. Has this hospital established written policies and procedures, protocols, or other guidelines that define how clinical caregivers and other staff are to communicate with patients and families about serious unanticipated outcomes?

(Check One)

☐₁ Yes, for ALL clinical caregivers and other staff

☐₂ Yes, for SOME clinical caregivers and other staff

☐₃ No

151

23. How often does this hospital conduct a formal review of its practices for communicating about serious unanticipated outcomes? If this hospital conducts reviews at differing frequencies, or constantly reviews its practices, use the most frequent response applicable.

(Check One)

☐1 Monthly or more often

☐2 Quarterly

☐3 Twice a year

☐4 Yearly

☐5 Every two years

☐6 Only when an event occurs

☐7 Never

24. Has this hospital established a support system to give clinical caregivers and other staff the skills and emotional support for managing events with unanticipated outcomes?

(Check One)

☐1 Yes, for ALL clinical caregivers and other staff

☐2 Yes, for SOME clinical caregivers and other staff

☐3 No

INFORMATION TRANSPARENCY ACROSS CONTINUUM OF CARE

The next questions are about labeling of diagnostic studies.

25. Which of the following actions does this hospital routinely perform for the labeling of imaging studies, laboratory specimens, or other diagnostic studies?

(Check One Answer for Each Item a-e)

	Yes	No
a. Label laboratory specimen containers at the time of use and in the presence of the patient	☐1	☐2
b. Identify the patient and match the intended service or treatment to that patient	☐1	☐2
c. Use at least two patient identifiers for blood samples or other specimens	☐1	☐2
d. Label imaging studies with correct patient information close to the imaging device	☐1	☐2
e. Mark "Left" or "Right" on each radiographic image	☐1	☐2

26. Does this hospital review its practices for labeling of the following diagnostic studies as part of its standard performance improvement (quality assurance) program?

(Check One Answer for Each Item a-c)

	Yes	No
a. Imaging studies	□₁	□₂
b. Laboratory specimens	□₁	□₂
c. Other diagnostic studies	□₁	□₂

27. Has this hospital established an intervention to improve issues regarding labeling of the following diagnostic studies?

(Check One Answer for Each Item a-c)

	Yes	No
a. Imaging studies	□₁	□₂
b. Laboratory specimens	□₁	□₂
c. Other diagnostic studies	□₁	□₂

The next questions are about the use of abbreviations.

28. Has this hospital prohibited use of ALL abbreviations, acronyms, symbols, and dose designations in the Joint Commission's list of "do not use" abbreviations?

(Check One)

□₁ Yes

□₂ No ➔ SKIP TO Q.30

29. Does this hospital routinely review AND enforce compliance with the Joint Commission's "do not use" abbreviation list?

(Check One)

□₁ Yes

□₂ No

30. Does this hospital use the metric system to communicate all doses on prescription orders (with the exception of therapies that use standard units, e.g. insulin or vitamins)?

(Check One)

□₁ Yes

□₂ No

153

The next questions are about this hospital's policies and procedures, protocols, or other guidelines for patient discharge.

31. A discharge plan lists the care, treatment and services a patient received, as well as his/her condition at discharge. The plan includes medical issues and tests or studies that require follow-up.

    Has this hospital established written policies and procedures, protocols, or other guidelines requiring a discharge plan for each patient?

    (Check One)

    ☐₁ Yes

    ☐₂ No ➜ SKIP TO Q.33

32. Which of the following provisions are included in the hospital's discharge policies and procedures, protocols, or other guidelines?

    (Check One Answer for Each Item a-g)

		<u>Yes</u>	<u>No</u>
a.	Delineation of roles and responsibilities in the discharge process	☐₁	☐₂
b.	Preparation for discharge occurs throughout the hospitalization	☐₁	☐₂
c.	Standardized information flow across clinical caregivers within and outside the hospital from admission through discharge	☐₁	☐₂
d.	Preparation of discharge summaries before discharge	☐₁	☐₂
e.	Preparation of discharge plan before discharge	☐₁	☐₂
f.	Patient or family perception of coordination of discharge care	☐₁	☐₂
g.	Performance measurement and improvement of the discharge process	☐₁	☐₂

33. Does this hospital provide a written discharge plan to each patient at the time of discharge?

    (Check One)

    ☐₁ Yes

    ☐₂ No

34. Does this hospital provide a discharge summary to all clinical caregivers who accept the patient's care after hospital discharge?

    (Check One)

    ☐₁ Yes

    ☐₂ No

The next questions are about the Universal Protocol established by the Joint Commission for eliminating wrong site, wrong procedure, wrong person surgery.

35. Has this hospital implemented the following components of the Universal Protocol for eliminating wrong site, wrong procedure, wrong person surgery?

(Check One Answer for Each Item a-c)

	Yes, Implemented and in Maintenance	Yes, In Process of Implementing	No
a. Preoperative verification process to ensure readiness for surgery.....	☐ 1	☐ 2	☐ 3
b. Marking the operative site for procedures in which incision site might be ambiguous...	☐ 1	☐ 2	☐ 3
c. Conducting a "time out" to verify correct patient, procedure, and other relevant actions	☐ 1	☐ 2	☐ 3

36. How often does this hospital conduct a formal review of its adherence to the Universal Protocol for eliminating wrong site, wrong procedure, wrong person surgery? If this hospital conducts reviews at differing frequencies, or constantly reviews its adherence to the Universal Protocol, use the most frequent response applicable.

(Check One)

☐ 1 Monthly or more often

☐ 2 Quarterly

☐ 3 Twice a year

☐ 4 Yearly

☐ 5 Less often than once a year

☐ 6 Never

155

The next questions are about evaluation of patients for risk of an acute ischemic perioperative cardiac event.

37. Surgical patients are at risk of an acute perioperative cardiac event if they have required beta blockers, have symptomatic arrhythmias or hypertension, or are undergoing vascular surgery and have a finding of ischemia on preoperative testing. Vascular surgery includes vascular repairs and reconstruction as well as amputations for peripheral vascular disease.

    Has this hospital established written policies and procedures, protocols, or other guidelines to evaluate surgery patients for risk of an acute ischemic perioperative cardiac event?

    (Check One)

    ☐₁ Yes

    ☐₂ No ➔ SKIP TO Q.39

38. Do these policies and procedures, protocols, or other guidelines regarding risk of cardiac events for surgical patients include the following provisions:

    (Check One Answer for Each Item a-d)

	Yes	No
a. Perform a cardiac risk assessment of at-risk surgery patients	☐₁	☐₂
b. Document results of cardiac risk assessment in patient's record	☐₁	☐₂
c. Establish guidelines for prevention of perioperative myocardial ischemia	☐₁	☐₂
d. Incorporate use of clinical judgment regarding use of beta blockade....	☐₁	☐₂

39. Does this hospital review its performance in the prevention of perioperative ischemic events as part of its standard performance improvement (quality assurance) program?

    (Check One)

    ☐₁ Yes

    ☐₂ No

MEDICAL EVALUATION AND PREVENTION

The next questions are about immunization of patients, clinical caregivers and other staff.

40. Does this hospital operate a patient influenza immunization program based on current Centers for Disease Control and Prevention (CDC) recommendations regarding which PATIENTS should be immunized?

    (Check One)

    ☐₁ Yes

    ☐₂ No

41. Does this hospital operate a program for the immunization of CLINICAL CAREGIVERS AND OTHER STAFF for influenza?

    (Check One)

    ☐₁ Yes, for ALL clinical caregivers and other staff

    ☐₂ Yes, for SOME clinical caregivers and other staff

    ☐₃ No

42. Does this hospital maintain current records on the influenza vaccination status of clinical caregivers and other staff?

    (Check One)

    ☐₁ Yes, for ALL clinical caregivers and other staff

    ☐₂ Yes, for SOME clinical caregivers and other staff

    ☐₃ No

The next questions are about evaluation of pressure ulcers.

43. As each patient is admitted to the hospital, is an assessment done to identify if the patient is at risk of developing pressure ulcers?

    (Check One)

    ☐₁ Yes

    ☐₂ No ➜ SKIP TO Q.45 ON PAGE 14

44. Are the assessment results AND a prevention plan documented in each patient's medical record?
(Check One)

☐₁ Yes

☐₂ No

45. When an individual is identified as being at risk for pressure ulcers, does the clinical caregiver routinely reevaluate the integrity of a patient's skin?
(Check One)

☐₁ Yes

☐₂ No ➔ SKIP TO Q.47

46. Are the results of skin reevaluations documented in the patient's medical record?
(Check One)

☐₁ Yes

☐₂ No

47. Has this hospital established written policies and procedures, protocols, or other guidelines regarding the prevention of pressure ulcers?
(Check One)

☐₁ Yes

☐₂ No

48. How often does this hospital perform prevalence studies to evaluate the effectiveness of its pressure ulcer prevention practices?
(Check One)

☐₁ Monthly or more often

☐₂ Quarterly

☐₃ Twice a year

☐₄ Yearly

☐₅ Less often than once a year

☐₆ Never

49. Does this hospital review its performance in preventing pressure ulcers as part of its standard performance improvement (quality assurance) program?

        (Check One)

☐₁ Yes

☐₂ No

The next questions are about evaluation for the risk of venous thromboembolism/deep vein thrombosis (VTE/DVT),

50. Has this hospital established written policies and procedures, protocols, or other guidelines regarding the prevention of venous thromboembolism/deep vein thrombosis (VTE/DVT)?

(Check One)

☐₁ Yes

☐₂ No ➔ SKIP TO Q.52

51. Do these policies and procedures, protocols, or other guidelines on prevention of VTE/DVT include the following provisions:

(Check One Answer for Each Item a-d)

	Yes	**No**
a. Evaluate all patients at admission to identify risk of VTE/DVT	☐₁	☐₂
b. Document risk assessment AND prevention plan in patient's record	☐₁	☐₂
c. Use evidence-based methods of thromboprophylaxis..........................	☐₁	☐₂
d. Regularly reassess risk during inpatient stay	☐₁	☐₂

52. Does this hospital review its performance in the prevention of VTE/DVT as part of its standard performance improvement (quality assurance) program?

(Check One)

☐₁ Yes

☐₂ No

The next question is about monitoring patients on long-term oral anticoagulants.

53. Has this hospital established written policies and procedures, protocols, or other guidelines for monitoring patients on a long-term oral anticoagulant?

    (Check One)

    ☐₁ Yes, for OUTPATIENT care only

    ☐₂ Yes, for INPATIENT care only

    ☐₃ Yes, for BOTH outpatient and inpatient care

    ☐₄ No

The next questions are about the prevention of contrast media-induced renal failure.

54. Has this hospital established written policies and procedures, protocols or other guidelines to prevent contrast media-induced renal failure?

    (Check One)

    ☐₁ Yes

    ☐₂ No ➔ SKIP TO Q.56

55. Do these policies and procedures, protocols, or other guidelines on prevention of contrast media-induced nephropathy include the following provisions?

    (Check One Answer for Each Item a-c)

	Yes	No
a. Evaluate patients at risk for contrast media-induced renal failure prior to contrast media administration	☐₁	☐₂
b. Use clinically appropriate methods for reducing risk of renal injury	☐₁	☐₂
c. Document risk assessment and prevention plan in patient's record	☐₁	☐₂

56. Does this hospital review its performance in the prevention of contrast media-induced nephropathy as part of its standard performance improvement (quality assurance) program?

    (Check One)

    ☐₁ Yes

    ☐₂ No

MEDICATION SAFETY MANAGEMENT

The next questions are about a computerized prescriber order entry (CPOE) system.

57. Does this hospital have a computerized prescriber order entry (CPOE) system for inpatient care?

(Check One)

☐₁ Yes, system is fully implemented ➜ SKIP TO Q.60 ON PAGE 18

☐₂ Yes, in the process of implementing a system ➜ SKIP TO Q.60 ON PAGE 18

☐₃ No, but plan to implement a system

☐₄ No, do not have plans to implement a system

58. Has this hospital performed an assessment to determine the feasibility of implementing a CPOE system and the possible impacts of doing so?

(Check One)

☐₁ Yes

☐₂ No ➜ SKIP TO Q.60 ON PAGE 18

59. Which of the following factors did this hospital examine in its assessment of a CPOE system?

(Check One Answer for Each Item a-g)

	Yes	**No**
a. The potential for CPOE to reduce patient safety risks and hazards	☐₁	☐₂
b. Adequacy of existing evidence-based care processes and workflow at the hospital	☐₁	☐₂
c. Capability of the hospital's clinical information infrastructure to support CPOE	☐₁	☐₂
d. Commitment of the hospital's governance and management staff	☐₁	☐₂
e. Commitment of the hospital's clinical personnel, including nursing, residents, independent practitioners, and other clinical staff	☐₁	☐₂
f. Costs and return-on-investment of CPOE for the hospital	☐₁	☐₂
g. Other, specify: _____	☐₁	☐₂

161

The next questions are about medication management systems.

60. As part of this hospital's medication management system, does the hospital pharmacist perform the following roles regularly?

(Check One Answer for Each Item a-i)

		Yes	No
a.	Select and maintain a formulary of medications chosen for safety and effectiveness, working with other health professionals	☐1	☐2
b.	Be available for consultation with prescribers on medication ordering, interpretation, and review of medical orders	☐1	☐2
c.	Provide medication safety recommendations and promote medication error prevention throughout the hospital	☐1	☐2
d.	Work with others to provide a work environment that promotes the accurate PRESCRIBING of medication orders	☐1	☐2
e.	Work with others to provide a work environment that promotes the accurate DISPENSING of medication orders	☐1	☐2
f.	Work with others to provide a work environment that promotes the accurate ADMINISTRATION of medication orders	☐1	☐2
g.	Review all non-emergent medication orders and patient medication profiles for appropriateness and completeness (when reviews do not create a medically unacceptable delay)	☐1	☐2
h.	Oversee the preparation of medications, including sterile products, to ensure they are safely prepared	☐1	☐2
i.	Inspect medication storage areas periodically to ensure that medications are stored properly	☐1	☐2

61. How does this hospital provide for 24-hour, 7-day availability of a pharmacist?

(Check One)

☐1 At least one pharmacist is available onsite all the time

☐2 A pharmacist is available onsite for some shifts, and whenever a pharmacist is not onsite, one is available by telephone or accessible at another location

☐3 Some other way - Specify: _____

☐4 This hospital does not provide for 24-hour, 7-day availability of a pharmacist

62. How often does this hospital conduct a formal review of its medication management process? If this hospital conducts reviews at differing frequencies, or constantly reviews its medication management process, use the most frequent response applicable.

    (Check One)

    ☐1 Monthly or more often

    ☐2 Quarterly

    ☐3 Twice a year

    ☐4 Yearly

    ☐5 Less often than once a year

    ☐6 Never

63. Is the hospital's medication management process reviewed as part of its standard performance improvement (quality assurance) program?

    (Check One)

    ☐1 Yes

    ☐2 No

The next questions are about medication reconciliation.

64. Which of the following actions does this hospital take to document and reconcile all the medications being taken by each patient admitted?

    (Check One Answer for Each Item a-h)

		Yes	**No**
a.	Developing a list of current medications at the start of an inpatient stay	☐1	☐2
b.	Active involvement by the patient, family or clinical caregiver in development of the initial medications list	☐1	☐2
c.	Documentation on the updated medication list of new medications prescribed by the first provider of service during the inpatient stay	☐1	☐2
d.	Communication of the updated medication list to subsequent providers of service	☐1	☐2
e.	Documentation on the updated list of new medications prescribed by subsequent providers of service	☐1	☐2
f.	Comparison of all newly prescribed medications to those already on the updated list and reconciliation of orders as necessary to ensure drug compatibility	☐1	☐2
g.	Communicate the updated medication list to the patient, family or clinical caregiver as the patient moves through levels of care within this hospital	☐1	☐2
h.	Communicate the updated medication list to the patient, family or clinical caregiver when the patient moves to another care setting	☐1	☐2

163

65. Has this hospital established a standardized process for developing, reconciling, and communicating an accurate medication list for each patient throughout an inpatient stay and referral to another care setting?

(Check One)

☐₁ Yes

☐₂ No

66. How often does this hospital conduct a formal review of its adherence to this standardized process for medication documentation, reconciliation, and communication? If this hospital conducts reviews at differing frequencies, or constantly reviews its adherence to this standardized process, use the most frequent response applicable.

(Check One)

☐₁ Monthly or more often

☐₂ Quarterly

☐₃ Twice a year

☐₄ Yearly

☐₅ Less often than once a year

☐₆ Never

67. Does this hospital review its adherence to this standardized process for documenting, reconciling, and communicating patients' medications as part of its standard performance improvement (quality assurance) program?

(Check One)

☐₁ Yes

☐₂ No

The next questions are about labeling and packaging of medications.

68. Which of the following provisions has this hospital implemented to ensure standardized labeling and packaging of medications?

(Check One Answer for Each Item a-e)

	Yes	No
a. Require a standardized labeling method to be used for all medications..	☐1	☐2
b. Require that all medications and solutions be labeled when transferred from the original package to another container...................	☐1	☐2
c. Provide appropriate labels for sterile procedure areas where the process of labeling containers is performed	☐1	☐2
d. Limit and standardize parenteral drug concentrations	☐1	☐2
e. Use ready-to-use parenteral drug products to the extent possible..........	☐1	☐2

69. Has this hospital established written policies and procedures, protocols, or other guidelines that standardize practices for labeling and packaging of medications?

   (Check One)

   ☐1 Yes
   ☐2 No

70. How often does this hospital conduct a formal review of its standardized medication labeling and packaging practices? If this hospital conducts reviews at differing frequencies, or constantly reviews its standardized medication labeling and packaging practices, use the most frequent response applicable.

   (Check One)

   ☐1 Monthly or more often
   ☐2 Quarterly
   ☐3 Twice a year
   ☐4 Yearly
   ☐5 Less often than once a year
   ☐6 Never

71. Is adherence to this hospital's standardized practices for labeling and packaging of medications reviewed as part of its standard performance improvement (quality assurance) program?

   (Check One)

   ☐₁ Yes

   ☐₂ No

The next questions are about high alert drugs.

72. High alert drugs include intravenous adrenergic agonists and antagonists, chemotherapy agents, anticoagulants and anti-thrombotics, concentrated parenteral electrolytes, general anesthetics, neuromuscular blockers, insulin and oral hypoglycemics, and opiates.

   Which of the following actions has this hospital taken for the appropriate management of high alert drugs?

   (Check One Answer for Each Item a-f)

	Yes, ALL High Alert Drugs	Yes, SOME High Alert Drugs	No
a. Create a multidisciplinary team that regularly reviews safeguards for high alert drugs	☐₁	☐₂	☐₃
b. Designate a list of high alert drugs	☐₁	☐₂	☐₃
c. Identify tools for optimizing safe use of designated high alert drugs	☐₁	☐₂	☐₃
d. Follow a defined process to identify new medications to add to the high alert list	☐₁	☐₂	☐₃
e. Centralize or outsource error-prone processes (e.g., intravenous admixtures)	☐₁	☐₂	☐₃
f. Communicate information on high alert drugs to clinical caregivers	☐₁	☐₂	☐₃

73. Does this hospital ensure that staff who handle chemotherapy and anesthesia medications have appropriate qualifications or certifications?

   (Check One)

   ☐₁ Yes

   ☐₂ No

74. Has this hospital established written policies and procedures, protocols, or other guidelines regarding the management of high alert drugs?

   (Check One)

   ☐₁ Yes

   ☐₂ No

75. How often does this hospital conduct a formal review of its management of high alert drugs? If this hospital conducts reviews at differing frequencies, or constantly reviews its management of high alert drugs, use the most frequent response category applicable.

(Check One)

☐₁ Monthly or more often

☐₂ Quarterly

☐₃ Twice a year

☐₄ Yearly

☐₅ Less often than once a year

☐₆ Never

76. Is the appropriate handling and use of high alert drugs reviewed as part of this hospital's standard performance improvement (quality assurance) program?

(Check One)

☐₁ Yes

☐₂ No

The next questions are about dispensing medications in unit-dose or unit-of-use form.

77. Which of the following procedures does this hospital follow when dispensing medications to patient care areas?

(Check One Answer for Each Item a-c)

	Yes	No
a. Unit-dose (single-unit) or unit-of-use medications in patient care areas are packaged in the most ready-to-administer forms available from the manufacturer, or repackaged by the pharmacy or a licensed repackager	☐₁	☐₂
b. Every unit-dose or unit-of-use package label contains a machine-readable bar code or RFID tag identifying the product name, strength, and manufacturer	☐₁	☐₂
c. No more than a 24 hours supply of doses for most medications is delivered to the patient care area at any time	☐₁	☐₂

78. Has this hospital established written policies and procedures, protocols, or other guidelines for dispensing medications in unit-dose or unit-of-use packages?

(Check One)

☐₁ Yes

☐₂ No

167

79. How often does this hospital conduct a formal review of its use of medications in unit-dose or unit-of-use packages? If this hospital conducts reviews at differing frequencies, or constantly reviews its use of medications in unit-dose or unit-of-use of packages, use the most frequent response category applicable.

(Check One)

☐₁ Monthly or more often

☐₂ Quarterly

☐₃ Twice a year

☐₄ Yearly

☐₅ Less often than once a year

☐₆ Never

80. Is the appropriate use of unit-dose or unit-of-use medications reviewed as part of this hospital's standard performance improvement (quality assurance) program?

(Check One)

☐₁ Yes

☐₂ No

The next questions are about this hospital's workforce in its general ICU.

81. General ICUs include adult and pediatric ICUs, as well as medical, surgical or mixed ICUs. Is at least one critical care certified physician physically present and providing clinic care exclusively in this hospital's general ICU during daytime hours (at least 8 hours per day) seven days a week?

(Check One)

☐₁ Yes, at our SINGLE ICU ➔ SKIP TO Q.83 ON PAGE 25

☐₂ Yes, at ALL of our multiple ICUs ➔ SKIP TO Q.83 ON PAGE 25

☐₃ Yes, at SOME of our multiple ICUs

☐₄ No

82. If this hospital does not have full daytime coverage by a critical care certified physician, does it have a system to provide dedicated around-the-clock ICU telemonitoring by a critical care certified physician, with real-time access to patient information?

(Check One)

☐₁ Yes, at our SINGLE ICU

☐₂ Yes, at ALL of our multiple ICU's

☐₃ Yes, at SOME of our multiple ICU's

☐₄ No

168

83. When a certified, critical care physician is not physically present in the ICU, does this hospital provide for telephone coverage for the ICU by a critical care certified physician along with an appropriately trained clinician onsite?

 (Check One)

 ☐₁ Yes, at our SINGLE ICU

 ☐₂ Yes, at ALL of our multiple ICUs

 ☐₃ Yes, at SOME of our multiple ICUs

    ☐₄ No

The next questions are about this hospital's nursing workforce.

84. Staffing targets for nursing staff include the number, competency, and skill mix of staff needed to provide safe direct care to patients. Has this hospital established written policies and procedures, protocols, or other guidelines that set staffing targets for nursing staff?

 (Check One)

 ☐₁ Yes

 ☐₂ No ➔ SKIP TO Q.86

85. In developing the staffing target policies or guidelines, which of the following actions did this hospital take to seek input from frontline nurses regarding relevant issues and staffing needs?

(Check One Answer for Each Item a-d)

	Yes	No
a. Survey of nursing staff	☐₁	☐₂
b. Discussion sessions with nursing staff	☐₁	☐₂
c. Dissemination of draft policy or guideline to nursing staff for review and comment	☐₁	☐₂
d. Other, specify:_____	☐₁	☐₂

86. Has this hospital provided education regarding the impact of nursing on patient safety to any of the following groups?

(Check One Answer for Each Item a-d)

	Yes, ALL People In This Category	Yes, SOME People In This Category	No
a. Governing board (directors, trustees, or advisory)	☐₁	☐₂	☐₃
b. Senior management staff (e.g., CEO, vice presidents)	☐₁	☐₂	☐₃
c. Midlevel management staff (e.g., department directors)	☐₁	☐₂	☐₃
d. Front line managers (e.g., charge nurses)	☐₁	☐₂	☐₃

87. How often does this hospital conduct hospital-wide risk assessments to identify patient safety risks related to nurse staffing?

    (Check One)

    ☐₁ Monthly or more often

    ☐₂ Quarterly

    ☐₃ Twice a year

    ☐₄ Yearly

    ☐₅ Less often than once a year

    ☐₆ Never ➜ SKIP TO Q.89

88. How often are the results of these risk assessments related to nursing staffing reviewed by senior administrative management and the governing board (directors, trustees, or advisory) to assure that resources are allocated and performance improvement programs are implemented?

    (Check One)

    ☐₁ Monthly or more often

    ☐₂ Quarterly

    ☐₃ Twice a year

    ☐₄ Yearly

    ☐₅ Less often than once a year

89. Has this hospital implemented performance improvement interventions to close patient safety gaps related to nursing services?

    (Check One)

    ☐₁ Yes

    ☐₂ No

    The last few questions are about this hospital's NON-NURSING DIRECT CARE STAFF, which includes lab techs, radiology techs, pharmacy techs, respiratory therapists, physical therapists, other therapists, and nursing assistants.

90. Staffing targets for non-nursing direct care staff include the number, competency, and skill mix of staff needed to provide safe care to patients. Does this hospital have written policies and procedures, or other guidelines that set staffing targets for non-nursing direct care staff?

    (Check One)

    ☐₁ Yes, for ALL non-nursing direct care staff

    ☐₂ Yes, for SOME non-nursing direct care staff

    ☐₃ No

91. How often does this hospital conduct hospital-wide risk assessments to identify patient safety risks related to non-nursing staff that have direct care contact with patients?

> *(Check One)*

- ☐ 1 Monthly or more often
- ☐ 2 Quarterly
- ☐ 3 Twice a year
- ☐ 4 Yearly
- ☐ 5 Less often than once a year
- ☐ 6 Never → SKIP TO Q.93

92. How often are the results of these risk assessments related to non-nursing staff reviewed by senior administrative management and the governing board to assure that resources are allocated and performance improvement programs are implemented?

> *(Check One)*

- ☐ 1 Monthly or more often
- ☐ 2 Quarterly
- ☐ 3 Twice a year
- ☐ 4 Yearly
- ☐ 5 Less often than once a year
- ☐ 6 Never

93. Has this hospital implemented performance improvement interventions to close patient safety gaps for services by non-nursing direct care staff?

> *(Check One)*

- ☐ 1 Yes, for ALL non-nursing direct care staff
- ☐ 2 Yes, for SOME non-nursing direct care staff
- ☐ 3 No

THANK YOU FOR COMPLETING THIS SURVEY!

APPENDIX F.
RATIONALE FOR DESIGN OF THE SURVEY ITEMS

Item No.	Survey Question	NQF Safe Practice	Rationale
PATIENT SAFETY CULTURE			
1	An integrated patient safety program provides hospital-wide oversight and alignment of all activity to monitor and improve patient safety, and to ensure that all individuals working in the hospital are educated and participate in safety and quality initiatives. Has this hospital established an integrated patient safety program? Yes, implemented and in maintenance Yes, in process of implementing No	1 element 1	It was learned through cognitive interviews with hospital staff that a definition of an "integrated patient safety program" was needed. This definition appeared to work well in subsequent review of the draft questionnaire. The response options "implemented and in maintenance" and "in process of implementing" allow hospitals to show partial implementation progress, for which they spoke strongly in cognitive testing. The "in maintenance" phrase is intended to acknowledge that continuing work is needed even for a fully implemented practice.
2	Does this hospital have a SINGLE individual – regardless of their job title – who functions as a patient safety officer? Yes / No	1 element 1	Cognitive interviews identified the need to specify clearly that this question is asking if a hospital has one person as patient safety officer. We learned that some hospitals divide the functions of this role across more than one person, which is not consistent with the intent of the NQF practice.
3	Has this hospital implemented performance improvement interventions (e.g., teamwork skills, reducing falls) to address issues identified from analysis of patient safety performance or events? Yes, implemented and in maintenance Yes, in process of implementing No	1 element 1	This question addresses the NQF practice specification that performance improvement programs should be in place.

#	Question	Element	Rationale
4	The following question refers to the governing board of the hospital, which may be called the board of directors or board of trustees. If this hospital does not have a governing board with decision-making authority, but has an advisory board, the question applies to the advisory board. Which of the following actions does this hospital's governing board perform regularly in its oversight of the hospital's patient safety issues and activities? (*Answer choices:: Yes, No*) a. Review policies or guidelines on patient safety goals, priorities, and strategies b. Review reports on risks and hazards identified by hospital management c. Review reports from all patient safety culture survey or other culture measures d. Review progress in patient safety improvement activities e. Review level of participation by patients and families in the hospital's patient safety activities	1 element 1	It was learned through cognitive interviews with hospital staff that a definition of "governing board" was needed because some hospitals do not have a board of directors or trustees. If a hospital has no governing board, but has an advisory board, the definition allows it to apply this question to its advisory board. Positive answers to the components of this question indicate that the hospital is ensuring that all members are well versed in patient safety and that they have a critical impact on patient safety in their organization, per the NQF practice. The NQF language of "involvement of patients" was changed to "participation of patients" to alleviate confusion about the meaning of "involvement" that was identified in the cognitive interviews.
5	Does this hospital's governing board (directors, trustees, or advisory), or one of its standing committees, include the review of patient safety issues and improvements in a standing agenda item for every board meeting, either as a separate agenda item on safety or as part of a larger agenda item? Yes, done by the board Yes, done by a standing committee. (Specify) No	1 element 1	The safe practice states that the organizational leadership should be kept knowledgeable and engaged about patient safety issues present within the organization. It states that patient safety risk, hazards, and progress towards improvement should be addressed at every board meeting and documented by meeting agendas and minutes. We added "standing committee" as a result of hospital feedback in the cognitive testing.
6	Has this hospital conducted a standardized survey of its staff to assess its patient safety culture? Yes / No	1 element 2	The term "standardized survey" was used to make it more clear that the question refers to a closed-ended survey, in response to cognitive interviews.
7	How often does this hospital conduct a patient safety culture survey? Monthly or more often Quarterly Twice a year Yearly Less often than once a year	1 element 2	The NQF practice specifies that the survey should be conducted "at least annually." This question allows hospitals to report their survey frequency directly, which they indicated they want to be able to do. Responses can be used to construct an item indicating yes/no for whether the survey is conducted at least annually.

#	Question	Element	Notes
8	Which patient safety culture survey did this hospital use for its MOST RECENT survey? Hospital Survey on Patient Safety Culture (AHRQ survey) Patient Safety Climate in Healthcare Organizations (Sara Singer survey) Safety Attitudes Questionnaire (Sexton/Helmriech survey) Survey developed by the hospital (i.e., "homegrown") Other, specify	1 element 2	This question will yield responses that can be used to judge the integrity of surveys fielded, and also to obtain nationally representative data on use of the AHRQ patient safety culture survey.
9	How many units or departments did the MOST RECENT patient safety culture survey include? All units or departments Some units or departments None	1 element 2	The NQF practice specifies that critical care areas and services, and high-volume and high-risk areas should be surveyed. We found that it was impossible to capture high risk areas consistently due to differing perceptions of hospitals regarding what constitutes "high risk." Although this question does not capture that level of specificity, it does give useful information on the reach of the survey across the hospital.
10	Has this hospital taken any of the following actions based on the results of the MOST RECENT culture survey results? *(Answer choices: Yes, No)* a. Changed policies and procedures to support patient safety culture b. Implemented specific performance improvement interventions c. Disseminated survey results to all clinical caregivers and other staff d. Held education/training for staff on patient safety principles and practices e. Worked with management to create a safe environment for staff f. Other, Specify		This question was included to address the portion of this safe practice that focuses on what is done with the survey results. The hospitals we interviewed felt particularly strongly that this question should be included as an indicator of hospitals' commitment to action.
11	In TEAM-BASED CARE, all clinical caregivers and other staff in a particular clinical area function as a team, with all team members responsible and empowered to work as partners using a shared mental model of care, clear communications, mutual support for prevention of incidents, effective handoffs of patients	1 element 3	The definition introduces the components of team-based care and the teamwork improvement that achieves team-based care. In the answer choices, hospital can indicate the extent to which it has taken teamwork actions across

175

#	Question	Explanation
	across shifts and functions, and debriefs of care experiences to further strengthen TEAMWORK. Has this hospital taken specific actions to improve teamwork in ANY units or departments? Yes, ALL units or departments; Yes, SOME units or departments; No	units or departments, which helps to provide a more accurate picture of commitment to and reach of action. The phrase "units or departments" is used because hospitals informed us that these are different components of a hospital organization.
12 element 3	For units or departments in which this hospital has taken actions to improve teamwork, which training model was used to help staff develop teamwork and communications skills? TeamSTEPPS (AHRQ); MedTeams; Flight team training model; NASCAR training model; A formal team training program developed by this hospital; Frontline coaching on team practices during service provision (on-the-job training); Other, specify	This question is intended to measure the extent to which TeamSTEPPS is being used by hospitals, relative to their use of other models. It also can offer some insight into the approaches and rigor of training being used. The frontline coaching was included as a response option as a result of discussions with hospitals during the validation of the questionnaire, in which we learned that some are using a "learning by doing" and coaching without providing much formal training.
13 element 3	Has this hospital taken actions to improve teamwork in any of the following high-risk units? (*Answer choices: Yes, implemented and in maintenance; Yes, in process of implementing; No*) a. Critical care unit(s) b. Emergency department c. Surgical operating room d. Labor and delivery unit e. Outpatient procedural care units (e.g., same day surgery, dialysis unit) f. Other, specify	For the outpatient units, we focused only on procedural care units because, in the cognitive testing, the hospitals pushed for specificity, remarking that they have numerous types of outpatient services, which may vary widely in their efforts to improve their teamwork practices. The response options "implemented and in maintenance" and "in process of implementing" allow hospitals to show partial implementation progress, for which they spoke strongly in cognitive testing. The "in maintenance" phrase is intended to acknowledge that continuing work is needed even for a fully implemented practice.
14 element 4	Has this hospital provided basic training on issues and skills related to team-based care for any of the following groups? Executive managers; Governing board members (directors, trustees, or advisory)	This question is drawn directly from the provision in the NQF practice for basic training on team-based care.

	Medical staff members Midlevel managers (e.g., department heads, nursing managers) Frontline nurses Other, specify: No basic teamwork training has been provided to any groups		
15	In the last 2 years, which of the following has the hospital used to RETROSPECTIVELY identify patient safety risks and hazards? *(Answer choices: Yes, No, Not familiar with tool)* a. Sentinel event reporting and analysis b. Event reporting c. Root cause analysis d. Analysis of closed claims e. Analysis of hospital-level system failures f. Monitoring of Patient Safety Indicators (PSI) g. Tracking retrospective triggers h. External reporting of adverse events i. Other, specify	1 element 4	This question lists the techniques identified in the NQF practice, with yes/no response options. There also is a response option for "don't recognize it" that hospitals can use when they do not know what one of the items is. Item 13e uses "hospital level system failures" to emphasize that it is asking about individual hospitals, which are the intended respondents for the survey. During cognitive interviews, some hospitals were interpreting "enterprise system failures" (the phrase used in the practice) to mean a failure across the larger system that includes more than one hospital.
16	In the last 2 years, which of the following has this hospital used to identify patient safety risks and hazards in REAL TIME OR NEAR REAL TIME? *(Answer choices: Yes, No, Not familiar with tool)* a. Trigger tools, manually or technology enabled b. Tools for direct observation of processes in high-risk areas c. Technology tools, such as electronic health records d. Real time risk identification tools e. Other, specify	1 element 4	This question lists the techniques identified in the practice, with yes/no response options. There also is a response option for "not familiar with tool" that hospitals can use if they do not know what one of the items is.
17	In the last 2 years, which of the following has this hospital used to PROSPECTIVELY identify potential patient safety risks and hazards? *(Answer choices: Yes, No, Not familiar with tool)* a. Failure Mode and Effects Analysis (FMEA) b. Probabilistic Risk Assessment (PRA) c. Other, specify	1 element 4	This question lists the techniques identified in the practice, with yes/no response options. There also is a response option for "not familiar with tool" that hospitals can use if they do not know what one of the items is.
18	Hospital-wide risk assessments integrate information -- across service lines and departments -- on patient safety risks, in order to	1 element 4	We added "and departments" in the definition per cognitive interviews during which hospitals

No.	Question		Comment
	prevent systems failures. Does this hospital use hospital-wide risk assessments to identify system-level patient safety risks and hazards? Yes / No		emphasized that that the term "service lines" alone does not include pharmacy.

COMMUNICATION WITH PATIENTS OR FAMILIES

No.	Question	Rating	Comment
19	Does this hospital have written policies and procedures, protocols, or other guidelines, for ensuring that written documentation of each patient's preferences for life sustaining treatment is prominently displayed in his or her medical chart? Yes / No	3	This question, and several others that ask about policies and procedures, is stated as "written policies and procedures, protocols or other guidelines". During cognitive interviews, hospital reported that many of their policies are not in the corporate policy documents, but are in written clinical protocols or guidelines. The question was expanded to include protocols and guidelines to be sure that it captured all formal hospital policies.
20	Does this hospital review its adherence to this policy or guideline as part of its standard performance improvement (quality assurance) program? Yes / No	3	This question, and several others like it, is a way of gauging the extent to which a hospital is truly integrating a practice into its routine operation. If the practice and related measures are considered regularly (on a periodic basis) in the hospital quality assurance program, it may be inferred that the hospital is working to make the practice routine. Both "performance improvement" and "quality assurance" are used because we learned from cognitive interviews that hospitals vary in the terms they use, and both terms (and probably others) are commonly used.
21	Serious unanticipated outcomes include sentinel events, serious reportable events, and other unanticipated outcomes that require provision of substantial additional care. Which of the following actions are part of hospital practice for communication about serious unanticipated outcomes with patients and families? *(Answer choices: Yes, No)* a. Initiate conversations with the patient and family within 24 hours of the event b. Provide an explicit statement of "the facts" about what	4	The question is addressing a hospital's standard practice for communicating with patients and families about events. It is not possible to use a survey to assess how well a hospital actually complies with its standard practice as an event occurs; this would require direct observation. The practice uses the term "caregiver" for clinical personnel, which can be confused with family caregivers who are caring for a relative. The term "clinical caregiver" is used throughout the survey to

	c. happened and why the event occurred Express regret explicitly and empathically that the outcome was not as expected d. Make a commitment to investigate the event and take action to prevent future occurrences e. Provide detailed feedback of results of the investigation f. Provide an apology if the event is found to be the result of error or system failures g. Provide emotional support for patient and family by trained clinical caregivers h. Provide emotional support for clinical caregivers and other staff involved in the event i. Other, specify		make it clear that it is referring to clinical staff.
22	Has this hospital established written policies and procedures, protocols, or other guidelines that define how clinical caregivers and other staff are to communicate with patients and families about serious unanticipated outcomes? Yes, for ALL clinical caregivers and other staff Yes, for SOME clinical caregivers and other staff No	4	As described for Q19, this question includes the phrase "protocols and guidelines" to be sure that it captured all formal hospital policies, wherever they may be written.
23	How often does this hospital conduct a formal review of its practices for communicating about serious unanticipated outcomes? If this hospital conducts reviews at differing frequencies, or constantly reviews its practices, use the most frequent response applicable. Monthly or more often Quarterly Twice a year Yearly Every two years Only when an event occurs Never	4	The practice specifies that the communication practices should be reviewed and updated annually. This question allows hospitals to report their review frequency directly, which they indicated they want to be able to do. Responses can be used to construct an item indicating yes/no for whether the review is done at least annually.
24	Has this hospital established a support system to give clinical caregivers and other staff the skills and emotional support for managing events with unanticipated outcomes? Yes, for ALL clinical caregivers and other staff	4	The practice uses the term "caregiver" for clinical personnel. The term "clinical caregiver" is used throughout the survey to make it clear that it is referring to clinical staff (versus other types of

#	Question		Notes
	caregivers such as family members).		
	Yes, for SOME clinical caregivers and other staff No		
INFORMATION TRANSPARENCY ACROSS CONTINUUM OF CARE			
25	Which of the following actions does this hospital routinely perform for the labeling of imaging studies, laboratory specimens, or other diagnostic studies? *(Answer choices: Yes, No)* a. Label laboratory specimen containers at the time of use and in the presence of the patient b. Identify the patient and match the intended service or treatment to that patient c. Use at least two patient identifiers for blood samples or other specimens d. Label imaging studies with correct patient information close to the imaging device e. Mark "Left" or "Right" on each radiographic image	10	
26	Does this hospital review its practices for labeling of the following diagnostic studies as part of its standard performance improvement (quality assurance) program? *(Answer choices: Yes, No)* a. Imaging studies b. Laboratory specimens c. Other diagnostic studies	10	This question, and several others like it, is a way of gauging the extent to which a hospital is truly integrating a practice into its routine operation. Both "performance improvement" and "quality assurance" are used because hospitals vary in the terms they use, and both terms (and probably others) are commonly used. The item asks for separate responses for each type of study listed in the practice in response to hospitals' reports that their labeling status differs by type of study.
27	Has this hospital established an intervention to improve issues regarding labeling of the following diagnostic studies? *(Answer choices: Yes, No)* a. Imaging studies b. Laboratory specimens c. Other diagnostic studies	10	The item asks for separate responses for each type of study listed in the practice in response to hospitals' reports that their labeling status differs by type of study.
28	Has this hospital prohibited use of ALL abbreviations, acronyms, symbols, and dose designations in the Joint Commission's list of	13	The practice directly prohibits use of terms known to lead to misinterpretation. The practice mirrors the

#	Question	Page	Notes
	"do not use" abbreviations? Yes / No		Joint Commission "do not use" abbreviations, so this question refers to that list, which should enhance consistency in hospital responses to the question.
29	Does this hospital routinely review AND enforce compliance with the Joint Commission's "do not use" abbreviation list? Yes / No	13	This question is a way of gauging the extent to which a hospital is truly integrating a practice into its routine operation.
30	Does this hospital use the metric system to communicate all doses on prescription orders (with the exception of therapies that use standard units, e.g. insulin or vitamins)? Yes / No	13	
31	A discharge plan lists the care, treatment and services a patient received, as well as his/her condition at discharge. The plan includes medical issues and tests or studies that require follow-up. Has this hospital established written policies and procedures, protocols, or other guidelines requiring a discharge plan for each patient? Yes / No	11	This question is introduced by a definition of a discharge plan, in response to hospitals' requests for a clear description of what was meant by a "discharge plan."
32	Which of the following provisions are included in the hospital's discharge policies and procedures, protocols, or other guidelines? (Answer choices:: Yes, No) a. Delineation of roles and responsibilities in the discharge process b. Preparation for discharge occurs throughout the hospitalization c. Standardized information flow across clinical caregivers within and outside the hospital from admission through discharge d. Preparation of discharge summaries before discharge e. Preparation of discharge plan before discharge f. Patient or family perception of coordination of discharge care g. Performance measurement and improvement of the discharge process	11	As described for Q19, this question includes the phrase "protocols and guidelines" to be sure that it captured all formal hospital policies, wherever they may be written. Item 32c explicitly references "clinical caregivers within and outside the hospital" to clarify that the intent is coordinated preparation for discharge with all relevant staff involved. Separate items are provided for "preparation of discharge summaries" (32d) and "preparation of discharge plan" (32e) before discharge because hospitals reported that these two documents often are handled differently in the discharge process.
33	Does this hospital provide a written discharge plan to each patient at the time of discharge?	11	

#		#	
	Yes / No		
34	Does this hospital provide a discharge summary to all clinical caregivers who accept the patient's care after hospital discharge? Yes / No	11	
SURGERY PROCEDURES			
35	Has this hospital implemented the following components of the Universal Protocol for eliminating wrong site, wrong procedure, wrong person surgery? *(Answer choices: Yes, implemented and in maintenance; Yes, in process of implementing; No)* a. Preoperative verification process to ensure readiness for surgery b. Marking the operative site for procedures in which incision site might be ambiguous c. Conducting a "time out" to verify correct patient, procedure, and other relevant actions	25	Two options were considered as references for this item: the Joint Commission Universal Protocol, or the Association of Perioperative Registered Nurses (AORN) protocol. The latter was considered because not all hospitals are Joint Commission accredited. In cognitive interviews, hospitals did not like use of the AORN protocol because it could be interpreted to focus on nursing, leading to potentially negative reactions by physicians. The response options "implemented and in maintenance" and "in process of implementing" allow hospitals to show partial implementation progress, for which they spoke strongly in cognitive testing. The "in maintenance" phrase is intended to acknowledge that continuing work is needed even for a fully implemented practice.
36	How often does this hospital conduct a formal review of its adherence to the Universal Protocol for eliminating wrong site, wrong procedure, wrong person surgery? If this hospital conducts reviews at differing frequencies, or constantly reviews its adherence to the Universal Protocol, use the most frequent response applicable. Monthly or more often Quarterly Twice a year Yearly Every two years Only when an event occurs Never	25	This question allows hospitals to report their review frequency directly, which they want to be able to do. It is a way of gauging the extent to which a hospital is truly integrating a practice into its routine operation.
37	Surgical patients are at risk of an acute perioperative cardiac event	26	In response to cognitive interviews results, a

182

#	Question		Comment
	if they have required beta blockers, have symptomatic arrhythmias or hypertension, or are undergoing vascular surgery and have a finding of ischemia on preoperative testing. Vascular surgery includes vascular repairs and reconstruction as well as amputations for peripheral vascular disease. Has this hospital established written policies and procedures, protocols, or other guidelines to evaluate surgery patients for risk of an acute ischemic perioperative cardiac event? Yes / No		definition is provided for when surgical patients are at risk of an acute perioperative cardiac event. The definition of vascular surgery provided is the one given in the practice.
38	Do these policies and procedures, protocols, or other guidelines regarding risk of cardiac events for surgical patients include the following provisions: *(Answer choices: Yes; No)* a. Perform a cardiac risk assessment of at-risk surgery patients b. Document results of cardiac risk assessment in patient's record c. Establish guidelines for prevention of perioperative myocardial ischemia d. Incorporate use of clinical judgment regarding use of beta blockade	26	
39	Does this hospital review its performance in the prevention of perioperative ischemic events as part of its standard performance improvement (quality assurance) program? Yes / No	26	This question, and several others like it, is a way of gauging the extent to which a hospital is truly integrating a practice into its routine operation. Both "performance improvement" and "quality assurance" are used because hospitals vary in the terms they use, and both terms (and probably others) are commonly used.
MEDICAL EVALUATION AND PREVENTION			
40	Does this hospital operate a patient influenza immunization program based on current Centers for Disease Control and Prevention (CDC) recommendations regarding which PATIENTS should be immunized? Yes / No	23	
41	Does this hospital operate a program for the immunization of CLINICAL CAREGIVERS AND OTHER STAFF for influenza?	23	Although the practice uses the term "healthcare workers," we used "clinical caregivers and other

#	Question	Ref	Comment
	Yes, for ALL clinical caregivers and other staff Yes, for SOME clinical caregivers and other staff No		"staff" for more specificity and consistency in terminology across the survey items.
42	Does this hospital maintain current records on the influenza vaccination status of clinical caregivers and other staff? Yes, for ALL clinical caregivers and other staff Yes, for SOME clinical caregivers and other staff No	23	This item addresses the practice provision to "document the immunization status of all employees," using "clinical caregivers and other staff" for specificity and consistency.
43	As each patient is admitted to the hospital, is an assessment done to identify if the patient is at risk of developing pressure ulcers? Yes / No	27	This item addresses the practice provision to "evaluate each patient upon admission," with the wording crafted in response to hospital feedback in cognitive interviews seeking clarity regarding both "admission" and evaluation of patients.
44	Are the assessment results AND a prevention plan documented in each patient's medical record? Yes / No	27	
45	When an individual is identified as being at risk for pressure ulcers, does the clinical caregiver routinely reevaluate the integrity of a patient's skin? Yes / No	27	This item addresses the practice provision to "assess and periodically reassess each patient's risk for developing a pressure ulcer."
46	Are the results of skin reevaluations documented in the patient's medical record? Yes / No	27	
47	Has this hospital established written policies and procedures, protocols, or other guidelines regarding the prevention of pressure ulcers? Yes / No	27	As described for Q19, the question includes the phrase "protocols and guidelines" to be sure that it captured all formal hospital policies, wherever they may be written.
48	How often does this hospital perform prevalence studies to evaluate the effectiveness of its pressure ulcer prevention practices? Monthly or more often Quarterly Twice a year Yearly Less often than once a year	27	This question allows hospitals to report their prevalence study frequency, which they want to be able to do. It is a way of gauging the extent to which a hospital is truly integrating a practice into its routine operation.

#	Question	Page	Notes
	Never		
49	Does this hospital review its performance in preventing pressure ulcers as part of its standard performance improvement (quality assurance) program? ? Yes / No	27	This question, and several others like it, is a way of gauging the extent to which a hospital is truly integrating a practice into its routine operation. Both "performance improvement" and "quality assurance" are used because hospitals vary in the terms they use, and both terms (and probably others) are commonly used.
50	Has this hospital established written policies and procedures, protocols, or other guidelines regarding the prevention of venous thromboembolism/deep vein thrombosis (VTE/DVT)? ? Yes / No	28	As described for Q19, the question includes the phrase "protocols and guidelines" to be sure that it captured all formal hospital policies, wherever they may be written.
51	Do these policies and procedures, protocols, or other guidelines on prevention of VTE/DVT include the following provisions: *(Answer choices: Yes, No)* a. Evaluate all patients at admission to identify risk of VTE/DVT b. Document risk assessment AND prevention plan in patient's record c. Use evidence-based methods of thromboprophylaxis d. Regularly reassess risk during inpatient stay	28	
52	Does this hospital review its performance in the prevention of VTE/DVT as part of its standard performance improvement (quality assurance) program? ? Yes / No	28	This question, and several others like it, is a way of gauging the extent to which a hospital is truly integrating a practice into its routine operation. Both "performance improvement" and "quality assurance" are used because hospitals vary in the terms they use, and both terms (and probably others) are commonly used.
53	Has this hospital established written policies and procedures, protocols, or other guidelines for monitoring patients on a long-term oral anticoagulant? Yes, for OUTPATIENT care only Yes, for INPATIENT care only Yes, for BOTH outpatient and inpatient care No	29	As described for Q19, the question includes the phrase "protocols and guidelines" to be sure that it captured all formal hospital policies, wherever they may be written.

185

54	Has this hospital established written policies and procedures, protocols or other guidelines to prevent contrast media-induced renal failure? Yes / No	30	As described for Q19, the question includes the phrase "protocols and guidelines" to be sure that it captured all formal hospital policies, wherever they may be written.
55	Do these policies and procedures, protocols, or other guidelines on prevention of contrast media-induced nephropathy include the following provisions? *(Answer choices: Yes; No)* a. Evaluate patients at risk for contrast media-induced renal failure prior to contrast media administration b. Use clinically appropriate methods for reducing risk of renal injury c. Document risk assessment and prevention plan in patient's record	30	
56	Does this hospital review its performance in the prevention of contrast media-induced nephropathy as part of its standard performance improvement (quality assurance) program? ? Yes / No	30	This question, and several others like it, is a way of gauging the extent to which a hospital is truly integrating a practice into its routine operation. Both "performance improvement" and "quality assurance" are used because hospitals vary in the terms they use, and both terms (and probably others) are commonly used.
MEDICATION SAFETY MANAGEMENT		
57	Does this hospital have a computerized prescriber order entry (CPOE) system for inpatient care? Yes, system is fully implemented Yes, in the process of implementing a system No, but plan to implement a system No, do not have plans to implement a system	12	
58	Has this hospital performed an assessment to determine the feasibility of implementing a CPOE system and the possible impacts of doing so? Yes / No	12	
59	Which of the following factors did this hospital examine in its assessment of a CPOE system? *(Answer choices: Yes; No)* a. The potential for CPOE to reduce patient safety risks and hazards	12	

186

	b. Adequacy of existing evidence-based care processes and workflow at the hospital c. Capability of the hospital's clinical information infrastructure to support CPOE d. Commitment of the hospital's governance and management staff e. Commitment of the hospital's clinical personnel, including nursing, residents, independent practitioners, and other clinical staff f. Costs and return-on-investment of CPOE for the hospital g. Other, specify		
60	As part of this hospital's medication management system, does the hospital pharmacist perform the following roles regularly? *(Answer choices: Yes; No)* a. Select and maintain a formulary of medications chosen for safety and effectiveness, working with other health professionals b. Be available for consultation with prescribers on medication ordering, interpretation, and review of medical orders c. Provide medication safety recommendations and promote medication error prevention throughout the hospital d. Work with others to provide a work environment that promotes the accurate PRESCRIBING of medication orders e. Work with others to provide a work environment that promotes the accurate DISPENSING of medication orders f. Work with others to provide a work environment that promotes the accurate ADMINISTRATION of medication orders g. Review all non-emergent medication orders and patient medication profiles for appropriateness and completeness (when reviews do not create a medically unacceptable delay) h. Oversee the preparation of medications, including sterile products, to ensure they are safely prepared	15	Items for prescribing, dispensing, and administration of medication orders (63d through 63f) are listed separately in response to feedback from hospitals in cognitive interviews that their status is likely to differ for each of these three steps of the medication management process.

		This item addresses the practice provision that when a full-time pharmacist is not available onsite, a pharmacist is available by telephone or is accessible at another location that has 24-hour pharmacy services.
i. Inspect medication storage areas periodically to ensure that medications are stored properly		
61	How does this hospital provide for 24-hour, 7-day availability of a pharmacist? At least one pharmacist is available onsite all the time A pharmacist is available onsite for some shifts, and whenever a pharmacist is not onsite, one is available by telephone or accessible at another location Some other way - Specify This hospital does not provide for 24-hour, 7-day availability of a pharmacist	15
62	How often does this hospital conduct a formal review of its medication management process? If this hospital conducts reviews at differing frequencies, or constantly reviews its medication management process, use the most frequent response applicable. Monthly or more often Quarterly Twice a year Yearly Every two years Only when an event occurs Never	15	This question allows hospitals to report their prevalence study frequency, which they want to be able to do. It is a way of gauging the extent to which a hospital is truly integrating a practice into its routine operation.
63	Is the hospital's medication management process reviewed as part of its standard performance improvement (quality assurance) program? ? Yes / No	15	This question, and several others like it, is a way of gauging the extent to which a hospital is truly integrating a practice into its routine operation. Both "performance improvement" and "quality assurance" are used because hospitals vary in the terms they use, and both terms (and probably others) are commonly used.
64	Which of the following actions does this hospital take to document and reconcile all the medications being taken by each patient admitted? *(Answer choices: Yes; No)* a. Developing a list of current medications at the start of an inpatient stay b. Active involvement by the patient, family or clinical	16	

	c. Documentation on the updated medication list of new medications prescribed by the first provider of service during the inpatient stay d. Communication of the updated medication list to subsequent providers of service e. Documentation on the updated list of new medications prescribed by subsequent providers of service f. Comparison of all newly prescribed medications to those already on the updated list and reconciliation of orders as necessary to ensure drug compatibility g. Communicate the updated medication list to the patient, family or clinical caregiver as the patient moves through levels of care within this hospital h. Communicate the updated medication list to the patient, family or clinical caregiver when the patient moves to another care setting		caregiver in development of the initial medications list
65	Has this hospital established a standardized process for developing, reconciling, and communicating an accurate medication list for each patient throughout an inpatient stay and referral to another care setting? Yes / No	16	As described for Q19, the question includes the phrase "protocols and guidelines" to be sure that it captured all formal hospital policies, wherever they may be written.
66	How often does this hospital conduct a formal review of its adherence to this standardized process for medication documentation, reconciliation, and communication? If this hospital conducts reviews at differing frequencies, or constantly reviews its adherence to this standardized process, use the most frequent response applicable. Monthly or more often Quarterly Twice a year Yearly Less often than once a year Never	16	This question allows hospitals to report their prevalence study frequency, which they want to be able to do. It is a way of gauging the extent to which a hospital is truly integrating a practice into its routine operation.
67	Does this hospital review its adherence to this standardized process for documenting, reconciling, and communicating	16	This question, and several others like it, is a way of gauging the extent to which a hospital is truly

189

#	Question		Notes
	patients' medications as part of its standard performance improvement (quality assurance) program? ? Yes / No		integrating a practice into its routine operation. Both "performance improvement" and "quality assurance" are used because hospitals vary in the terms they use, and both terms (and probably others) are commonly used.
68	Which of the following provisions has this hospital implemented to ensure standardized labeling and packaging of medications? (*Answer choices: Yes; No*) a. Require a standardized labeling method to be used for all medications b. Require that all medications and solutions be labeled when transferred from the original package to another container c. Provide appropriate labels for sterile procedure areas where the process of labeling containers is performed d. Limit and standardize parenteral drug concentrations e. Use ready-to-use parenteral drug products to the extent possible	14	In the cognitive interviews, hospitals raised a number of definitional issues for this item. Thus, we crafted the wording carefully to ensure clarity and consistent responses by hospitals, with many of the wording choices diverging from the exact language in the practice: Use of "at the start of an inpatient stay" instead of "beginning of each episode of care at a facility" Use of "clinical caregiver" instead of "caregiver" Use of "updated medication list" instead of "medication list"; Use of "first provider of service" instead of "provider" Use of separate questions for patient moving through levels of care and patient moving to another care setting. Q30f addresses drug reconciliation in a general way, using "as necessary" to motivate actions. The practice handles this element using the phrase "transitions in care," which also confused hospitals in the cognitive interviews.
69	Has this hospital established written policies and procedures, protocols, or other guidelines that standardize practices for labeling and packaging of medications? ? Yes / No	14	This addresses the provision in the practice that "reconciliation must occur any time the organization requires that orders be rewritten and any time the patient changes services, setting, provider, or level of care and new medication orders are written…"
70	How often does this hospital conduct a formal review of its standardized medication labeling and packaging practices? If this hospital conducts reviews at differing frequencies, or constantly reviews its standardized medication labeling and packaging practices, use the most frequent response applicable.	14	This question allows hospitals to report their review frequency directly, which they want to be able to do. It is a way of gauging the extent to which a hospital is truly integrating a practice into its routine operation.

#	Question		Notes
	Monthly or more often Quarterly Twice a year Yearly Less often than once a year Never		
71	Is adherence to this hospital's standardized practices for labeling and packaging of medications reviewed as part of its standard performance improvement (quality assurance) program? ? Yes / No	14	This question, and several others like it, is a way of gauging the extent to which a hospital is truly integrating a practice into its routine operation. Both "performance improvement" and "quality assurance" are used because hospitals vary in the terms they use, and both terms (and probably others) are commonly used.
72	High alert drugs include intravenous adrenergic agonists and antagonists, chemotherapy agents, anticoagulants and anti-thrombotics, concentrated parenteral electrolytes, general anesthetics, neuromuscular blockers, insulin and oral hypoglycemics, and opiates. Which of the following actions has this hospital taken for the appropriate management of high alert drugs? *(Answer choices: Yes, ALL high alert drugs; Yes, SOME high alert drugs; No)* a. Create a multidisciplinary team that regularly reviews safeguards for high alert drugs b. Designate a list of high alert drugs c. Identify tools for optimizing safe use of designated high alert drugs d. Follow a defined process to identify new medications to add to the high alert list e. Centralize or outsource error-prone processes (e.g., intravenous admixtures) f. Communicate information on high alert drugs to clinical caregivers	17	The definition of high alert drugs used in this section of the survey comes directly from the practice.
73	Does this hospital ensure that staff who handle chemotherapy and anesthesia medications have appropriate qualifications or	17	

#	Question		Notes
	certifications? Yes / No		
74	Has this hospital established written policies and procedures, protocols, or other guidelines regarding the management of high alert drugs? Yes / No	17	As described for Q19, the question includes the phrase "protocols and guidelines" to be sure that it captured all formal hospital policies, wherever they may be written.
75	How often does this hospital conduct a formal review of its management of high alert drugs? If this hospital conducts reviews at differing frequencies, or constantly reviews its management of high alert drugs, use the most frequent response category applicable. Monthly or more often Quarterly Twice a year Yearly Less often than once a year Never	17	This question allows hospitals to report their prevalence study frequency, which they want to be able to do. It is a way of gauging the extent to which a hospital is truly integrating a practice into its routine operation.
76	Is the appropriate handling and use of high alert drugs reviewed as part of this hospital's standard performance improvement (quality assurance) program? Yes / No	17	This question, and several others like it, is a way of gauging the extent to which a hospital is truly integrating a practice into its routine operation. Both "performance improvement" and "quality assurance" are used because hospitals vary in the terms they use, and both terms (and probably others) are commonly used.
77	Which of the following procedures does this hospital follow when dispensing medications to patient care areas? *(Answer choices: Yes; No)* a. Unit-dose (single-unit) or unit of use medications in patient care areas are packaged in the most ready-to-administer forms available from the manufacturer, or repackaged by the pharmacy or a licensed repackager b. Every unit-dose or unit of use package label contains a machine-readable bar code or RFID tag identifying the product name, strength, and manufacturer c. No more than a 24 hours supply of doses for most	18	

192

#	Question		Notes
	medications is delivered to the patient care area at any time		
78	Has this hospital established written policies and procedures, protocols, or other guidelines for dispensing medications in unit-dose or unit of use packages? ? Yes / No	18	As described for Q19, the question includes the phrase "protocols and guidelines" to be sure that it captured all formal hospital policies, wherever they may be written.
79	How often does this hospital conduct a formal review of its use of medications in unit-dose or unit of use packages? If this hospital conducts reviews at differing frequencies, or constantly reviews its use of medications in unit-dose or unit use of packages, use the most frequent response category applicable. Monthly or more often Quarterly Twice a year Yearly Less often than once a year Never	18	This question allows hospitals to report their prevalence study frequency, which they want to be able to do. It is a way of gauging the extent to which a hospital is truly integrating a practice into its routine operation.
80	Is the appropriate use of unit-dose or unit of use medications reviewed as part of this hospital's standard performance improvement (quality assurance) program? Yes / No	18	This question, and several others like it, is a way of gauging the extent to which a hospital is truly integrating a practice into its routine operation. Both "performance improvement" and "quality assurance" are used because hospitals vary in the terms they use, and both terms (and probably others) are commonly used.
WORKFORCE			
81	General ICUs include adult and pediatric ICUs, as well as medical, surgical or mixed ICUs. Is at least one critical care certified physician physically present and providing clinic care exclusively in this hospital's general ICU during daytime hours (at least 8 hours per day) seven days a week? Yes, at our SINGLE ICU Yes, at ALL of our multiple ICUs Yes, at SOME of our multiple ICUs No	7	The practices references "general ICU, both adult and pediatric." In cognitive interviews, hospitals emphasized the diversity of ICUs they operate and sought clarification on which types the question is addressing. In response, we added "as well as medical, surgical, or mixed ICUs" to the definition.
82	If this hospital does not have full daytime coverage by a critical	7	

193

#	Question		
	care certified physician, does it have a system to provide dedicated around-the-clock ICU telemonitoring by a critical care certified physician, with real-time access to patient information? Yes, at our SINGLE ICU Yes, at ALL of our multiple ICUs Yes, at SOME of our multiple ICUs No		
83	When a certified, critical care physician is not physically present in the ICU, does this hospital provide for telephone coverage for the ICU by a critical care certified physician along with an appropriately trained clinician onsite? Yes, at our SINGLE ICU Yes, at ALL of our multiple ICUs Yes, at SOME of our multiple ICUs No	7	
84	Staffing targets for nursing staff include the number, competency, and skill mix of staff needed to provide safe direct care to patients. Has this hospital established written policies and procedures, protocols, or other guidelines that set staffing targets for nursing staff? Yes / No	5	
85	In developing the staffing target policies or guidelines, which of the following actions did this hospital take to seek input from frontline nurses regarding relevant issues and staffing needs? *(Answer choices: Yes; No)* a. Survey of nursing staff b. Discussion sessions with nursing staff c. Dissemination of draft policy or guideline to nursing staff for review and comment d. Other, specify		The practice states that a health care organization should "implement explicit organizational policies and procedures, with input from nurses at the unit level, regarding effective staffing targets." The answer choices provided explicitly list possible ways in which nursing input can be obtained, to enhance clarity for respondents.
86	Has this hospital provided education regarding the impact of nursing on patient safety to any of the following groups? *(Answer choices: Yes, ALL people in this category; Yes, SOME people in this category; No)* a. Governing board (directors, trustees, or advisory)	5	The practice provision is to "ensure that the governance board and senior, midlevel, and line managers are educated regarding the impact of nursing on patient safety." In cognitive interviews, hospitals sought clarification of what was meant by

#	Question		Comments
	b. Senior management staff (e.g., CEO, vice presidents) c. Midlevel management staff (e.g., department directors) d. Front line managers (e.g., charge nurses)		each group. We responded by providing examples for each one.
87	How often does this hospital conduct hospital-wide risk assessments to identify patient safety risks related to nurse staffing? Monthly or more often Quarterly Twice a year Yearly Less often than once a year Never	5	This question allows hospitals to report their risk assessment frequency, which they want to be able to do. It is a way of gauging the extent to which a hospital is truly integrating a practice into its routine operation.
88	How often are the results of these risk assessments related to nursing staffing reviewed by senior administrative management and the governing board (directors, trustees, or advisory) to assure that resources are allocated and performance improvement programs are implemented? Monthly or more often Quarterly Twice a year Yearly Less often than once a year Never	5	This question allows hospitals to report their reporting frequency, which they want to be able to do. It is a way of gauging the extent to which a hospital is truly integrating a practice into its routine operation.
89	Has this hospital implemented performance improvement interventions to close patient safety gaps related to nursing services? Yes / No	5	
90	The last few questions are about this hospital's NON-NURSING DIRECT CARE STAFF, which includes lab techs, radiology techs, pharmacy techs, respiratory therapists, physical therapists, other therapists, and nursing assistants. Staffing targets for non-nursing direct care staff include the number, competency, and skill mix of staff needed to provide safe care to patients. Does this hospital have written policies and procedures, or other guidelines that set staffing targets for non-	6	The practice gives the definition of the staffing targets. In response to hospital feedback in cognitive interviews, a list of the types of non-nursing direct care staff was added to the introductory statement. As described for Q19, the question includes the phrase "protocols and guidelines" to be sure that it captured all formal hospital policies, wherever they may be written.

195

#	Question		Explanation
	nursing direct care staff? Yes, for ALL non-nursing direct care staff Yes, for SOME non-nursing direct care staff No		
91	How often does this hospital conduct hospital-wide risk assessments to identify patient safety risks related to non-nursing staff that have direct care contact with patients? Monthly or more often Quarterly Twice a year Yearly Less often than once a year Never	6	This question allows hospitals to report their risk assessment frequency, which they want to be able to do. It is a way of gauging the extent to which a hospital is truly integrating a practice into its routine operation.
92	How often are the results of these risk assessments related to non-nursing staff reviewed by senior administrative management and the governing board to assure that resources are allocated and a performance improvement programs are implemented? Monthly or more often Quarterly Twice a year Yearly Less often than once a year Never	6	This question allows hospitals to report their reporting frequency, which they want to be able to do. It is a way of gauging the extent to which a hospital is truly integrating a practice into its routine operation.
93	Has this hospital implemented performance improvement interventions to close patient safety gaps for services by non-nursing direct care staff? Yes, for ALL non-nursing direct care staff Yes, for SOME non-nursing direct care staff No	6	

REFERENCES

Agency for Healthcare Research and Quality, *AHRQ Quality Indicators—Guide to the Patient Safety Indicators*, Version 2.1, Rev. 3, Rockville, Md: AHRQ No. 03-R203, 2005a.

Agency for Healthcare Research and Quality, *Patient Safety Indicators: Technical Specifications*, Version 3.1, Rockville, Md., March 12, 2007a.

Agency for Healthcare Research and Quality, *Hospital Survey on Patient Safety Culture*, Rockville, Md., April 2005b. As of July 27, 2009:
http://www.ahrq.gov/qual/patientsafetyculture/

Agency for Healthcare Quality and Research, *National Healthcare Quality Report: 2007*, Rockville, Md: Department of Health and Human Services, AHRQ No. 08-0040, 2008a.

Agency for Healthcare Research and Quality, *Log of Revisions to PSI Documentation and Software*, March 10, 2008b. As of July 27, 2009:
<http://www.qualityindicators.ahrq.gov/downloads/psi/psi_change_log.pdf

Agency for Healthcare Research and Quality, *Medical Expenditure Panel Survey*, 2009. As of August 3, 2009:
http://www.meps.ahrq.gov/mepsweb/about_meps/survey_back.jsp

Agency for Healthcare Research and Quality, *TeamSTEPPS*. As of September 2007c:
http://www.ahrq.gov/qual/teamstepps/
As of July 27, 2009:
http://teamstepps.ahrq.gov/abouttoolsmaterials.htm

Agency for Healthcare Research and Quality Website, Data Tables appendix page, "Detailed Data Tables," March 2008c. As of July 19, 2008:
http://www.ahrq.gov/qual/nhrq87/Safety

Ansett S. "Boundary Spanner: The Gatekeeper of Innovation in Partnerships," *Accountability Forum*, Vol. 6, April 2005, pp. 36–44.

Barach, P., and S. Small, "Reporting and Preventing Medical Mishaps: Lessons from Non-Medical Near Miss Reporting Systems," *British Medical Journal*, Vol. 320, March 2000, pp. 759–763.

Beckett Megan K., Donna Fossum, Connie S. Moreno, Jolene Rae Galegher, and Richard Marken, *A Review of Current State-Level Adverse Medical Event Reporting Practices: Toward National Standards*. Santa Monica CA: RAND Corporation, TR-383-AHRQ, 2006. As of July 27, 2009:
http://www.rand.org/pubs/technical_reports/TR383/

Bradshaw LK, "Principles as Boundary Spanners: Working Collaboratively to Solve Problems," *NASSP Bulletin* 83, Vol. 611, 1999, pp. 38–47.

Center for Studying Health System Change, *Community Tracking Study (CTS), CTS Site Visits*,. As of July 27, 2009:
http://www.hschange.org/index.cgi?data=06

Centers for Medicare and Medicaid Services (CMS), *Medicare Patient Safety Monitoring System*, Baltimore, Md., 2009. As of August 3, 2009:
http://www.cms.hhs.gov/QualityInitiativesGenInfo/15_MQMS.asp

CMS, *Quarterly Summary Statistics for MDS 2.0 Public Quality Indicators Measures.* As of August 2008:
http://www.cms.hhs.gov/MDSPubQIandResRep/02_qmreport.asp#TopOfPage

CMS, *CMS Long Term Care Facility Resident Assessment Instrument User's Manual 2.0*, Version 2.0, Baltimore, Md., December 2008.

Farley D. O.,A. M. Haviland, S. Champagne, A. L. Jain, J. B. Battles, W. B. Munier, and J. M. Loeb, "Adverse Event Reporting Practices by U.S. Hospitals: Results of a National Survey," *Quality and Safety in Health Care*, Vol.17, 2008a, pp. 416–423.

Farley D. O., S. C. Morton, C. Damberg, A. Fremont, S. Berry, M. Greenberg, et al., *Assessment of the National Patient Safety Initiative: Context and Baseline, Evaluation Report I*, Santa Monica, Calif.: RAND Corporation, TR-203-AHRQ, 2005.
As of July 27, 2009: http://www.rand.org/pubs/technical_reports/TR203/

Farley D. O., S. C. Morton, C. Damberg, S. Ridgely, A. Fremont, M. Greenberg, et al., *Assessment of the National Patient Safety Initiative: Moving from Research to Practice, Evaluation Report II (2003–2004)*, Santa Monica, Calif.: RAND Corporation, TR-463-AHRQ, 2007a.
As of July 27, 2009: http://www.rand.org/pubs/technical_reports/TR463/

Farley D. O., C. Damberg, S. Ridgely, M. E. Sorbero, Greenberg, et al., *Assessment of the AHRQ Patient Safety Initiative: Focus on Implementation and Dissemination, Evaluation Report III (2004 – 2005)* , Santa Monica, Calif.: RAND Corporation, TR-508-AHRQ, 2007b.
As of July 27, 2009: http://www.rand.org/pubs/technical_reports/TR508/

Farley D. O., C. Damberg, S. Ridgely, M. E. Sorbero, M. Greenberg, et al., *Assessment of the National Patient Safety Initiative: Final Report, Evaluation Report IV*, Santa Monica, Calif.: RAND Corporation, TR-563-AHRQ, 2008b.
As of July 27, 2009: http://www.rand.org/pubs/technical_reports/TR563/

Farley, D. O., M. D. Greenberg, A. M Haviland, and S. Lovejoy, *Prioritizing Patient Safety Outcomes Measures: Results of An Expert Consensus Process.* Santa Monica, CA: RAND Corporation, WR-601-AHRQ, 2008c.

Greenberg M. D., A. M. Haviland, H. Yu, and D. O. Farley, "Safety Outcomes in the United States: Trends and Challenges in Measurement," *Health Services Research* 44, No. 2, Part II: April 2009, pp. 739–755.

Hicks, R.W., S. C. Becker, and D. D. Cousins, *MEDMARX Data Report: A Chartbook of Medication Error Findings from the Perioperative Settings from 1998 – 2005,* Rockville, Md.: U.S. Pharmacopeia (USP) Center for the Advancement of Patient Safety, 2006

Hicks, R. W., S. C. Becker, and D. D. Cousins, *MEDMARX Data Report: A Report on the Relationship of Drug Names and Medication Errors in Response to the Institute of Medicine's Call for Action*, Rockville, Md.: USP Center for the Advancement of Patient Safety, 2008.

Institute of Medicine, *To Err Is Human: Building a Safer Health System*, L. T. Kohn, J. M. Corrigan, and M. S. Donaldson, eds., Washington, D.C.: National Academy Press, 2000.

Joint Commission, *Sentinel Event Policies and Procedures*, July 2007. As of May 13, 2009: http://www.jointcommission.org/SentinelEvents/PolicyandProcedures/se_pp.htm

Joint Commission, *Specifications Manual for National Hospital Inpatient Quality Measures, Version 2.6b*, Oakbrook, Ill., 2009. As of August 3, 2009: http://www.jointcommission.org/PerformanceMeasurement/PerformanceMeasurement/ Current+NHQM+Manual.htm

Jones, B. L, D. Nagin, and K. Roeder, "A SAS Procedure Based on Mixture Models for Estimating Developmental Trajectories." *Sociological Research and Methods*, Vol. 29: 2001, pp. 374–393.

The Leapfrog Group. As of July 19, 2009: www.leapfroggroup.org/media/file/leapfrogreportfinal.pdf

McDonald, K., P. Romano, J. Geppert, et al., *Measures of Patient Safety Based on Hospital Administrative Data: The Patient Safety Indicators,* Technical Review 5 (prepared by University of California at San Francisco–Stanford Evidence-based Practice Center, under Contract No. 290-97-0013), Rockville, Md.: Agency for Healthcare Research and Quality, AHRQ Publication No. 02-0038, 2002.

Mendel, P., C. L. Damberg, M. E. S. Sorbero, D. M. Varda, and D. O. Farley, "The Growth of Partnerships to Support Patient Safety Practice Adoption," *Health Services Research* Vol. 44, No. 2, Part II, April 2009, pp. 717–738.

Miller, M. R., A. Elixhauser, C. Zhan, and G. S. Meyer, "Patient Safety Indicators: Using Administrative Data to Identify Potential Patient Safety Concerns," *Health Services Research*, Vol. 36, No. 6, Pt 2: 2001, pp. 110–132.

Nagin, Daniel, *Group-Based Modeling of Development.* Cambridge, Mass: Harvard University Press, 2005.

National Center for Control of Infectious Diseases (NCCID), *National Nosocomial Infections Surveillance System*, Centers for Disease Control and Prevention Atlanta, Ga.: 2009. As of August 3, 2009: http://www.cdc.gov/ncidod/dhqp/nnis.html

National Center for Health Statistics (NCHS), *International Classification of Diseases, 9th Revision, Clinical Modification (ICD-9-CM), Sixth Edition*, Centers for Disease Control and Prevention, Hyattsville, Md.: 2008. As of August 3, 2009: http://www.cdc.gov/nchs/about/otheract/icd9/abticd9.htm

National Quality Forum (NQF), *National Voluntary Consensus Standards for Nursing Home Care: A Consensus Report*, Washington, D.C., No. NQFCR-06-04, 2004.

NQF, *Safe Practices for Better Healthcare, A Consensus Report*, Washington, D.C., No. NQFCR-05-03, 2003.

NQF, *Safe Practices for Better Healthcare–2006 Update: A Consensus Report*, Washington, D.C., No. NQFCR-17-07, 2007.

NQF, *Safe Practices for Better Healthcare–2009 Update: A Consensus Report*, Washington, DC: NQF, 2009.

Public Law 109-41, Patient Safety and Quality Improvement Act of 2005, Washington, D.C. As of July 27, 2009:
http://web.lexis-nexis.com/congcomp/.

Rosen, A. K., P. Rivard, S. Zhao, S. Loveland, D. Tsilimingras, C. L. Christiansen, et al., "Evaluating the Patient Safety Indicators: How Well Do They Perform on Veterans Health Administration Data?" *Medical Care*, Vol. 43, No. 9, 2005, pp. 873–84.

Sedman, A., J. M. Harris, 2nd, K. Schulz, E. Schwalenstocker, D. Remus, M. Scanlon, et al., "Relevance of the Agency for Healthcare Research and Quality Patient Safety Indicators for Children's Hospitals," *Pediatrics*, Vol. 115, No. 1, 2005, pp. 135–45.

Sorra J, T. Famolaro, N. Dyer, D. Nelson, and K. Khanna, *Hospital Survey on Patient Safety Culture: 2008 Comparative Database Report*, AHRQ Publication No. 08-0039. (Prepared by Westat, Rockville, Md., under contract No. 233-02-0087, Task Order No. 18), Rockville, Md.: Agency for Healthcare Research and Quality, March, 2008.

Sorra J, V. Nieva, T. Famolaro, and N. Dyer, *Hospital Survey on Patient Safety Culture: 2007 Comparative Database Report*, AHRQ Publication No. 07-0025 (Prepared by Westat, Rockville, Md., under contract No. 233-02-0087, Task Order No. 18), Rockville, Md.: Agency for Healthcare Research and Quality, March, 2007.

South Carolina General Assembly, Hospital Infections Disclosure Act, 2006.

Stufflebeam, D, W. J. Gephart, E. G. Guba, R. L. Hammond, H. O. Merriman, and M. M. Provus, *Educational Evaluation and Decision Making*, Itasca, Ill.: F. E. Peacock Publishers, Inc., 1971.

Stufflebeam, D. L., G. F. Madaus, and T. Kellaghan, *Evaluation Models: Viewpoints on Educational and Human Services Evaluation.* Norwell, Mass.: Kluwer Academic Publishers, 2000.

U.S. Pharmacopeia, *MEDMARX 5th Anniversary Data Report: A Chartbook of 2003 Findings and Trends 1999–2003*, Rockville, MD: USP Center for the Advancement of Patient Safety, 2004.

U.S. Pharmacopeia, *MEDMARX Data Report: A Report on the Relationship of Drug Names and Medication Errors in Response to the Institute of Medicine's Call for Action.* Rockville, MD: USP Center for the Advancement of Patient Safety, 2008.

Utah Department of Health, *Patient Safety Grant: Utah/Missouri Adverse Event ICD-9-CM Classification, Final 2008 Version*, last updated 2008. As of May 13, 2009:
http://health.utah.gov/psi/ps_grant.htm

Williams, Paul, "The Competent Boundary Spanner," *Public Administration*, Vol. 80, No. 1, 2002, pp. 103–124.

Yu H., M. D. Greenberg, A. M. Haviland, and D. O. Farley, "Canary Measures Among the AHRQ Patient Safety Indicators," *American Journal of Medical Quality*, forthcoming.

Zwanziger, J., and G. Melnick, "The Effects of Hospital Competition and the Medicare PPS Program on Hospital Cost behavior in California," *Journal of Health Economics*, Vol. 7, 1988, pp. 301–320.